LINES ON THE UNDERGROUND

LINES ON THE UNDERGROUND

An Anthology
for London Travellers

Compiled by

DOROTHY MEADE & TATIANA WOLFF

Illustrated by Basil Cottle
and Jonathan Newdick

CASSELL

Cassell Publishers Limited
Villiers House, 41/47 Strand
London WC2N 5JE

in association with the London Transport Museum

Introduction and selection
copyright © Dorothy Meade and Tatiana Wolff 1994
Extracts copyright authors and publishers (see Acknowledgements)
Illustrations copyright © Basil Cottle and Jonathan Newdick 1994

First published 1994

British Library Cataloguing in Publication Data
A catalogue record for this book is available from the British Library

ISBN 0-304-34451-6

Distributed in the United States by
Sterling Publishing Co, Inc.
387 Park Avenue South, New York, NY 10016-8810

Distributed in Australia by
Capricorn Link (Australia) Pty Ltd
PO Box 665, Lane Cove, NSW 2066

Designed by Ronald Clark
Cover calligraphy by Joy Cuff
Underground map reproduced by permission of
London Transport
Typeset in Meridien by Ronald Clark
Printed and bound in Great Britain by
Martins The Printers Ltd, Berwick upon Tweed

To Joe, Dora, Anna and Ben

*

And in memory of
M. M. W.

CONTENTS

INTRODUCTION

Nearly fifty years ago, when we were two young students waiting for our exam results in wartime London, we thought we had a brilliant idea for an anthology. The Underground was a war hero then, providing travel out of danger from raids by day and safe sleeping space on the platforms by night. Surely all those people, with plenty of time on their hands and nothing much to see or read, would be glad of an anthology about this mysterious labyrinthine haven and the world around and above it.

The war over, the project began to take shape. From the start we felt that the book was on the point of publication, and we must hurry. We wrote hectic letters to each other from strange locations: June 1947: 'Yesterday I spent in the B.M. by whose Reading Room I was greatly impressed. . . . Am off to Guildhall tomorrow for books on London.' September 1948, Bolton: 'I have the anthology with me and intend to start all sorts of new ideas going.' February 1949, Sweden: 'I feel the anthology has been hanging fire, and we must make a supreme effort with it. So many other things distract one – but let's have a consultation about it before I whizz up to Stoke-on-Trent.' In June 1949 a possible illustrator turned up in Bristol: 'Cottle is *v*. enthusiastic, is coming tomorrow with a list of silhouettes, can get them done in a week's time, thinks the whole thing *most* exciting and will co-operate to the full!!! . . . Let me have suggestions quickly. He's a man of action.' We agreed to keep him informed.

We finished the Inner Circle in a hurry, the deceptively easy part, a short line and plenty of literature to choose from – a bit bookish we can now see, though it didn't strike us that way at the time. In 1949, it was nearly, but not quite, accepted by a publisher, who started costing it and then got cold feet. In a letter of December 1949 we imagined the deciding factor at the board meeting, the younger members pressing for publication but the aged director muttering: 'Too many London anthologies already', 'just a feeble stunt', 'What, compiled by two young dilettantes?' Nothing daunted, we pressed on.

But now other priorities took over. Teaching children, or having children, writing books and articles, eased the anthology onto a high shelf. We kept adding to the collection, with occasional frenzied flutters when an agent or publisher showed interest. And, more important, and the reason we went on so long, was the fun we had in finding people and events, real and fictional, to enliven those anonymous names on the map.

It must have been thrilling to travel on the world's first underground train when in 1863 the Metropolitan steam railway opened, running between Paddington and Farringdon Street. It was greeted by a frenzy of excitement (and many complaints and jokes about the smoke in tunnels). The Central line, opening in 1900 and known as the 'tuppenny tube' because of its flat-rate fare, was described by the *Daily Mail*: 'All London seems to be pleased with its latest novelty as a child would be with a toy.' The main attraction now was the first escalator, with long queues forming to try the strange new moving stairs; there were lunch parties on platforms, first-day offers of free tickets. It was a splendid source of fun for *Punch* cartoons (with captions like mini-essays); W.S. Sullivan reset a lyric to include a 'Tuppenny Tube young man'. Galsworthy's Forsytes were devotees of this intriguing new-fangled method of travel, 'for everyone today went underground'.

The whole network has continued to expand. Since we began there have been numerous line extensions and two totally new lines, with many new stations in the suburbs. At first we worried about them, some named only when the tube arrived, as the lines stretched ever further out. When time allowed, we set off to consult distant libraries and archivists and to investigate places strange to us like Snaresbrook, Cockfosters, Colliers Wood. Then gradually they came to life, nearly all of them. We luckily found that Pepys had visited many a stately home on the outskirts of London, and written about them with his inimitable gusto; Trollope lived in Harrow, John Drinkwater in Leytonstone, Clement Attlee in Stanmore (until he moved to 10 Downing Street). We were delighted to discover Dickens saying: 'Chigwell, my dear fellow, is the greatest place in the world', and wished he'd said more about remoter outskirts too. Following the Great Fire in 1666 the wind blew pages of burnt books to Acton.

INTRODUCTION

We read many wartime novels – greyish paperbacks on recycled paper, with narrow margins – providing records of wartime exploits. Swiss Cottage underground shelterers published their own bulletins, 'De Profundis', with advice for platform sleepers and complaints about snorers. We alighted often ourselves at the same platform which Henry Moore recalls when describing his method of recording the rows of sleeping figures for his wartime sketches.

Since the system's inception the lives of Londoners have been punctuated by tube journeys, our own among them. Underground adventures set in trains and tunnels, dark, disused stations flashing by, stories of ghosts and hide-outs have a special fascination for children. Excerpts from children's stories crop up throughout the book, from Mole and Badger discussing the advantages of underground river life in *The Wind in the Willows* to schoolchildren singing their way round the Inner Circle in the holidays; and races to see who could break the speed record for travelling the full extent of every line, parents waiting at line ends to ferry their offspring to the next terminus. Julian Barnes, who wasn't yet born when our anthology began, describes all the short-cut travel tricks on his daily journey to school in his novel *Metroland*, taking the name from John Betjeman, the acknowledged Poet of the Suburbs, who brought his inimitable magic to the Metropolitan line. Philippa Pearce describes a young boy with a very small imaginary dog, his constant underground companion, always up to tricks in carriages and on escalators.

Now, despite the grumbles, the bad press about delays, power cuts, ageing rolling stock in the wake of the recession, the magic of the Underground refuses to go away. Undaunted, contemporary writers, including Ruth Rendell, Doris Lessing and Philip Howard, still find a magnetism down there, and a place in this book.

We started active work again when we retired, overhauling the text, preparing a dummy issue, contacting all likely outlets, with the added incentive that now all our London Transport journeys were free. And we have become aware of subtle changes taking place below ground. We noticed that posters, once short and punchy, are now longer and more informative, and people read them carefully; word games are appearing; buskers penetrate the passages, would-be pop stars and classical music students alike. As stations are newly decorated, local associations are turning up – Sherlock Holmes at Baker Street, and Tate Gallery treasures on the tiles at Pimlico. Everyone seems to be reading, instead of just waiting blankly to arrive at their destination. There are poems in the carriages, and passengers reading and memorising them. It's as if you can't stop culture seeping along the corridors.

Then suddenly, that early sense of urgency of ours was back again with the arrival of a firm contract from an enterprising publisher who also felt a change afoot on the Underground. And thanks to our stubborn persistence and the 'never throw anything away' filing system of ours, almost all the material we needed was at hand. Now our pre-war portable typewriter had been succeeded by a computer with mouse and laser printer, and it was possible to deliver the entire text on one high-dendensity floppy disk, a concept beyond our wildest imagination when we first set out. It just needed a promised phone call to our 'man of action' illustrator of 48 years ago, who, a little surprised, was nonetheless happy to renew the earlier collaboration. Sadly, he died before this book was published.

We would like to have included longer quotations, but they are necessarily brief to allow space for so many entries. We hope that those you most enjoy will tempt you to library or bookshop to read further. We have included general information for remoter stations where literary gems have escaped us. If you feel your special station has been undervalued, and you think you can offer a better alternative, we shall be very glad to hear from you.

Use the book as you like, either following your route by way of quotations (we remind you when to change trains, and provide a map), or just dipping in anywhere you choose. Indexes for authors and editors as well as station names are included, to help find your way around our writers and the network.

So this abiding obsession of ours is out in the open at last, like a tube train coming up for air at Golders Green or Arnos Grove. It has been fun to prepare over the years. We hope you find it fun to read.

The map of the London Underground, which can be seen inside every train, on all stations, on the back of the London A–Z guide, on tea-cloths on sale at the London Transport Museum, on posters, in diaries and in sundry other places, has been called a model of its kind, a work of art.

It was designed by Henry Beck and first used by London Transport on posters in 1933. They paid him five guineas, or £5.25 for it. It has been reproduced in millions and has served as the model for metro maps all over the world.

The last to carry the signature Henry C. Beck in the lower lefthand corner was issued in 1959. . . . . It presents the underground network as a geometric grid . . .

The tube lines do not, of course, lie at right angles to one another like the streets of Manhattan. Nor do they branch off at acute angles or form perfect oblongs. A true map of the London Underground shows the central complex as a shape suggestive of a swimming dolphin, its snout being Aldgate, its forehead Old Street, the crown of its head King's Cross, its spine Paddington, White City and Acton, its tail Ealing Broadway and its underbelly the stations of Kensington. The outer configurations branch out in graceful tentacles. The seal has become a medusa, a jellyfish. Its extremities touch Middlesex and Hertfordshire, Essex and Surrey. A claw penetrates Heathrow.

BARBARA VINE, *King Solomon's Carpet*, 1991

BAKERLOO LINE

Elephant & Castle

Change for Northern line

In the south suburbs at the Elephant
Is best to lodge.

WILLIAM SHAKESPEARE, *Twelfth Night*, 1601

The Elephant and Castle Underground Station (Northern and Bakerloo
Lines) is haunted by the sound of running footsteps. These are
frequently heard by maintenance staff working there after services
have stopped, especially on wintry nights. When the Victoria Line was
being built it was necessary to make a new tunnel beneath the Thames
close to Vauxhall Bridge. The navvies who excavated this in 1968
firmly believed in the ghost many of them met in the dark gloom.
Irishmen working on the project called him 'The Quare Feller' and one
described him as being at least seven feet tall, with outstretched, men-
acing, hands and arms. They believed that they had disturbed one of
the Plague pits of 1665.

J.A. BROOKS, *Ghosts of London*, 1982

Lambeth North

This was the London of my childhood, of my moods and awakenings:
memories of Lambeth in the spring; of trivial incidents and things; of
riding with Mother on top of a horse-bus trying to touch passing lilac-
trees – of the many coloured bus tickets, orange, blue, pink and green,
that bestrewed the pavement where the trams and buses stopped – of
rubicund flower-girls at the corner of Westminster Bridge, making gay

Waterloo
Change for Northern line

boutonnières, their adroit fingers manipulating tinsel and quivering fern
– of the humid odour of freshly watered roses that affected me with a
vague sadness – of melancholy Sundays and pale-faced parents and
their children escorting toy windmills and coloured balloons over
Westminster Bridge; and the maternal penny steamers that softly
lowered their funnels as they glided under it. From such trivia I believe
my soul was born.

CHARLIE CHAPLIN, *My Autobiography*, 1964

Every man has his Moscow. Suppose he [John Brown] did fail, every
man meets his Waterloo at last.

WENDELL PHILLIPS, Speech on Harper's Ferry, 1 November 1859

. . . on Waterloo Bridge . . . The wind has blown up the waves. The
river races beneath us, and the men standing on the barges have to
lean all their weight on the tiller. A black tarpaulin is tied down over a
swelling load of gold. Avalanches of coal glitter blackly. As usual,
painters are slung on planks across the great riverside hotels, and the
hotel windows have already points of light in them. On the other side
the city is white as if with age; St. Paul's swells white above the fretted,
pointed, or oblong buildings beside it. The cross alone shines rosy-gilt.

VIRGINIA WOOLF, *Jacob's Room*, 1922

Embankment
Change for Circle, District and Northern lines

Here was the city, the world. I waited for the flowering to come to me.
The trams on the Embankment sparked blue. The river was edged and
pierced with reflections of light, blue and red and yellow. Excitement!

V.S. NAIPAUL, *The Mimic Men*, 1967

. . . they set off resolutely along the desolate Embankment homeward.
    But indeed the Thames was a wonderful sight that year! Ice-fringed
along either shore, and with drift-ice in the middle reflecting a lumi-
nous scarlet from the broad red setting sun, and moving steadily, inces-

santly seaward. A swarm of mewing gulls went to and fro, and with them mingled pigeons and crows. The buildings on the Surrey side were dim and grey and very mysterious, the moored, ice-blocked barges silent and deserted, and here and there a lit window shone warm. The sun sank right out of sight into a bank of blue, and the Surrey side dissolved in mist save for a few insoluble spots of yellow light, that presently became many. And after our lovers had come under Charing Cross Bridge the Houses of Parliament rose before them at the end of a great crescent of golden lamps, blue and faint, halfway between the earth and sky. And the clock on the Tower was like a November sun.

H.G. WELLS, *Love and Mr Lewisham*, 1900

Charing Cross
Change for Jubilee and Northern lines

That the First Charles does here in triumph ride,
See his son reign'd where he a martyr died . . .

EDMUND WALLER, 'On the Statue of King Charles I at
Charing Cross, in the year 1674'

. . . Comely and calm, he rides
Hard by his own Whitehall:
Only the night wind glides:
No crowds, nor rebels, brawl.

LIONEL JOHNSON, 'By the statue of King Charles I at
Charing Cross', *Poems*, 1895

. . . upon thy so sore loss
Shall shine the traffic of Jacob's ladder
Pitched betwixt Heaven and Charing Cross . . .

FRANCIS THOMPSON, 'The Kingdom of God',
The Works, 1913

Out of the dark sky a noise was coming, a droning sound. The streets were empty, there was no light. Leaves blown across the pavement brushed our ankles and moved on, fleeing along the wind.

'Charing Cross Underground. Let's go there,' I said, urgently. Grasping our blankets we stumbled across the forecourt of Charing Cross

Station, and down the side street. Suddenly our path was brilliantly lit, bathed in icy white light. . . .

'What's happening?' she cried to me.

'Those enemy flares, parachute flares, shot out by our gunners. They are trying to get light to bomb by. Come on, come quickly now!' . . . It was full there, crowded with people even on the District Line platforms and approaches, which weren't really deep enough to be safe.

JILL PATON WALSH, The Fireweed, 1969

Piccadilly Circus
Change for Piccadilly line

If the present ballooning mania should be carried much further, it will become necessary for the Police Commissioners to issue regulations as to the taking up and setting down, in the same way as they now do with regard to carriages. . . . It is difficult to go down Piccadilly after six o'clock p.m., without getting your eyes filled with sand thrown out by the occupants of a balloon car, who, making themselves as jolly as sand-boys, sprinkle London with their discharged ballast.

Punch, 1849

Then a sentimental passion of a vegetable fashion must excite your
> languid spleen,
An attachment *à la* Plato for a bashful young potato, or a not too
> French French bean!
Though the Philistines may jostle, you will rank as an apostle in the
> high aesthetic band,
If you walk down Piccadilly with a poppy or a lily in your mediaeval
> hand.

W.S. GILBERT, Patience, 1881

Piccadilly! Shops, palaces, bustle, and breeze,
The whirring of wheels, and the murmur of trees;
By night or by day, whether noisy or stilly,
Whatever my mood is, I love Piccadilly.

F. LOCKER-LAMPSON, *London Lyrics,* 1857

Oxford Circus
Change for Central and Victoria lines

So then, Oxford-street, stonyhearted stepmother! thou that listenest to
the sighs of orphans, and drinkest the tears of children, at length I was
dismissed from thee: . . .
. . . oftentimes on moonlight nights, during my first mournful abode
in London, my consolation was (if such it could be thought) to gaze
from Oxford-street up every avenue in succession which pierces
through the heart of Marylebone to the fields and the woods.

THOMAS DE QUINCEY, *Confessions of an English Opium-Eater,* 1822

Regent's Park

'Verily I cannot get this mighty street out of my head,' said the Doctor.
'And then there is the new park – what do you call it? Mary-le-bone –
no, the Regent's Park: it seems to be an elegant, well-plannned place,
methinks, and will have a fine effect, no doubt, with its villas and what
not, when the shrubs and trees have shot up a little. But I shall not live
to see it, and I care not; for I remember those fields in their natural,
rural garb, covered with herds of kine, when you might stretch across
from old William's farm there a-top of Portland Street, right away
without impediment to Saint John's Wood, where I have gathered
blackberries when a boy – which pretty place, I am sorry to see, these
brick and mortar gentry have trenched upon. Why, Ephraim, your
metropolitans will have half a day's journey, if you proceed at this rate,
ere you can get a mouthful of fresh air.'

EPHRAIM HARDCASTLE, *Wine and Walnuts;*
or, After Dinner Chit-Chat, 1823

They were by this time outside the lovely gate; they went legging it down the short serpentine road that, with trees, railings and air of a private avenue, runs downhill from the Inner into the Outer Circle. Ahead one had still an illusion of wooded distance, out of whose blue and bronzy ethereality rose the tops of Regency terraces – these, in their semi-ruin, just less pale than the sky. . . . This moment of walking to meet the houses seemed to have its place in no given hour of time – though across it, in contradiction, St. Marylebone clock began striking eight.

ELIZABETH BOWEN, *The Heat of the Day*, 1949

Baker Street

Change for Circle, Hammersmith & City, Jubilee and Metropolitan lines

For those of us who did not live in it, the London of the eighties and nineties of last century is simply the London of Holmes and we cannot pass down Baker Street without thinking of him and trying to locate his lodgings. Of whom but Holmes has a literature sprung up solely concerned with the question of where he lived?

HESKETH PEARSON, *Conan Doyle: His Life and Art*, 1943

Marylebone

. . . we abroad to Marrowbone and there walked in the garden, the first time I ever there, and a pretty place it is; and here we eat and drank and stayed till 9 at night; and so home by moonshine . . .

SAMUEL PEPYS, *Diary*, 7 May 1668

PEACHUM: The Captain keeps too good company ever to grow rich. Marybone* and the chocolate-houses are his undoing . . .
MACHEATH: There will be deep play to-night at Marybone, and consequently money may be picked up upon the road. Meet me there, and I'll give you the hint who is worth setting.

* The Marylebone Pleasure Gardens.

JOHN GAY, *The Beggar's Opera*, 1728

Advertisement of Marylebone gardens: 'Mr. Trusler's daughter begs leave to inform the Nobility and Gentry, that she intends to make fruit-tarts during the fruit season; and hopes to give equal satisfaction as with the rich cakes, and almond cheesecakes. The fruit will always be fresh gathered, having great quantities in the garden; and none but loaf sugar used, and the finest Epping butter.'

The Daily Advertiser, 6 May 1760, quoted in
J.T. SMITH, *A Book for a Rainy Day*, 1845

That afternoon Hetta trusted herself all alone to the mysteries of the Marylebone underground railway,* and emerged with accuracy at King's Cross . . .

* The Metropolitan underground railway, which had opened in 1863.

ANTHONY TROLLOPE, *The Way We Live Now*, 1875

Between 1871 and 1872, openings were made in the crown of the long tunnel, venting through iron grilles at the centre of Euston and Marylebone Roads. . . . The author's father . . . used to recall that these grilles afforded a lunchtime diversion for the younger clerks, whose custom was to keep them under close surveillance. The reason for this was that should any lady be unwise enough to stand over them whilst a train was passing below, the force of the blast would raise her skirts in a satisfyingly revealing fashion.

ALAN A. JACKSON, *London's Metropolitan Railway*, 1986

Edgware Road

. . . 'tis certain, that this was formerly the only or the main Road from London to *St Alban's*, being the famous high Road call'd *Watling-street*, which reached from *London* to *Shrewsbury*, and on towards Wales.*

*In a later edition this sentence was added: 'The remains of this road are still to be seen here, and particularly in this, that from Hide-Park Corner, just where Tyburn stands, the road makes one straight line without any turning, even to the very town of St Albans.'

DANIEL DEFOE, *A Tour thro' the Whole Island of Great Britain*, 1742

I'm sure if anyone had told me as I could be whisked away from Moorfields to Marrybone in ten minutes I should have said, 'Go along with your rubbish' . . . just as a train as was a-goin' to start, and afore as I'd time to wink, as the sayin' is, I was shoved head foremost into a carriage and away we went under them dark arches . . .

. . . I set a-waitin' till a party put his head in at the winder and said, 'Change here for Kensington.'

I says, 'I shan't do nothin' of the sort, for I'm a-goin' to Baker-street.' 'Then,' says he, 'you've come past it; you must go upstairs and get a ticket to go back.'

I says, 'What a shame to bring parties out of their way like this.' He says, 'Can't you read nor got no ears, for,' he says, 'the names of the stations is wrote up.' . . .

I must say as we was not long in bein' whisked to Baker Street, where the train put us out, tho' in that 'urried way, as it's a mercy I didn't fall out thro' a-ketchin' my foot in a party's crinoline as was next the door.

ARTHUR SKETCHLEY, 'Mrs Brown on the Underground Railway', *The Brown Papers*, second series, reprinted from 'Fun', 1870

Paddington
Change for Circle, District and Hammersmith & City lines

I am a broken-hearted milkman, in grief I'm arrayed,
Through keeping of the company of a young servant maid,
Who lived on board wages to keep the house clean
In a gentleman's family near Paddington Green.

Chorus:

> She was as beautiful as a butterfly
> And as proud as a Queen .
> Was pretty Polly Perkins of
> Paddington Green.

Her eyes were as black as the pips of a pear,
No rose in the garden with her cheeks could compare,
Her hair hung in ringlets so beautiful and long,
I thought that she loved me but I found I was wrong.
. . .
In six months she married, this hard-hearted girl,
But it was not a wicount, and it was not a nearl,
It was not a baronite, but a shade or two wuss,
It was a bow-legged conductor of a Twopenny Bus.

Victorian Street Ballads edited by W. Henderson, 1937

Warwick Avenue

Little Venice [served by Warwick Avenue station]. The canal surrounded by trees . . . [is] one of the most unexpected beauty spots in London. Though both Robert Browning* and Lord Byron compared it to Venice, the name seems not to have been generally used until after the 2nd World War.

* Robert Browning lived at 19 Warwick Crescent between 1861 and 1887.

The London Encyclopaedia edited by Ben Weinreb
and Christopher Hibbert, 1983

Maida Vale

> I know where Maida Vale receives
> The night dews on her summer leaves,
> Nor less my settled spirit cleaves
> To Bloomsbury.

ANON., 'To Bloomsbury' quoted in *London in Verse*
edited by Christopher Logue, 1982

Kilburn Park

. . . 'Don't you ever get bored?' Toni once asked as we were adding up the months and years of our lives we had spent on trains. He only had a ten-stop ride round the Circle Line: uneventful, all underground, no chance of rape or abduction.

'Nah. Too much going on.'

'Tunnels, bridges, telegraph poles?'

'That sort of thing. No, actually, things like Kilburn. It's Doré; it really is.'

The next half-day, Toni came to try it out. Between Finchley Road and Wembley Park the train goes over a high viaduct system at Kilburn. . . . The value of Kilburn depended on not knowing particularities, because it changed to the eye and the brain according to yourself, your mood and the day. On a late afternoon in winter, with the egg-white lamps faintly beginning to show, it was melancholy and frightening, the haunt of acid-bath murderers. On a clear, bright morning in summer, with almost no smog and lots of people visible, it was like a brave little slum in the Blitz: you half expected to see George VI poking around the few remaining bomb-sites with his umbrella. . . .

Toni and I got off at Wembley Park, changed platforms, and went back over the area. Then we did the same again.

JULIAN BARNES, *Metroland*, 1980

Queen's Park

. . . so low were the finances [of Queen's Park Rangers] in these early days that the club's gear consisted of four uprights and two pieces of tape used as cross-bars! The question of shorts was also acute, but one supporter who maintained riding stables at Maida Vale came to the rescue by giving all the players a pair of riding pants in which they played their first match! . . .

The Kensal Rise ground was requisitioned for allotments, but salvation came when in 1917 Shepherd's Bush amateur club disbanded and Rangers took over their ground at Loftus Road. They were 'home' at last. . . .

R.J. HAYTER, *Official History of Queen's Park Rangers*, 1948

Kensal Green

My friends, we will not go again or ape an ancient rage,
Or stretch the folly of your youth to be the shame of age,
But walk with clearer eyes and ears this path that wandereth,
And see undrugged in evening light the decent inn of death;
For there is good news yet to hear and fine things to be seen,
Before we go to Paradise by way of Kensal Green.

G.K. CHESTERTON, 'The Rolling English Road', 1914

Willesden Junction

Willesden Junction Station. . . . There is here almost as great a network of railways as at Clapham Junction, the lines radiating hence to almost all parts of London both north and south of the Thames; and the arrangement of the station is, if possible, more consummately bewildering to the unhappy traveller who has to 'change'.

E. WALFORD, *Greater London*, 1882–4

. . . the pilgrimage to *Our Lady of Willesden*, a popular pilgrimage resembling the more famous one to Our Lady of Walsingham . . . and to it the Londoners of both sexes flocked in great numbers, it being in the 15th century their most favourite resort. But the pilgrims were, at least in the later years, often persons of immoral character; and the pilgrimage itself was the occasion of much scandal. 'Ye men of London,' said the Scottish friar Father Donald, in a sermon he preached at St Paul's Cross . . . 'gang you yourselves with your wives to Willesden, in the Devyl's name, or else keep them at home with you with sorrow.' The pilgrimage was suppressed and the miraculous image of Our Lady of Willesden was destroyed at Chelsea, along with the shrine of Our Lady of Walsingham, in 1548.

JAMES THORNE, *Handbook to the Environs of London*, 1876

Harlesden

Harlesden was recorded as *Herulvestune* in Domesday Book and comes from the personal name of the Saxon *Heoruwulf* . . . and Old English tun, 'a farm' – . . . being on a site where he and his family once lived. It was recorded as *Herlesdon* in 1291.

CYRIL M. HARRIS, What's in a Name?, 1977

Stonebridge Park

It was here that the Harrow Road was carried across the River Brent and the local inn – the Coach and Horses – was frequented by the painter, Morland, at the end of the 18th century. . . . The development of the Stonebridge Park estate in the 1870s and 1880s was intended to set the tone of the area. . . .

The London Encyclopaedia edited by Ben Weinreb
and Christopher Hibbert, 1983

Wembley Central

When melancholy Autumn comes to Wembley
And electric trains are lighted after tea
The poplars near the Stadium are trembly
With their tap and tap and whispering to me,
Like the sound of little breakers
Spreading out along the surf-line
When the estuary's filling
With the sea.

JOHN BETJEMAN, 'Harrow-on-the-Hill',
A Few Late Chrysanthemums, 1954

Oh bygone Wembley! Where's the pleasure now?
The temples stare, the Empire passes by.
This was the grandest Palace of them all.

The British government pavilion and the famous Wembley lions.
Now they guard an empty warehouse site.

JOHN BETJEMAN, 'Metro-land' (TV programme), 1973, quoted in
The Best of Betjeman selected by John Guest, 1978

North Wembley

Gentle Brent, I used to know you
Wandering Wembley-wards at will,
Now what change your waters show you
In the meadowlands you fill!
Recollect the elm-trees misty
And the footpath climbing twisty
Under cedar-shaded palings,
Low laburnum-leaned-on railings,
Out of Northolt on and upwards to the heights of Harrow hill.

JOHN BETJEMAN, 'Middlesex',
A Few Late Chrysanthemums, 1954

South Kenton

. . . on the northern part of Kenton lane in 1933 . . . the builder of the houses, a man named Jefferies, would go round on a Sunday, when people came to visit the site, and offer to lend them the £5 deposit money! 'Houses on gently moulded hills, surrounded by verdant lanes and age-old trees, giving quiet, pastoral beauty. This is the ideal setting for one's home.' Even today some of this sylvan beauty remains.

DENNIS EDWARDS AND RON PIGRAM,
London's Underground Suburbs, 1986

Kenton

Since I had the pleasure of seeing you last I have been almost wholly in the country at a farmer's house quite alone trying to write a Comedy [*She Stoops to Conquer*]. It is now finished but when or how it will be acted, or whether it will be acted at all are questions I cannot resolve.

OLIVER GOLDSMITH, letter to Bennet Langton, 4 September 1771,
quoted in *The Collected Letters of Oliver Goldsmith* edited by
Katharine C. Balderston, 1928

The farmhouse still stands on a gentle eminence in what is called Hyde-Lane, leading to Kenton . . . and looking over a pretty country in the direction of Hendon; and when a biographer of the poet went in search of it some years since . . . he found traditions of Goldsmith surviving too . . . how Reynolds and Johnson and Sir William Chambers had been entertained there, and he had taken the young folks of the farm in a coach to see some strolling players at Hendon; how he had come home one night without his shoes, having left them stuck fast in a slough; and how he had an evil habit of reading in bed, and of putting out his candle by flinging his slipper at it. It was certain he was fond of this humble place.

JOHN FORSTER, *The Life and Adventures of Oliver Goldsmith*, 1848

There's a storm cloud to the westward over Kenton,
There's a line of harbour lights at Perivale,
Is it rounding rough Pentire in a flood of sunset fire
The little fleet of trawlers under sail?
Can those boats be only roof tops
As they stream along the skyline
In a race for port and Padstow
With the gale?

JOHN BETJEMAN, 'Harrow-on-the-Hill',
A Few Late Chrysanthemums, 1954

Harrow & Wealdstone

Then Harrow-on-the-Hill's a rocky island
And Harrow churchyard full of sailors' graves
And the constant click and kissing of the trolley buses hissing
Is the level to the Wealdstone turned to waves
And the rumble of the railway
Is the thunder of the rollers
As they gather up for plunging
Into caves.

JOHN BETJEMAN, 'Harrow-on-the-Hill',
A Few Late Chrysanthemums, 1954

Anthony Trollope and his family once lived in a farmhouse in Harrow Weald. . . . Trollope has nothing good to say about Harrow, to which he tramped day after day, at first from the Weald, then from Orley Farm – 12 miles through the lanes. . . .

BAKERLOO LINE

. . . Grimsdyke . . . containing a Norman Shaw mansion, formerly the home of W.S. Gilbert . . . Gilbert loved this place; he was passionately fond of birds and animals; game birds flourished here, and he would not allow his keepers to shoot even a squirrel . . . he enjoyed the seclusion of his fine library (into which bullfinches and even deer would penetrate), and the splendour of the music room, with its minstrels gallery. When the great house was sold, dozens of pictures of characters from the Savoy operas were found, and the headman's block and the axe from the *Yeoman of the Guard*.

BRUCE STEVENSON, *Middlesex*, 1972

CENTRAL LINE

The Central Line holds the distinction of providing the longest possible train journey on the Underground without a change, from Epping to West Ruislip, a journey of 34.1 miles (54.9 km). With 51 stations spread along the 52 route miles of track it is also unusual in embracing one of the most heavily used sections of the Underground (Liverpool Street to Stratford) with the most lightly used (Epping to Ongar).

M.A.C. HORNE, *The Central Line*, 1987

West Ruislip

Oak from the woods [around Ruislip Common] was used in the 14th century for work on the Tower of London, in 1344 for Windsor Castle, and in 1346 and 1347 for Westminster Palace.

The London Encyclopaedia edited by Ben Weinreb
and Christopher Hibbert, 1983

Ruislip Gardens

Gaily into Ruislip Gardens
   Runs the red electric train,
With a thousand Ta's and Pardon's
   Daintily alights Elaine;
Hurries down the concrete station
With a frown of concentration,
Out into the outskirt's edges
Where a few surviving hedges
Keep alive our lost Elysium – rural Middlesex again.

JOHN BETJEMAN, 'Middlesex',
A Few Late Chrysanthemums, 1954

South Ruislip

The village [Ruislip] with its church, almshouses, and moated farm is now so closely surrounded on all sides by suburban developments that the small and fairly completely preserved nucleus of old building comes as a surprise from whatever direction it is approached. . . . The parish is richer in good farmhouses than any other in the county.

NIKOLAUS PEVSNER, *The Buildings of England: Middlesex,* 1951

Northolt

[Northolt] Airport was a base of Fighter Command and played a considerable part in the Battle of Britain. . . . On the afternoon of 29th September 1940, over 200 high explosive bombs fell in the Greenford area. . . . Churchill left here to inspect the crossing of the Rhine.

BRUCE STEVENSON, *Middlesex,* 1972

Greenford

. . . Parish of enormous hayfields
    Perivale stood all alone,
And from Greenford scent of mayfields
    Most enticingly was blown
Over market gardens tidy,
Taverns for the *bona fide,*
Cockney anglers, cockney shooters,
Murray Poshes, Lupin Pooters
Long in Kensal Green and Highgate silent under soot and stone.

JOHN BETJEMAN, 'Middlesex',
A Few Late Chrysanthemums, 1954

Perivale

She Peryvale perceiv'd prank'd up with wreaths of wheat,
'Why should not I be coy, and of my beauties nice,
Since this my goodly grain is held of greatest price?'*

* Peryvale, or Pure-vale, yieldeth the finest meal of England.

MICHAEL DRAYTON, *The Poly-olbion* Part I,
the Sixteenth Song, 1612

Hanger Lane

Turn to page 33 for North Acton

Hanger Vale Lane. An ancient way . . . there is widespread misunder-
standing of the name. It is sometimes fondly supposed that the name
has to do with hangmen or gibbets or . . . with aeroplane sheds. This
kind of hanger is in fact a wood on a hillside, where the trees may be
said to hang on by their roots.

R.N.G. ROWLAND, *The Street-names of Acton, Middlesex,* 1977

What is the matter with Hanger Lane?
I'm late and it's dark and it's pouring with rain,
The traffic is bumper to bumper again,
What *is* the matter with Hanger Lane?
Answer: Too many cars: take a train.

ANON.

Ealing Broadway

Change for District line

There was a young lady of Ealing
Who walked up and down on the ceiling;
   She shouted: 'Oh heck!
   I've broken my neck,
And it is a peculiar feeling.'

ANON., *Penguin Book of Limericks*
edited by E.O. Parrott, 1983

West Acton

To the west of Acton High Street . . . lived Bulwer Lytton, the novelist
and statesman. Another prominent resident of Acton was Henry
Fielding, the novelist.

HAROLD P. CLUNN, *The Face of London,* 1932

North Acton

Great was my joy with London at my feet –
All London mine, five shillings in my hand
And not expected back till after tea!
Great was our joy, Ronald Hughes Wright's and mine,
To travel by the Underground all day
Between the rush hours, so that very soon
There was no station north to Finsbury Park,
To Barking eastwards, Clapham Common south,
No temporary platform in the west
Among the Actons and the Ealings, where
We had not once alighted. Metroland
Beckoned us out to lanes in beechy Bucks –
Goldschmidt and Howland (in a wooden hut
Beside the station): 'Most attractive sites
Ripe for development'; Charrington's for coal;
And not far off the neo-Tudor shops.

JOHN BETJEMAN, *Summoned by Bells*, 1960

East Acton

The wells at Acton are seldom remembered . . . but they were uncommonly popular in their own time, even though to reach them from London involved a rather arduous ride. The Acton wells were 'rediscovered' in the reign of Queen Anne. . . . The spa achieved its greatest popularity during the reign of George III. The water was said with relish to be 'more powerfully cathartic than any other in the Kingdom of the same quality except that of Cheltenham', with the added inducement that the quantity of salts in each pound weight of the Acton water was forty-four grains. It must have been a powerful draught which attracted not only permanent residents to East Acton and Friar's Place, which adjoined the hamlet of East Acton, but thousands of visitors for the day from London.

CHRISTOPHER TRENT, *Greater London*, 1965

White City

On 14 May 1908 the Central London Railway (the original 'tuppeny Tube') was extended from Shepherd's Bush to Wood Lane to serve the Franco-British Exhibition which opened that year at White City.

DENNIS EDWARDS AND RON PIGRAM,
London's Underground Suburbs, 1986

Shepherd's Bush
Change for Hammersmith & City line station

Shepherd's Bush Common. Triangular open space of 8 acres acquired by Act of Parliament 1871. It was formerly called Gagglegoose Green. Its present name is from the shepherd's practice of watching his sheep whilst lying in a thorn bush. The highwayman 'Sixteen String Jack' was finally captured here.

The London Encyclopaedia edited by Ben Weinreb
and Christopher Hibbert, 1983

I had been waiting now at Holland Park for a long time . . . the saving grace of the Central Line [was] the way that beyond Shepherd's Bush and Liverpool Street, it veered off at either end to outlying towns to the north. I stood for a minute or more with my toes over the platform's edge, looking down into the concrete gully where a whole family of nervous, sooty little mice shot back and forth as if themselves operated by electricity.

ALAN HOLLINGHURST, *The Swimming Pool Library,* 1988

Holland Park

[Holland] Park was once the grounds of Holland House, built in 1605–7 for Sir Walter Cope, whose daughter married the first Earl of Holland . . . [It] enjoyed a long heyday as a centre of political and literary society, for the third Earl's widow married Joseph Addison, the statesman and essayist, and, in 1768, the property passed to the Fox family. Charles James Fox spent his childhood here, and his nephew, the third Baron Holland, entertained brilliantly, numbering among his guests Talleyrand, Madame de Staël, Ugo Foscolo, Sir Walter Scott,

Wordsworth, Thomas Moore, Fenimore Cooper, and his neighbour, the historian Lord Macaulay, who lived in Holly Lodge on Campden Hill.

ANN SAUNDERS, *The Art and Architecture of London,* 1984

Notting Hill Gate
Change for Circle and District lines

Nature puts on a disguise when she speaks to every man; to this man she put on the disguise of Notting Hill. Nature would mean to a poet born in the Cumberland hills, a stormy sky-line and sudden rocks. Nature would mean to a poet born in the Essex flats, a waste of splendid waters and splendid sunsets. So Nature meant to this man Wayne a line of violet roofs and lemon lamps, the chiaroscuro of the town.

G.K. CHESTERTON, *The Napoleon of Notting Hill,* 1904

The little cosmopolis of Notting Hill, its littered streets, its record exchanges, its international newsagents, late-night cinemas, late-night delis, was to hand. The elegant vacancy of the Park was admirably near; you could walk to the museums, to Knightsbridge even, and a little later in the year, to the Proms. And at the back, a block away, you were in Carnival country.

ALAN HOLLINGHURST, *The Swimming Pool Library,* 1988

I am an old and valuable customer of the Underground. It is by far the quickest and most efficient way of getting around central London, apart from walking, or possibly bicycling. The lines have their familiar idiosyncrasies, from the swift thrust of the Central to the heart of the City, to the perversity of the Northern, which sends six Edgwares when what you want is a High Barnet. The names of the stations are poetry, from Theydon Bois to Cockfosters. . . .

My daily journey to work from Notting Hill Gate to Tower Hill is the farthest you can go on the inner zone, making me feel smug that I am getting value for money. Over the years I have spent hundreds of pounds on the Underground. When it comes to getting around London, I am a mole.

PHILIP HOWARD, *The Times*

Queensway

Since Roman times London has sunk fifteen feet. Severe weather, combined with an abnormally high tide, threatened to engulf forty-five square miles of the centre, including most of Westminster, the City and London's valleys. John Stow's rivers would have surfaced once again. The Cabinet would have moved to Holborn, Parliament to Queensway, and the Ministry of Defence to Lacon House in Theobald's Road.

It never happened, and at a cost of £460m, a monster flood barrier . . . was built between 1975 and 1982 to protect the capital . . . it is the largest flood barrier in the world.

RICHARD TRENCH AND ELLIS HILLMAN,
London Under London, 1984, revised 1993

Lancaster Gate

In their house in Lancaster Gate or some country house which they took for the summer she [Lady Strachey] would sit at the head of the table around which her five sons and five daughters together with a certain number of their wives or husbands argued at the top of their Stracheyan voices with Stracheyan vehemence. Lady Strachey seemed entirely oblivious to or unaware of the terrific din. She delighted to tell one about the vanishing literary world in which she had been the intimate friend of Lord Lytton, Browning and Tennyson.

Leonard Woolf in *Coming to London* edited by John Lehmann, 1957

W. Gunn Gwennet, an illustrator of railway advertisements, complained of the poor quality and large number of advertisements in the Underground:– It is as though the guards on the Central London Railway shouted out: 'Next Station Pear's Soap, Beecham's Pills, Marblarch, Bovril.'

HUGH DOUGLAS, *The Underground Story*, 1963

Marble Arch

If you walk from Newgate Street . . . to Marble Arch, you will be crossing the same ground that for five hundred years, from the thirteenth century until 1783, the death cart took carrying condemned criminals

from Newgate prison to their hanging at Tyburn: . . . the procession
. . . began the steep ascent of Holborn Hill, which was sometimes called
Heavy Hill. To 'ride up Heavy Hill' meant that a man's misbehaviour
might one day lead him to Tyburn, while 'going west' meant that he
was literally on the way there.

There were several other gallows in London and at first Tyburn was
reserved for the upper classes, though not for long. The first hangings
at Tyburn were a little to the west of the later site of the gallows,
where the western tributary of the Tyburn river crossed what is now
the Bayswater Road. The brook was lined with elm trees and the first
recorded hanging was on one of these trees, when Roger de Mortimer,
a lover of Edward II's wife, Queen Isabella, was dragged there on a
hurdle, hanged, drawn and quartered and left there for several days.
Later the place of execution was moved to the end of the Edgware
Road, where today the Marble Arch stands.

MARY CATHCART BORER, *London Walks and Legends,* 1981

. . . they tell me that So-and-So, who does not write prefaces, is no
charlatan. Well, I am. I first caught the ear of the British public on a
cart in Hyde Park, to the blaring of brass bands, and this . . . because
like all dramatists and mimes of genuine vocation, I am a natural-born
mountebank.

GEORGE BERNARD SHAW, Preface to *Three Plays for Puritans,* 1901

Bond Street
Change for Jubilee line

What sauntering indifference is displayed in the steps of the well-
dressed pedestrians, who at the accustomed moment commence their

daily pilgrimage from the top of Bond-street to the end of Pall Mall! Some stop at the fruit-shops, and, careless of consequences, run up a bill for early strawberries, forced peaches, and pine-apple ices. . . . Some empty their purses in bidding for useless baubles at the splendid auction-rooms of Phillips and Christie. Some are attracted by the grotesque prints exhibited at the windows of the caricature-sellers . . . scarcely any can resist the varied temptations which shops of every possible kind hold out to the vanity or the wants of the passers by.

MARQUIS DE VERMOND, 1823, quoted by
D.J. Olsen in *The City as a Work of Art*, 1986

Oxford Circus
Change for Bakerloo and Victoria lines

The women who walk down Oxford Street
Have bird-like faces and brick-like feet;
Floppity flop go 'tens' and 'elevens'
Of Easiphit into D.H. Evans.
The women who walk down Oxford Street
Suffer a lot from nerves and heat,
But with Bovril, Tizer and Phospherine
They may all become what they might have been.
They gladly clatter with bag in hand
Out of the train from Metroland,
And gladly gape, when commerce calls,
At all the glory of plate-glass walls,
And gladly buy, till their bags are full,
'Milton' cleaner and 'Wolsey' wool,
'Shakespeare' cornflour, a 'Shelley' shirt,
'Brighto', 'Righto' and 'Moovyerdirt'.
Commerce pours on them gifts like rain;
Back in Metroland once again,
Wasn't it worth your weary feet –
The colourful bustle of Oxford Street?

JOHN BETJEMAN, 'Civilized Woman',
Uncollected Poems, 1982

Tottenham Court Road

Change for Northern line

LUNARDI'S SECOND VOYAGE

The most pompous, absurd, and ridiculous advertisements and paragraphs, had, for six weeks, announced to the publick, the glorious ascension of the Italian philosopher. Large bills, printed on pea green paper, for eight days, ornamented all the corners of the streets. . . . The GRAND BRITISH BALLOON, covered thick with paint, represented the arms of England, upon a ground of red and blue, imitating the St. George's flag.

Signor Lunardi had promised to elevate with him a young lady, without doubt, in emulation of Miss Simonet [of a rival's ascent]; but Miss Simonet weighed only eighty-three pounds, and Mr. Lunardi's lady two hundred and fifty. A scientifick gentleman, furnished with barometers, thermometers, hydrometers, sextants, quadrants, telescopes, time-pieces, etc. etc. etc. was to complete the philosophick cargo. The great citizen of Lucca was to *direct the machine*, the scientifick gentleman was to *take the altitudes*, and the lady of two hundred and a half, was to make *'interesting observations on the general appearances.'*

Each of these aeronauts had a separate department, and in case they met with the sea, the sea was to be crossed. These were the solemn engagements made to the publick; we now proceed to the result of them.

On Friday, to accomplish all these fair promises, at twenty minutes after one, the GRAND BRITISH BALLOON, plastered with four coats of colour, and appearing in the form of a flattened orange, elevated with great difficulty a gallery of 112 pounds, two or three bags of ballast, and Signor Lunardi *only*. The fat lady, who had swallowed a few spoonfuls of brandy, to recruit her *'heroism'*, and to dispose her *'liberal mind for the reflections she intended to make for the benefit of her fair country-*

women', finding herself left behind, made a national reproach to Lunardi for his neglect of her. . . .

It was fortunate, that the fat lady and the scientifick gentleman, did not accompany this new Icarus in his voyage, for having neglected, at the moment of his ascension, to open the appendices of his balloon, the dilatation produced by the heat of the sun, caused it to burst, at the distance of a mile from the place where he set out, and the pilot and the vessel descended, with considerable velocity, and landed at the skettle ground of the Adam and Eve publick-house, in Tottenham Court Road.

Morning Chronicle, 17 May 1785

Opinion was that Tottenham Court Road was the best pitch, the Central Line area. Tom didn't know that at that station you had to book your pitch in advance, add your name or the name of your band to the list under the No Smoking sign . . . busking was not what his grandmother and a lot of others seemed to think, just another kind of begging, but a real musical *means of living, something you had to book and arrange like giving a concert in a concert hall. Unlike the noise made by the strummers who called it pop or country, his was serious music.*

That day he committed himself to being a busker. He was a professional musician and the concourses of the Underground were his auditorium.

BARBARA VINE, *King Solomon's Carpet,* 1991

Holborn
Change for Piccadilly line and Aldwych link

By the seventeenth century there was another stopping place on the way to the gallows, although only for the more gentlemanly prisoners. This was the Blue Boar [later the George and Blue Boar], on the south side of High Holborn, a stopping place on the way from Newgate prison to the gallows, where they were offered a glass of sherry. . . . Today, Number 285 High Holborn stands on the site.

MARY CATHCART BORER, *London Walks and Legends,* 1981

As clever *Tom Clinch,* while the Rabble was bawling,
Rode stately through Holbourn to die in his Calling;
He stopt at the *George* for a Bottle of Sack,
And promis'd to pay for it when he'd come back.

His Waistcoat and Stockings, and Breeches were white,
His Cap had a new Cherry Ribbon to ty't;
The Maids to the Doors and the Balconies ran,
And said, lack-a-day! he's a proper young Man.

JONATHAN SWIFT, 'Clever Tom Clinch Going
to be Hanged. Written in the year 1726'

Near to the spot on which Snow Hill and Holborn meet, there opens, upon the right hand as you come out of the City, a narrow and dismal alley, leading to Saffron Hill. In the filthy shops are exposed for sale huge bunches of second-hand silk handkerchiefs, of all sizes and patterns; for here reside the traders who purchase them from pick pockets. Hundreds of these handkerchiefs hang dangling from pegs outside the windows or flaunting from the doorposts; and the shelves, within, are piled with them.

CHARLES DICKENS, *Oliver Twist*, 1837–8

Chancery Lane

LONDON. Michaelmas Term lately over, and the Lord Chancellor sitting in Lincoln's Inn Hall. Implacable November weather. . . . Fog everywhere. Fog up the river, where it flows among green aits and meadows; fog down the river, where it rolls defiled among the tiers of shipping, and the waterside pollutions of a great (and dirty) city. Fog on the Essex marshes, fog on the Kentish heights. Fog creeping into the cabooses of collier-brigs; fog lying out on the yards, and hovering in the rigging of great ships; fog drooping on the gunwales of barges and small boats. Fog in the eyes and throats of ancient Greenwich pensioners, wheezing by the firesides of their wards; fog in the stem and bowl of the afternoon pipe of the wrathful skipper, down in his close cabin; fog cruelly pinching the toes and fingers of his shivering little 'prentice boy on deck. Chance people on the bridges peeping over the parapets into a nether sky of fog, with fog all round them, as if they were up in a balloon, and hanging in the misty clouds. . . .

The raw afternoon is rawest, and the dense fog is densest, and the muddy streets are muddiest, near that leaden-headed old obstruction, appropriate ornament for the threshold of a leaden-headed old corporation: Temple Bar. And hard by Temple Bar, in Lincoln's Inn Hall, at the very heart of the fog, sits the Lord High Chancellor in his High Court of Chancery.

CHARLES DICKENS, *Bleak House,* 1852–3

St. Paul's

. . . the stones of St. Paul's flew like granados, ye mealting lead running downe the streetes in a streame, and the very pavements glowing with fiery rednesse, so as no horse nor man was able to tread on them.

JOHN EVELYN, *Diary, 4 September 1666,* on the Great Fire of London

. . . I had just extinguished my candle and lain down, when a deep, low, mighty tone swung through the night. At first I knew it not; but it was uttered twelve times, and at the twelfth colossal hum and trembling knell, I said: 'I lie in the shadow of St. Paul's.'

CHARLOTTE BRONTË, *Villette,* 1853

. . . St Paul's Cathedral is the finest building that ever I did see,
There's no building can surpass it in the city of Dundee . . .

WILLIAM MCGONAGALL (1825/30–1902),
'Descriptive Jottings of London', *Poetic Gems,* 1953

The Thames nocturne of blue and gold
   Changed to a Harmony in grey:
   A barge with ochre-coloured hay
Dropt from the wharf: and chill and cold

The yellow fog came creeping down
   The bridges, till the houses' walls
   Seemed changed to shadows and St. Paul's
Loomed like a bubble o'er the town. . . .

> OSCAR WILDE, 'Impression du Matin',
> *Poems*, 1881

Sir Christopher Wren
Said, 'I am going to dine with some men.
If anybody calls
Say I am designing St. Paul's.'

> E. CLERIHEW BENTLEY,
> *Biography for Beginners*, 1905

Initial adoption of the universal fare of 2d immediately attracted to the railway the friendly nickname of the 'Two-penny Tube'. The name was used by the Daily Mail *as early as 4 August 1900, and within a month had appeared in the New York press, where it was said that 'all London seems to be as pleased with its latest novelty as a child would be with a toy.' London newspapers showed real enthusiasm in recording that 'the crowds swayed and surged to get on to the trains . . .'*

   . . . In the revival of the Gilbert and Sullivan comic opera 'Patience', the 'very delectable, highly respectable, three-penny bus young man' of the original 1881 performance, became the 'Twopenny Tube young man'.

> CHARLES E. LEE, *The Central Line*, 1974

Bank

Change for Northern line and for escalator
to Monument for Circle and District lines

The first reference to tea by a Briton is in a letter dated June 27th, 1615. It was written by a Mr. Wickham, and is in the archives of the Old East India Company. It appeared in the September 2nd–9th, 1658 issue of *Commonwealth Mercury*, 'That excellent . . . by all physitians approved, China drink, called by the Chineans, tcha, by other nations, tay or tee, is sold at the Sultaness Head, a cophee house in Sweetings Rents by the Royal Exchange, London.'

In this same issue of the *Commonwealth Mercury* was a report of the death of Oliver Cromwell.

WILLIAM KENT, *London in the News,* 1954

The world's first electric tube of the completely modern type was the Central London, opened in 1900 – as a brass-plate in a subway at Bank Station still commemorates – by Albert Edward, Prince of Wales, K.G., in the last year before he succeeded to the throne. This was the famous 'Tuppeny Tube', so called from the uniform fare which was charged for any distance up to a total of its five miles run from the Bank to Shepherd's Bush.

MICHAEL HARRISON, *London Beneath the Pavement,* 1961

Liverpool Street
Change for Circle, Hammersmith & City and Metropolitan lines

> Dear Mary,
>   Yes, it will be bliss
>   To go with you by train to Diss,
>   Your walking shoes upon your feet;
>   We'll meet, my sweet, at Liverpool Street.

JOHN BETJEMAN, letter to Lady Wilson, 'A Mind's
Journey to Diss', *A Nip in the Air,* 1974

. . . The Central London from Bank to Wood Lane, extended to Liverpool Street in 1912, was the highest class line because it went by Bond Street to the City. It was also regarded as a sort of health resort, because it was ventilated by the Ozonair system, which was meant to smell like the sea, and certainly did smell of something. Air came out of grilles at the ends of huge aluminium pipes and sent a health-giving breeze down the platforms which caused the crinkly glass shades which hung over the white tiled stations to move slightly. . . .

JOHN BETJEMAN, 'Coffee, Port and Cigars
on the Inner Circle', *The Times,* 24 May 1963

Bethnal Green

. . . and I by coach to Bednall green to Sir W. Riders to dinner – where a fine place, good lady, and their daughter Mrs. Middleton, a fine woman. A noble dinner and a fine merry walk with the ladies alone, after dinner in the garden, which is very pleasant. The greatest Quantity of Strawberrys I ever saw, and good. . . . This very house* was built by the blinde beggar of Bednall greene, so much talked of and sang in ballats (sic); but they say it was only some of the out-houses of it.

* Kirby Castle or Bethnal Green House. The blind beggar was reputed to be the son of Simon de Montfort.

SAMUEL PEPYS, *Diary, 26 June 1663*

It was a blind beggar, had long lost his sight,
He had a faire daughter of bewty most bright;
And many a gallant brave suiter had shee,
For none was so comely as pretty Bessee.

'The Beggar's Daughter of Bednall-Green', T. Percy's
Reliques of Ancient English Poetry, 1765

Rattling through the tunnel of the Central Line, I looked out furtively, affectionately, at my fellow passengers. Some had their eyes closed, some toyed with papers, some looked abstractedly upwards as if they were doing sums in their heads. Walls of black moss streamed past inches from the windows; looped cables, tool boxes. Each time the doors sighed open at a lighted station they let in a gust of subterranean wind. It tasted metallic, of burned carbon and newsprint – a warm, industrial mistral, as particular to the city as Big Ben or red buses. . . . Everyone aboard the carriage had mastered the trick of looking as if they were alone in an empty room. Everyone was travelling under sealed orders to a separate destination. In a fleeting conceit, I saw us all as members of the Underground, moving in secret through Occupied London, and for the first time on the trip, the city felt like home again.

JONATHAN RABAN, *Coasting, 1986*

Mile End

Change for District line

Being past Whitechappell and having left faire London . . . multitudes of Londoners left not me; but eyther to keepe a custome which many holde, that Mile-end is no walke without a recreation at Stratford Bow with Creame and Cakes, or else for love they beare toward me, or per-happes to make themselves merry.

Kemp's nine daies wonder. Performed in a daunce from London to Norwich . . . Written by himself to satisfie his friends, 1600

. . . we are, not absolutely in Whitechapel itself, but at the entrance of that peculiar and characteristic district, which I take to be bounded by Mile-end gate on the east, and by the establishment of Messrs. Moses and Son on the west.

First, Moses. Gas, splendour, wealth, boundless and immeasurable, at a glance. Countless stories of gorgeous show-rooms, laden to reple-tion with rich garments. Gas everywhere. Seven hundred burners, they whisper to me. The tailoring department; the haberdashery department; the hat, boots, shawl, outfitting, cutlery department. Hundreds of departments. Legions of 'our young men' in irreproach-able coats, and neckcloths void of reproach. Corinthian columns, enriched cornices, sculptured panels, arabesque ceilings, massive chan-deliers, soft carpets of choice patterns, luxury, elegance, the riches of a world, the merchandize of two, everything that anybody ever could want, from a tin shaving-pot to a Cashmere shawl. Astonishing cheap-ness – wonderful celerity – enchanting civility! Great is Moses of the Minories!

G.A. SALA, *Humorous Papers,* 1872

Stratford

Ther was also a Nonne, a Prioresse,
That of hir smylyng was ful symple and coy;
Her gretteste ooth was but by Seinte Loy;
And she was cleped madame Eglentyne.

Ful weel she soong the service dyvyne,
Entuned in hir nose ful semely;
And Frenssh she spak ful faire and fetisly,
After the scole of Stratford atte Bowe,
For Frenssh of Parys was to hire unknowe.

GEOFFREY CHAUCER, General Prologue to
The Canterbury Tales, c. 1387

Leyton

It . . . was generally accepted that Leyton is the same as the ancient Roman station called Darolitum, though some antiquaries fix that at Romford. The discovery of coins, bricks, and pottery of Roman work here would seem to show that it was a place of some importance during the period of the Roman occupation.

E. WALFORD, *Greater London,* 1882–4

Leytonstone
Change for Epping branch

John Drinkwater (1882–1937), poet and dramatist, was born in Leytonstone.

HAINAULT BRANCH
Turn to page 52 for Snaresbrook

Wanstead

I went to see *Sir Josiah Childs* prodigious cost in planting walnut trees about his seate [Wanstead House], and making fish-ponds, many miles in circuit, in *Epping Forest*, in a barren spot, as oftentimes these suddainly monied men seate themselves.

JOHN EVELYN, *Diary, 16 March 1683*

[Wanstead House] . . . having added to the Advantage of its Situation innumerable Rows of Trees, planted in curious Order for Avenues and

Vista's, all leading up to the Place where the old House stood as to a Centre. . . . The Green-House is an excellent Building fit to entertain a Prince, 'tis furnish'd with Stoves, and artificial Places for Heat from an Apartment, in which are a Bagnio, and other Conveniences, which render it both useful and pleasant; and these Gardens have been so much the just Admiration of the Publick. . . . The House is built since these Gardens have been finish'd: the Building is all of *Portland* Stone in the front, which makes it look extremely splendid and Magnificent at a Distance; it being the particular Property of that Stone, except in the Streets of London, where it is tainted and ting'd with the Smoke of the City, to grow Whiter and Whiter the longer it stands in the open Air.

DANIEL DEFOE, *A Tour thro' the Whole Island of Great Britain*, 1738

Redbridge

Redbridge gets its name from the old red bridge over the River Roding.

Gants Hill

The most striking feature [of Gants Hill Station] occurs at the foot of the escalators, at platform level where the 'Moscow' concourse used for the Metropolitan at Kings Cross was again a major inspiration. . . . The work had been planned by Oliver Hill, and it earned him the Festival of Britain award for architectural merit in 1951.

LAURENCE MENEAR, *London's Underground Stations*, 1983

Newbury Park

A man went to Newbury Park
Expecting a bit of a lark.
'It's one of those places
I thought would have races –
I see I'm quite wide of the mark.'

JOHN GRIMSHAW, 1994

Barkingside

Barkingside is an altogether charming station. One can sit here on a misty day hearing nothing but birdsong and almost imagine that the peace will only be disturbed by the arrival of a steam train. Those illusions are shattered by the appearance of a standard tube train fresh from its journey under the centre of London.

LAURENCE MENEAR, *London's Underground Stations*, 1983

Fairlop

The Fairlop fair was founded by Daniel Day, who was born in Southwark in 1683 and was the owner of a small estate at Hainault. An eccentric extrovert, Day used to visit his estate on the first Friday in July for the purpose of collecting the rents from his tenants. He invariably took the opportunity provided by this occasion to entertain his friends, whom he regaled with beans and bacon under the spreading canopy of the Fairlop oak in Hainault Forest. This annual function developed into the Fairlop fair, and long before Day's death had ceased to be a private affair. The oak itself had a girth of thirty-six feet and was virtually destroyed by fire in June, 1805, the gutted trunk finally yielding to the elements when it was blown down by a gale in February 1820. . . . The timber from the old tree still survives, for from it was fashioned the pulpit of St. Pancras Church. As for Day himself, he died in 1767 and was buried in a coffin also made from a bough of the celebrated oak.

KENNETH NEALE, *Discovering Essex in London*, 1970

Hainault

With human bellow, bovine blare,
Glittering trumpery, gaudy ware,
The life of Romford market-square
Set all our pulses pounding:
The gypsy drover with his stick,
The huckster with his hoary trick,
The pork with fat six inches thick
And sausages abounding:

Stalls of apples, stacks of cake,
Piles of kippers, haddocks, hake,
Great slabs of toffee that men make,
Which urchins eye and pray for:
Divine abundance! glorious day!
We stayed as long as we could stay,
Then upped our loads and went our way
With all that we could pay for. . . .

Threading the silent, mist bedewed
And darkening thicks of Hainault Wood,
We reached that cottage, low and rude,
Which was so dear a dwelling;
By the black yew, solemn and still,
Under the brow of Crabtree Hill;
Ah dear it was, and ever will
Be dear beyond all telling.

Dry hornbeam twigs roared up in flame,
The kettle quivered to the same,
When home the weary parents came
The sausages were frying;
The tea was brewed, the toast was brown –
We chattered of our day in town;
Outside the leaves went whispering down,
And autumn owls were crying. . . .

RUTH PITTER, 'Romford Market',
Poems 1926–66

Grange Hill

. . . passing that part of the Great Forest which we now call Heinault Forest [near Grange Hill], came into that which is now the Great Road, a little on this side the Whalebone; a Place on the Road so called, because a Rib-bone of a great Whale, which was taken in the River of Thames the Year that Oliver Cromwel died, 1658, was fixed there for a Monument of that monstrous Creature, it being at first about eight and twenty Foot long.

DANIEL DEFOE, *A Tour thro' the Whole Island of Great Britain*, 1738

Chigwell

Chigwell, my dear fellow, is the greatest place in the world. Name your day for going. Such a delicious old inn opposite the churchyard – such a lovely ride, such beautiful forest scenery – such an out-of-the-way, rural, place – such a sexton! I say again, name your day.

CHARLES DICKENS, letter to John Forster, 25 March 1841

The day was named at once. . . . His promise was exceeded by our enjoyment; and his delight in the double recognition, of himself and of *Barnaby*, by the landlord of the nice old inn, far exceeded any pride he would have taken in what the world thinks the highest sort of honour.

JOHN FORSTER, *The Life of Charles Dickens*, 1872–4

Roding Valley

Ilford Bridge was the limit of commercial navigation on the Roding. . . . A considerable trade was done in timber, coal, gravel, cement and sand, but this declined sharply in the 1920s and the barge traffic ceased about 1930.

The London Encyclopaedia edited by Ben Weinreb
and Christopher Hibbert, 1983

EPPING BRANCH

It was a cold, dry, and dusty morning, and that the huntsmen of the east were all abroad by nine o'clock, trotting, fair and softly, down the road, on great nine-hand skyscrapers, nimble daisy-cutting nags, flowing-tailed chargers, and ponies no bigger than the learned one at Astley's. . . . Every gentleman was arrayed after his own particular taste, in blue, brown, or black – in dress-coats, long coats, short coats, frock coats, great coats, and no-coats; in drab-slacks, and slippers; – in gray tights, and black-spurred Wellingtons; in nankeen bomb-balloons; – in city-white cotton-cord unmentionables, with jockey toppers, and in Russian-drill down-belows, as a memento to the late czar. The ladies all wore a goose-skin under-dress, in compliment to the north-easter.

At that far-famed spot, the brow above Fairmead bottom, by twelve o'clock, there were not less than three thousand merry lieges then and there assembled . . . Fair dames 'in purple and in pall', reposed in vehicles. . . .

But where the deuce is the stag all this while? One o'clock, and no stag. TWO o'clock, and no stag! . . . *Precisely at half-past two o'clock the stag-cart was seen coming over the hill by the Baldfaced Stag, and hundreds of horsemen and gig-men rushed gallantly forward to meet and escort it to the top of Fairmead bottom, amidst such whooping and hallooing, as made all the forest echo again.* . . . *For a moment, all was deep, silent, breathless anxiety; and the doors of the cart were thrown open, and out popped a strapping four-year-old red buck, fat as a porker with a chaplet of flowers round his neck, a girth of divers coloured ribbons, and a long pink and blue streamer depending from the summit of his branching horns.* . . .

Presently, he caught a glimpse of the hounds and the huntsmen, waiting for him at the bottom, and in an instant off he bounded. . . . *Then might be seen, gentlemen running about without their horses, and horses galloping about without their gentlemen; and hats out of number brushed off their owners' heads by the rude branches of the trees; and everybody asking which way the stag was gone and nobody knowing anything about him; and ladies beseeching gentlemen not to be too venturesome; and gentlemen gasping for breath at the thoughts of what they were determined to venture; and myriads of people on foot running hither and thither in search of little eminences to look from, and yet nothing at all to be seen, though more than enough to be heard; for every man, and every woman too, made as loud a noise as possible. Meanwhile the stag followed by the keepers and about six couple of hounds, took away through the covers towards Woodford. Finding himself too near the haunts of his enemy, man, he there turned back, sweeping down the bottom for a mile or two, and away up the enclosures towards Chingford; where he was caught nobody knows how, for everybody returned to town, except those who stopped to regale afresh, and recount the glorious perils of the day. Thus ended the* Easter Hunt *of 1826.*

'SIMON YOUNGBUCK', *Morning Herald,* Easter Monday, 1826, describing the
Epping Hunt, quoted in William Hone, *The Everyday Book,* 1830

Snaresbrook

[Snaresbrook] has retained its identity largely because in 1856 the Great Eastern Railway gave that name to its new station at the bottom of Wanstead High Street. The earlier focal point had been the Spread Eagle coaching inn on the Woodford Road. . . . Now the Eagle, it still retains something of its former elegance.

The London Encyclopaedia edited by Ben Weinreb
and Christopher Hibbert , 1983

South Woodford

We have all been through much together, and I am honoured to have represented you in Parliament [for Wanstead and Woodford] for so long. You have all shown a kindness and a support to my wife and myself through the years of war and peace that have been a joy, a comfort and a source of strength. We are both very proud to be Freemen of this great Borough. Long may it prosper in peace and happiness.

SIR WINSTON CHURCHILL to his constituents on the occasion of the Borough's Silver Jubilee, September 1962

Woodford

Change for Hainault branch
Turn to page 51 for Roding Valley

About the year 1629, and the 34th of his Age, Mr. *Herbert* was seized with a sharp *Quotidian Ague*, and thought to remove it by the change of Air; to which end, he went to *Woodford* in Essex, but thither more chiefly, to enjoy the company of his beloved Brother, Sir *Henry Herbert*, and other Friends then of that Family. In his House he remain'd about Twelve Months and there became his own Physitian, and cur'd himself of his Ague, by forbearing Drink, and not eating any Meat, no not Mutton, nor a Hen, or Pidgeon, unless they were salted.

IZAAK WALTON, *The Life of Mr George Herbert*, 1670

Buckhurst Hill

I love the Forest and its airy bounds,
Where friendly Campbell takes his daily rounds;
I love the breakneck hills, that headlong go,
And leave me high, and half the world below,
I love to see the Beech Hill mounting high,
The brooks without a bridge, and nearly dry,
There's Bucket's Hill, a place of furze and clouds,
Which evening in a golden blaze enshrouds.

JOHN CLARE, 'A Walk in the Forest' from poems
written at High Beech, Epping, 1837–41

Loughton

The parishers of Loughton were given the right by Queen Elizabeth I to lop wood from trees seven feet from the ground (the lower branches being left for deer to feed on) from the 11th November till 23rd April for winter fuel.

To retain this right they had to lop a bough before midnight on 11th November – failing to do so would lose them their lopping rights for ever.

On the 11th of November 1859 an agent for the Lord of the Manor named Richardson (also called The Bulldog) ordered a dinner at the King's Head Loughton and invited all the loppers. The wine flowed freely and all got drunk, all except old Thomas Willingale who had been warned by a lawyer, Mr. Buxton, not to touch any drink. Tom took his axe with him, went to Staples Road, lopped the bough and returned to the King's Head on the stroke of midnight, thereby saving the lopping rights.

For 16 years old Tom defied the Lord of the Manor and lopped wood, which he sold the parishers, from his woodyard in Whitaker Way, Baldwyns Hill. . . . Willingale Road and School are named after old Tom.

WALTER BULLEN, great-grandson of Thomas Willingale, 'The condensed history of Epping Forest & the Willingale Family' quoted in Barbara Pratt, *The Loppers of Loughton*, 1981

Debden

Debden, variously recorded in bygone days, in different chronicles, as Depden, Deepden, Depdon, Dependon, Dependana, Dependin, from Saxon words all of which mean 'a valley'.

W.G. RAMSEY with R.L. FOWKES, *Epping Forest Then and Now*, 1986

Debden is recorded as Deppendana in the Domesday Book. It is derived from the Old English *deb* 'deep' and *den* 'valley' – which means simply 'the deep valley'.

CYRIL M. HARRIS, *What's in a Name?*, 1977

Theydon Bois

I was born and bred in its neighbourhood, and when I was a boy and young man I knew it yard by yard from Wanstead to the Theydons and from Hale End to the Fairlop Oak. . . . The special character of it was derived from the fact that by far the greater part was a wood of horn-beams, a tree not common save in Essex and Herts. It was certainly the biggest hornbeam wood in these islands and I suppose in the world. . . . It has a peculiar charm not to be found in any other forest.

WILLIAM MORRIS quoted by J.W. Mackail in
The Life of William Morris, 1899

Epping

So we went to our Inn, and after eating of something, and kissed the daughter of the house, she being very pretty, we took leave; and so that night, the road pretty good but the weather rainy, to Eping. Where we sat and played a game at draughts; and after supper and some merry talk with a plain bold maid of the house, we went to bed.

Up in the morning. . . . Then to horse and for London through the Forrest, where we found the way good. . . .

SAMUEL PEPYS, *Diary, 27–8 February 1660*

Oh, take me from the busy crowd,
   I cannot bear the noise.
For Nature's voice is never loud;
   I seek for quiet joys. . . .

And quiet Epping pleases well,
   Where Nature's love delays;
I joy to see the quiet place,
   And wait for better days.

JOHN CLARE, 'Sighing for Retirement' from poems
written at High Beech, Epping, 1837–41

North Weald

There was a tube map on the station platform just as there had always
been on stations. Victor didn't bother to look at it because the indicator
informed him that the next train due would be going to Epping. It
wasn't quite at the extreme other end of the Central Line but almost.
A small subsidiary line went on to North Weald and Ongar during the
rush hours. He stood on the platform with a return ticket for Epping in
his pocket, waiting for the train that would go no further than Epping.
. . . The journey was long and slow, for the line soon entered the
tunnel, and would not emerge again till the eastern edge of London.
Victor had bought *Ellery Queen's Mystery Magazine* and *Private Eye* to
read. . . . The train finally emerged from the tunnel after Leyton.
Victor had never been this far along the line before. This was deepest
suburbia, the view being of the backs of houses with long gardens full
of grass and flowers and pear trees in bloom running down to the
track. Four more stations of this sort of thing and then, after Buckhurst
Hill, a burst of countryside, part of the Green Belt encircling London.
Loughton, Debden, and what seemed to be an enormous estate of
council houses with industrial areas. The train came out into more or
less unspoiled country again, slowed and drew to a stop. The station
was Theydon Bois.

RUTH RENDELL, *Live Flesh*, 1986

Ongar

The founder of Boodle's Club in St James's is buried outside the Norman church of Ongar, the composer of 'Twinkle Twinkle Little Star',
Jane Taylor, in the vestry.

And they disperse to places far out on the reaches of the Central Line –
places with unlikely names like Chipping On-gar – places presumably
out on the Essex marshes, totally uninhabited except for a few rather
rangy marsh birds mournfully pacing the primeval slime.

JONATHAN MILLER in 'Beyond the Fringe', 1960

Sir John Betjeman once expressed a wish to 'retire from all poetry and
journalism and become the station-master at Ongar'.

FRANK DELANEY, *Betjeman Country*, 1983

CIRCLE LINE

Round *about*
And round *about*
And round *about I go.*

A.A. MILNE, 'Busy', *Now We Are Six*, 1927

King's Cross St. Pancras
Change for Hammersmith & City, Metropolitan, Northern,
Piccadilly and Victoria lines

King's Cross!
What shall we do?
His Purple Robe
Is rent in two!
Out of his Crown
He's torn the gems!
He's thrown his Sceptre
Into the Thames!
The Court is shaking
In its shoe –
King's Cross!
What shall we do?
Leave him alone
For a minute or two.

ELEANOR FARJEON,
Nursery Rhymes of London Town, 1916

Farringdon

In mid-Victorian times [Farringdon Market] was celebrated for its cress. Mayhew paints a pathetic picture of the little watercress girls, some no more than seven years old, haggling with the saleswomen before dawn, then shivering in their cotton dresses and threadbare shawls as they tied up the bunches and washed the leaves at the pump before going out into the streets crying: 'Water-creases, four bunches a penny, water-creases!' On an average day they would make 3d or 4d.

The London Encyclopaedia edited by Ben Weinreb
and Christopher Hibbert, 1983

PUBLIC OPENING OF THE METROPOLITAN RAILWAY

On Saturday, from as early an hour as six o'clock in the morning until late at night, trains filled with people were running at short intervals of time between Paddington and Farringdon-street. It soon became apparent that the locomotive power and rolling stock at the disposal of the company was by no means in proportion to the requirements of the opening day. From eight o'clock or nine o'clock every station became crowded with intending travellers, who were admitted in sections; but poor were the chances of a place to those who ventured to take their tickets at any mid-way station, the occupants being, with but very rare exceptions, 'long distance' or terminus passengers. However, the crowding at King's-cross was immense. This station is certainly the finest on the line, throwing even the termini into the shade. Here the constant cry, as the trains arrived of 'No room!' appeared to have a very depressing effect upon those assembled. Between eleven and twelve at this station, and continuously for the space of an hour and a half, the money-takers refused to take money for passengers between King's-cross and Farringdon-street, but they issued tickets between that station and Paddington, and many, whose destination were Cityward, determined to ride on the railway on its first day of opening, took tickets for the opposite direction, in order to secure places for the return journey.

Daily Telegraph, 12 January 1863

Barbican

. . . under Henry III, the hostile Londoners built or strengthened several watch-towers, only to be forced to dismantle them after the king's triumph. . . . In 1377, with all the perils of a regency and a French invasion, it was decided to equip the gates with chains, portcullises and outer barbicans.

TIMOTHY BAKER, *Mediaeval London*, 1970

John Milton lived in the Barbican between 1645 and 1649. *L'Allegro* and *Comus* were probably written at this time. He was buried in St Giles without Cripplegate in the Barbican in 1674.

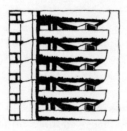

Moorgate
Change for Northern line

Often I longed to be in love; but I was already in love with London, and although too shy to go into pubs – and hating anyway the taste of beer – I would listen to the rattle of dominoes among the coffee tables of the Mecca as far north as Moorgate, and obscurely feel my passion.

V.S. PRITCHETT, *A Cab at the Door*, 1968

Snow falls in the buffet of Aldersgate station,
    Soot hangs in the tunnel in clouds of steam.
City of London! before the next desecration
    Let your steepled forest of churches be my theme. . . .

Snow falls in the buffet of Aldersgate station,
    Toiling and doomed from Moorgate Street puffs the train,
For us of the steam and the gas-light, the lost generation,
    The new white cliffs of the City are built in vain.

JOHN BETJEMAN, 'Monody on the Death of Aldersgate Street Station', *Collected Poems*, 1958

Liverpool Street
Change for Central, Hammersmith & City and Metropolitan lines

After leaving the office I would travel either to Sloane Square or to Liverpool Street to have a drink in the station buffet. In the whole extension of the Underground system those two stations are, as far as I've been able to discover, the only ones which have bars actually upon the platform. The concept of the tube station platform bar excited me. In fact the whole Underground region moved me, I felt as if it were in some sense my natural home. These two bars were not just a cosy after-the-office treat, they were the source of a dark excitement, places of profound communication with London, with the sources of life, with the caverns of resignation to grief and to mortality. Drinking there between six and seven in the shifting crowd of rush-hour travellers, one could feel on one's shoulders as a curiously soothing yoke the weariness of toiling London. . . . The uncertainty of the order of the trains. The dangerousness of the platform. (Trains are lethal weapons.) The resolution of a given moment (but which?) to lay down your glass and mount the next train. . . . the stations, each unique, the sinister brightness of Charing Cross, the mysterious gloom of Regent's Park, the dereliction of Mornington Crescent, the futuristic melancholy of Moorgate, the monumental ironwork of Liverpool Street, the twining *art nouveau* of Gloucester Road, the Barbican sunk in a baroque hole, fit subject for Piranesi. And in the summer, like an excursion into the country, the flowering banks of the Westbound District Line . . . I loved the Inner Circle best.

IRIS MURDOCH, *A Word Child*, 1975

Aldgate

Know ye that we, with unanimous will and assent, have granted and released by these presents unto Geoffrey Chaucer the whole of the dwelling house above the gate of Algate, with the rooms built over, and a certain cellar beneath, the same gate, on the South side of that gate, and the appurtenances thereof, unto the aforesaid Geoffrey, for the whole life of him, the said Geoffrey.

Corporation of London Records Office, Letter-Book G, Fo. cccxxi,
part of the lease granting the whole of the house above
Aldgate to the poet Chaucer in 1374

For when thy labour doon al ys,
And hast mad alle thy rekenynges,
In stede of reste and newe thynges,
Thy goost hom to thy hous anoon,
And, also domb as any stoon,
Thou sittest at another book
Tyl fully daswed ys thy look,
And lyvest thus as an heremite,
Although thyn abstynence ys lyte . . .

GEOFFREY CHAUCER, *The House of Fame*, describing his life in the house
above Aldgate between 1374 and 1385

Tower Hill
Change for District line

Jane called us up, about 3 in the morning, to tell us of a great fire they
saw in the City. . . . So I made myself ready presently, and walked to
the Tower and there got up upon one of the high places . . . and there I
did see the houses at that end of the bridge all on fire, and an infinite
great fire on this. . . . So down, with my heart full of trouble, to the
Lieutenant of the Tower, who tells me that it begun this morning in
the King's bakers house in Pudding Lane. . . . So I down to the water-
side and there got a boat and through the bridge, and there saw a lam-
entable fire. . . . Everybody endeavouring to remove their goods, and
flinging into the River or bringing them into lighters that lay off. Poor
people staying in their houses as long as till the very fire touched them,
and then running into boats or clambering from one pair of stairs by
the waterside to another. And among other things, the poor pigeons I
perceive were loath to leave their houses, but hovered about the windows and balconies till they were some of them burned, their wings

and fell down. . . . I observed that hardly one lighter or boat in three that had goods of a house in, but there was a pair of virginalls in it . . . I away to Whitehall by appointment . . . and walked to my boat, and there upon the water again, and to the fire up and down, it still increasing and the wind great. So near the fire as we could for smoke; and all over the Thames, with one's face in the wind you were almost burned with a shower of Firedrops . . . and saw the fire grow; and as it grow darker, appeared more and more, and in Corners and upon steeples and between churches and houses, as far as we could see up the hill of the City, in a most horrid malicious bloody flame, not like the fine flame of an ordinary fire. . . . We stayed till, it being darkish, we saw the fire as only one entire arch of fire from this to the other side of the bridge, and in a bow up the hill, for an arch of above a mile long. It made me weep to see it.

SAMUEL PEPYS, *Diary, Lords Day, 2 September 1666*

Monument

Change for escalator to Bank station for Central
and Northern lines

The Monument, designed by Christopher Wren, commemorates the great fire of London of 1666.

. . . After dinner I sauntered in a pleasing humour to London Bridge, viewed the Thames's silver expanse and the springy bosom of the surrounding fields. I then went up to the top of the Monument. This is a most amazing building. It is a pillar two hundred feet high. In the inside, a turnpike stair runs up all the way. When I was about half way up, I grew frightened. I would have come down again, but thought I would despise myself for my timidity. Thus does the spirit of pride get the better of fear. I mounted to the top and got upon the balcony. It was horrid to find myself so monstrous a way up in the air, so far above London and all its spires. I durst not look round me. There is no real danger, as there is a strong rail both on the stair and balcony. But I shuddered, and as every heavy wagon passed down Gracechurch Street, dreaded that the shaking of the earth would make the tremendous pile tumble to the foundation. . . .

JAMES BOSWELL, *London Journal*, 2 April 1763

In the churches about Mark-lane . . . there was a dry whiff of wheat; and I accidentally struck an airy sample of barley out of an aged hassock in one of them. From Rood-lane to Tower-street, and thereabouts, there was often a subtle flavour of wine: sometimes, of tea. One church near Mincing-lane smelt like a druggist's drawer. Behind the Monument, the service had a flavour of damaged oranges, which, a little further down towards the river, tempered into herrings, and gradually toned into a cosmospolitan blast of fish.

> CHARLES DICKENS in 'City of London Churches', *All the Year Round*,
> 5 May 1860, included in *The Uncommercial Traveller*, 1861

Cannon Street

Then his gaze swept over [London] bridge to what could be seen beyond . . . cavernous, immense, the great black arch of Cannon Street Station, and high above, far beyond, not in the city but in the sky and still softly shining in the darkening air, a ball and a cross. It was the very top of St Paul's, seen above the roof of Cannon Street Station.

> J.B. PRIESTLEY, *Angel Pavement*, 1930

Certainly London fascinates . . . the earth is explicable – from her we came, and we must return to her. But who can explain Westminster Bridge Road or Liverpool Street in the morning – the City inhaling – or the same thoroughfares in the evening – the City exhaling her exhausted air? . . .

The Londoner seldom understands his city until it sweeps him, too, away from his moorings.

> E.M. FORSTER, *Howards End*, 1910

Mansion House

There was a dinner preparing at the Mansion House, and when I* peeped in at the grated kitchen window . . . my heart began to beat with hope that the Lord Mayor . . . would look out of an upper apartment and direct me to be taken in.

*Charles Dickens is here recollecting his own experience as a hungry nine-year-old.

> CHARLES DICKENS, 'Gone Astray', *Household Words*, 1853

April 30. Perfectly astounded at receiving an invitation for Carrie and myself from the Lord and Lady Mayoress to the Mansion House, to 'meet the Representatives of Trades and Commerce'. My heart beat like that of a schoolboy's. Carrie and I read the invitation over two or three times. I could scarcely eat my breakfast. I said – and felt it from the bottom of my heart – 'Carrie darling. I was a proud man when I led you down the aisle of the church on our wedding day; that pride will be equalled if not surpassed, when I lead my dear, pretty wife up to the Lord and Lady Mayoress at the Mansion House.'

GEORGE AND WEEDON GROSSMITH, *The Diary of a Nobody*, 1892

Blackfriars

And did you not hear of a jolly young waterman,
　Who at Blackfriars Bridge used for to ply;
And he feather'd his oars with such skill and dexterity,
　Winning each heart, and delighting each eye.
He look'd so neat, and he row'd so steadily:
The maidens all flock'd in his boat so readily,
And he ey'd the young rogues with so charming an air,
That this waterman ne'er was in want of a fare.

CHARLES DIBDIN, 'The Waterman', *The Songs of Charles Dibdin*, 1837

One of the loveliest glimpses of London I have ever seen is that which unfolds itself at night through the jet black arches of Blackfriars Bridge . . . the pin points of the Embankment lights curving round to Westminster across an oily expanse of Thames, the lights wavering in the water, and in the background, grey and sleeping, the tall buildings of the Embankment . . . a little oblong yellow tramcar moving slowly in the darkness. . . .

H.V. MORTON, *The Nights of London*, 1926

Temple

We then walked into the City, and then strolled about the Temple, which is a most agreeable place. You quit all the hurry and bustle of the City in Fleet Street and the Strand, and all at once find yourself in a pleasant academical retreat. You see good convenient buildings, handsome walks, you view the silver Thames. You are shaded by venerable trees. Crows are cawing above your head. Here and there you see a solitary bencher sauntering about.

JAMES BOSWELL, *London Journal*, 6 April 1763

I was born, and passed the first seven years of my life, in the Temple. Its church, its halls, its gardens, its fountain, its river, I had almost said – for in those young years, what was this king of rivers to me but a stream that watered our pleasant places? – these are of my oldest recollections. I repeat, to this day, no verses to myself more frequently, or with kindlier emotion, than those of Spenser, where he speaks of this spot:

'There when they came, whereas those bricky towers,
The which on Themmes brode aged back doth ride,
Where now the studious lawyers have their bowers,
There whylome wont the Templar knights to bide,
Till they decayed through pride.'

Indeed, it is the most elegant spot in the metropolis. What a transition for a countryman visiting London for the first time – the passing from the crowded Strand or Fleet Street, by unexpected avenues, into its magnificent ample squares, its classic green recesses!

CHARLES LAMB, 'The Old Benchers of the Inner Temple',
Essays of Elia, 1823

Embankment
Change for Bakerloo and Northern lines

I went crosse the Thames on the ice, now become so thick as to beare not only streetes of boothes, in which they roasted meate, and had divers shops of wares, quite acrosse as in a towne, but coaches, carts, and horses, passed over. I went from *Westminster stayres* to *Lambeth*, and dined with the Archbishop.

JOHN EVELYN, *Diary, 9 January 1684*

I determined to make my way down to the Embankment, and rest my eyes and cool my head by watching the variegated lights upon the river. Beyond comparison the night is the best time for this place; a merciful darkness hides the dirt of the waters, and the lights of this transition age, red, glaring orange, gas-yellow, and electric white, are set in shadowy outlines of every possible shade between grey and deep purple. Through the arches of Waterloo Bridge a hundred points of light mark the sweep of the Embankment, and above its parapet rise the towers of Westminster, warm grey against the starlight. The black river goes by with only a rare ripple breaking its silence, and disturbing the reflections of the lights that swim upon its surface.

H.G. WELLS, 'The Diamond Maker', *The Stolen Bacillus and Other Incidents*, 1895

Westminster

We left London on Saturday morning at 1/2 past 5 or 6, the 31st of July . . . we mounted the Dover Coach at Charing Cross. It was a beautiful morning. The city, St. Paul's, with the river and a multitude of little boats, made a most beautiful sight as we crossed Westminster Bridge. The houses were not overhung by their cloud of smoke, and they were spread out endlessly, yet the sun shone so brightly, with such a fierce light, that there was even something like the purity of one of Nature's own grand spectacles.

DOROTHY WORDSWORTH, *The Journals*, 1802

CIRCLE LINE

Earth has not anything to show more fair:
Dull would he be of soul who could pass by
A sight so touching in its majesty:
This City now doth, like a garment, wear
The beauty of the morning; silent, bare,
Ships, towers, domes, theatres, and temples lie
Open unto the fields, and to the sky;
All bright and glittering in the smokeless air.
Never did sun more beautifully steep
In his first splendour, valley, rock, or hill;
Ne'er saw I, never felt, a calm so deep!
The river glideth at his own sweet will:
Dear God! the very houses seem asleep;
And all that mighty heart is lying still!

WILLIAM WORDSWORTH, 'Composed upon
Westminster Bridge, September 3, 1802'

The actors know their parts. The public crowd who wait for the Speaker's Procession which passes every day through the light Central Hall [of Westminster] have a homely and ludicrous look in this gay Gothic setting; for the defect of a Gothic background is that it makes twentieth-century man and woman look vulgar and pathetic. The scene may have been more tolerable in the Victorian age, when clothes were severer, or more elaborate than they are now; but even then one must have felt the human inadequacy in these surroundings. . . . But when, suddenly, a loud voice calls out, 'The Speaker', and another voice calls out sharply, 'Hats off', there is a silence in which one realizes that what is about to happen is not a joke at all. One is going to see the ghosts walk. One hears their rapid step. They go by in their black with the briskness of a dream and give a cold thrill for a second or two to the blood. Exactly at half past two, in perfect step, expressionless, chins a little raised, as if on some duty, exalted and exquisitely unnecessary, five men go by, dressed in black: the Sergeant-at-Arms; the mace-bearer, holding the mace before him; the wigged Speaker himself, in black silk knee-breeches and buckled shoes; his train-bearer, holding up his short robe; and his chaplain, bringing up the rear. A stir of air follows them. They have vanished. The strange moment, with no clowning in it, is eerie; it is one of London's brilliant little set pieces. In twenty seconds the 'thing' has been 'done'.

V.S. PRITCHETT, *London Perceived*, 1962

I love to think of bland Pall Mall
(Where Charles made love to pretty Nell)
And rich South Audley Street, and Wapping,
And Bond Street, and the Christmas shopping.
Knightsbridge, the Inner Circle train,
And Piccadilly and Park Lane.

DOUGLAS GOLDRING, 'In Praise of London',
Streets and Other Verses, 1920

St. James's Park

Me thinks I see the love that shall be made,
The Lovers walking in that Amorous shade,
The Gallants dancing by the Rivers side,
They bath in Summer, and in Winter slide.
Methinks I hear the Musick in the boats,
And the loud Eccho which returns the notes,
Whilst over head a flock of new sprung fowle
Hangs in the aire, and does the Sun controle:
Darkning the aire they hover o'er, and shrowd
The wanton Saylors with a feather'd cloud.
The Ladies angling in the Cristal lake,
Feast on the water with the prey they take.
A thousand Cupids on the billows ride,
And Sea-nimphs enter with the swelling tyde . . .

EDMUND WALLER, *A Poem on St James's Park*
As lately improved by his Maiesty, 1661

Victoria

Change for Victoria line

LADY BRACKNELL: Found!

JACK: The late Mr. Thomas Cardew, an old gentleman of a very charitable and kindly disposition, found me, and gave me the name of Worthing, because he happened to have a first-class ticket for Worthing in his pocket at the time. Worthing is a place in Sussex. It is a seaside resort.

LADY BRACKNELL: Where did the charitable gentleman who had a first-class ticket for this seaside-resort find you?

JACK (gravely): In a hand-bag.

LADY BRACKNELL: A hand-bag?

JACK (very seriously): Yes, Lady Bracknell. I was in a hand-bag – a somewhat large, black leather hand-bag, with handles to it – an ordinary hand-bag in fact.

LADY BRACKNELL: In what locality did this Mr James, or Thomas, Cardew come across this ordinary hand-bag?

JACK: In the cloakroom at Victoria Station. It was given to him in mistake for his own.

LADY BRACKNELL: The cloak-room at Victoria Station?

JACK: Yes. The Brighton line.

LADY BRACKNELL: The line is immaterial. Mr Worthing, I confess I feel somewhat bewildered by what you have just told me. To be born, or at any rate bred, in a hand-bag, whether it had handles or not, seems to me to display a contempt for the ordinary decencies of family life that reminds one of the worst excesses of the French Revolution. And I presume you know what that unfortunate movement led to? As for the particular locality in which the hand-bag was found, a cloak-room at a railway station might serve to conceal a social indiscretion – has probably, indeed, been used for that purpose before now – but it could hardly be regarded as an assured basis for a recognised position in good society. . . . You can hardly imagine that I and Lord Bracknell would dream of allowing our only daughter – a girl brought up with the utmost care – to marry into a cloak-room, and form an alliance with a parcel.

OSCAR WILDE, *The Importance of Being Earnest*, 1895

Sloane Square

Soames used the Underground again in going home. The fog was worse than ever at Sloane Square Station. Through the still, thick blur, men groped in and out; women, very few, grasped their reticules to their bosoms and handkerchiefs to their mouths; crowned with the weird excrescence of the driver, haloed by a vague glow of lamp-light that seemed to drown in vapour before it reached the pavement, cabs loomed dim-shaped ever and again, and discharged citizens bolting like rabbits to their burrows.

And these shadowy figures, wrapped each in his own little shroud of fog, took no notice of each other. In the great warren, each rabbit for himself, especially those clothed in the more expensive fur, who, afraid of carriages on foggy days, are driven underground.

JOHN GALSWORTHY, *The Man of Property*, 1906

They knew what they meant to do. They were going to have their money's worth, and far more than their money's worth, of underground travelling. Round and round and round and all for a penny fare. . . . This was a favourite occupation of theirs, a secret, morbid vice. They indulged in it at least twice every holidays. . . .

Sloane Square. Two penny fares. Down the stairs into the delicious, romantic, cool valley. The train thundered in. Inner Circle its style. A half empty compartment; there was small run on the underground this lovely August Sunday. Into it dashed the children; they had a corner seat each, next the open door. They bumped up and down on the seats, opposite each other. The train speeded off, rushing like a mighty wind. South Kensington station. More people coming in, getting out. Off again. Gloucester Road, High Street, Notting Hill Gate, Queen's Road. . . . The penny fare was well over. Still they travelled, and jogged up and down on the straw seats, and chanted softly, monotonously, so that they could scarcely be heard above the roaring of the train:

> *. . . Where great whales come sailing by,*
> *Sail and sail with unshut eye,*
> *Round the world for ever and aye,*
> *ROUND THE WORLD FOR EVER AND AYE . . .*

At Paddington they saw the conductor eyeing them, and changed their compartment. This should be done from time to time.

And so on, past King's Cross and Farringdon Street, towards the wild, romantic stations of the east: Liverpool Street, Aldgate, and so round the bend, sweeping west like the sun. Blackfriars, Temple, Charing Cross, Westminster, St James's Park, Victoria, SLOANE SQUARE. O joy! Sing for the circle completed, the new circle begun.

> *. . . Where great whales come sailing by . . .*
> *ROUND THE WORLD FOR EVER AND AYE . . .*

ROSE MACAULAY, *Told by an Idiot,* 1923

South Kensington
Change for Piccadilly line

It is no longer true to think of South Kensington as was the habit to think of it not long ago, as a region ineffably English, where afternoon tea, the Times crossword, dogs and dinner jackets each prevailed at their appointed hour; where military and civilian vertebrae from the backbone of the British Empire came to retirement in private hotels. . . .

NICOLAS BENTLEY in *Flower of Cities. A Book of London. Studies and Sketches by Twenty-two Authors,* 1949

. . . an elderly lady of ample proportions found it necessary to alight from a narrow 3rd class compartment in reverse, with her back to the platform. The guard saw her in this position, half in and half out of the compartment, and concluded that she was trying to board the train – so he gave her a helping push. It is said that she travelled the whole Inner Circle, being pushed back into the train at each station, before the guard realised his mistake.

HENRY HOWSON, *London's Underground,* 1951

Gloucester Road
Change for District and Piccadilly lines

Oh dear, and a very big 'oh dear' at that. Rumpole's occupation, that of making sure that citizens of all classes are not randomly convicted of crimes they didn't do just so that the prison statistics may look more impressive, seems to have fallen into disrepute. I felt more than usually unappreciated as I burrowed down the Gloucester Road tube on my mole-like journey to irritate the constabulary and pour sand in the gear-box of justice, and when I emerged, blinking, into the daylight of the Temple Station I was beginning to wonder if it was not time to abandon the up-hill struggle. Was it possible that Rumpole should retire from the Bar?

JOHN MORTIMER, 'Rumpole and the Age of Retirement',
The Trials of Rumpole, 1979

High Street Kensington

Where *Kensington* high o'er the neighb'ring lands
'Midst greens and sweets, a Regal fabrick stands,
And sees each spring, luxuriant in her bowers,
A snow of blossoms, and a wilde of flowers,
The Dames of Britain oft in crowds repair
To gravel walks, and unpolluted air.
Here, while the Town in damps and darkness lies,
They breathe in sun-shine, and see azure skies;
Each walk, with robes of various dyes bespread,
Seems from afar a moving Tulip-bed,
Where rich Brocades and glossy Damasks glow,
And Chints, the rival of the show'ry Bow.

THOMAS TICKELL, *Kensington Garden*, 1722

Notting Hill Gate
Change for Central line

'I'm glad you are so stalwart a defender of your old inviolate Notting Hill. Look up nightly to that peak, my child, where it lifts itself among the stars so ancient, so lonely, so unutterably Notting. So long as you are ready to die for the sacred mountain, even if it were ringed with all the armies of Bayswater – ' The King stopped suddenly, and his eyes shone.

'Perhaps,' he said, 'perhaps the noblest of all my conceptions. A revival of the arrogance of the old mediaeval cities applied to our glorious suburbs. Clapham with a city guard. Wimbledon with a city wall. Surbiton tolling a bell to raise its citizens. West Hampstead going into battle with its own banner. . . .'

G.K. CHESTERTON, *The Napoleon of Notting Hill*, 1904

Bayswater

A trick that everyone abhors
In Little Girls is slamming doors.
A Wealthy Banker's Little Daughter
Who lived in Palace Green, Bayswater
(By name Rebecca Offendort),
Was given to this Furious Sport.
She would deliberately go
And Slam the door like Billy-ho!
To make her Uncle Jacob start.
She was not really bad at heart,
But only rather rude and wild:
She was an aggravating child.

HILAIRE BELLOC, 'Rebecca, who slammed doors for fun and
perished miserably', *Cautionary Tales for Children*, 1907

Paddington
Change for Bakerloo and Hammersmith & City lines

The undergraduates of Oxford used Paddington; and so did Public
Schools at Eton, Radley, Marlborough, Shrewsbury, Malvern and the
now extinct Weymouth College; hunting people got out at Badminton;
carpet manufacturers at Kidderminster; coal owners at Cardiff, jewel-
lers at Birmingham; valetudinarians at Torquay, Leamington, Cheltenham, Tenbury Wells and Tenby, sailors at Plymouth, Devonport and
Falmouth; organists used it for the Three Choirs Festival at Worcester,
Hereford and Gloucester. The Welsh, who seem so often to be in trains,
use it all the time.

JOHN BETJEMAN, *London's Historic Railway Stations*, 1972

Mr. and Mrs. Brown first met Paddington on a railway platform. In
fact, that was how he came to have such an unusual name for a bear,
for Paddington was the name of the station.

The Browns were there to meet their daughter. . . . It was a warm
summer day and the station was crowded with people on their way to
the seaside. Trains were whistling, taxis hooting, porters rushing about
shouting at one another, and altogether there was so much noise that

Mr. Brown, who saw him first, had to tell his wife several times before she understood.

'A *bear*? On Paddington Station?' Mrs. Brown looked at her husband in amazement. 'Don't be silly, Henry. There can't be!' . . .

. . . The bear raised its hat politely – twice. 'I haven't really got a name,' he said. 'Only a Peruvian one which no one can understand.'

'Then we'd better give you an English one,' said Mrs. Brown. 'It will make things much easier.' She looked round the station for inspiration. 'It ought to be something special,' she said thoughtfully. As she spoke an engine standing in one of the platforms gave a loud whistle and let off a cloud of steam. 'I know what!' she exclaimed. 'We found you on Paddington Station so we'll call you Paddington!'

MICHAEL BOND, *A Bear Called Paddington*, 1958

. . . the fine flare of one of Mr W.H. Smith's bookstalls – a feature not to be omitted in my enumeration of the charms of Paddington and Euston. It is a focus of warmth and light in the vast smoky cavern; it gives the idea that literature is a thing of splendour, of a dazzling essence, of infinite gas-lit red and gold. A glamour hangs over the glittering booth and a tantalising air of clever new things. How brilliant must the books all be, how veracious and courteous the fresh, pure journals! Of a Saturday afternoon, as you wait in your corner of the compartment for the starting of the train, the window makes a frame for the glowing picture.

HENRY JAMES, *English Hours*, 1905

Edgware Road

Yesterday Mary Anne and I made our first trip down the 'Drain'. We walked to the Edgware Road and took first class tickets for King's Cross (6d each). We experienced no disagreeable odour, beyond the smell common to tunnels. The carriages hold ten persons, with divided seats, and are lighted by gas (two lights), they are also so lofty that a six footer may stand erect with his hat on. Trains run every 15 minutes from six in the morning till twelve at night (with some slight variation), and about 30,000 are conveyed on the line daily: shares have risen, and there is a prospect of a large dividend. Monday, 26 January 1863.

SIR WILLIAM HARDMAN, *A Mid-Victorian Pepys: The Letters and Memoirs of Sir William Hardman* edited by S.M. Ellis, 1923

Baker Street
Change for Bakerloo, Jubilee and Metropolitan lines

. . . At this moment there was a loud ring at the bell and I could hear Mrs. Hudson, our landlady, raising her voice in a wail of expostulation and dismay.

'By heavens, Holmes,' said I, half rising, 'I believe that they are really after us.'

'No, it's not quite so bad as that. It is the unofficial force – the Baker Street irregulars.'

As he spoke, there came a swift pattering of naked feet upon the stairs, a clatter of high voices, and in rushed a dozen dirty and ragged little street arabs. There was some show of discipline among them, despite their tumultuous entry, for they instantly drew up in line and stood facing us with expectant faces. One of their number, taller and older than the others, stood forward with an air of lounging superiority which was very funny in such a disreputable little scarecrow.

'Got your message, sir,' said he, 'and brought 'em on sharp. Three bob and a tanner for tickets.'

'Here you are,' said Holmes, producing some silver. 'In future they can report to you, Wiggins and you to me. I cannot have the house invaded in this way. . . .'

'. . . Look here, Watson; you look regularly done. Lie down there on the sofa, and see if I can put you to sleep.'

He took up his violin from the corner, and as I stretched myself out he began to play some low, dreamy, melodious air – his own, no doubt, for he had a remarkable gift for improvisation. I have a vague remembrance of his gaunt limbs, his earnest face and the rise and fall of his bow. Then I seemed to be floated peacefully away upon a soft sea of sound, until I found myself in dreamland. . . .

SIR ARTHUR CONAN DOYLE, *The Sign of Four*, 1890

During the Second World War, Baker Street housed the Headquarters of the SOE (Special Operations Executive), a secret service organisation from 1940 to 1946 organising underground warfare and sabotage against Germany and her allies.

Great Portland Street

. . . Another difficulty was ridding the tunnels of smoke from the steam engines which were used before the introduction of electric locomotion at the end of the century. Special engines were developed to condense the smoke, but the Metropolitan's cheery statement that the atmosphere in the tunnels was usually clear enough to enable drivers to see the signals cannot have been entirely reassuring. Nor did the general manager's suggestion that a visit to Great Portland Street station would bring instant relief to bronchitis sufferers carry much conviction.

ROBERT GRAY, *A History of London*, 1978

Euston Square

The ground behind the north-west end of Russell Street [i.e. Euston Square] was occupied by a farm occupied by two old maiden sisters of the name of Capper. They wore riding-habits, and men's hats; one rode an old grey mare, and it was her spiteful delight to ride with a large pair of shears after boys who were flying their kites, purposely to cut their strings; the other sister's business was to seize the clothes of the lads who trespassed on their premises to bathe.

J.T. SMITH, *A Book for a Rainy Day*, 1905 edition

It stood out . . . that when you came to look into things in a spirit of earnestness an immense deal could be done for very little more than your fare in the Underground.

HENRY JAMES, *What Maisie Knew*, 1897

DISTRICT LINE

Wimbledon

Great Wimbledon! You stand alone,
the queen of tennis on your throne,
with magic in your very name,
reaching world-wide with its fame,
history steeps your ivied walls,
echoing to the sound of balls . . .

And then at last the final roar
as one great player shuts the door
on his opponent, turns the latch
and wins triumphantly the match.
The crowd subsides, and peace descends
But not for long for soon it ends.
For soon again, with nerves strung taut,
Two other players walk on court.

H.W. 'BUNNY' AUSTIN* in *The BBC Book of Wimbledon Verse*
edited by Joanne Watson, 1987

*Wimbledon finalist twice and member of British Davis Cup Team, which won four times
in succession in the 1930's.

Wimbledon Park

. . . at last the great day dawned, with every Womble hard at work as
soon as the sun rose. . . . For the Midsummer party is the biggest, most
important and happiest occasion of the year.

At ten o'clock they all lined up outside the kitchen where Madame
Cholet, wearing a flowered apron, was doling out their party food. By
ten-thirty, with eyes shining and fur gleaming, they were lining up by
the main door, where Tomsk, looking very important, was on duty
with a list of names. At ten forty-five there was a rumbling noise and
Tobermory, wearing a flat cap, goggles and a long coat, appeared at the
wheel of the Silver Womble which bore the number plate: WOM 1.

He was shaking with excitement, but his face was dignified and grave as he picked up his first passengers, Great Uncle Bulgaria, Madame Cholet – now wearing a hat with flowers on it and a feather boa – Cousin Yellowstone, Bungo, Orinoco, Alderney and twenty-four of the youngest Wombles.

Slowly and very carefully the Silver Womble moved across Wimbledon Common beneath the golden light of the rising moon. Tobermory, who was always very thorough, had taken the time and trouble to study all the latest road maps, so he completed the journey to Battersea Park without a hitch, dropping his party at the gates at exactly midnight.

'Isn't it beautiful?' said Alderney.

'Not as good as Wimbledon though,' said Bungo.

ELISABETH BERESFORD, *The Wombles*, 1968

Underground overground wombling free
The Wombles of Wimbledon Common are we.

Wombles TV song

Southfields

George Eliot finished *The Mill on the Floss* whilst living at Holly Lodge, No. 31 Wimbledon Park Road [Southfields].

The London Encyclopaedia edited by Ben Weinreb
and Christopher Hibbert, 1983

East Putney

There was an Old Person of Putney,
Whose food was roast spiders and chutney,
  Which he took with his tea,
  Within sight of the sea,
That romantic Old Person of Putney.

EDWARD LEAR, *More Nonsense, Pictures,
Rhymes, Botany, etc.*, 1872

Putney Bridge

On the day appointed 'I came as one whose feet half linger'. It is but a few steps from the railway-station in Putney High Street to No. 2. The Pines. I had expected a greater distance to the sanctuary – a walk in which to compose my mind and prepare myself for initiation. I laid my hand irresolutely against the gate of the bleak trim front-garden. . . . Swinburne's entry was for me a great moment. Here, suddenly visible in the flesh, was the legendary being and divine singer . . . a strange small figure in grey, having an air at once noble and roguish, proud and skittish. My name was roared to him. In shaking his hand, I bowed low, of course – a bow *de coeur*; and he, in the old aristocratic manner, bowed equally low, but with such swiftness that we narrowly escaped concussion . . . he had the eyes of a god, and the smile of an elf. In figure, at first glance, he seemed almost fat; but this was merely because of the way he carried himself, with his long neck strained so tightly back that he all receded from the waist upwards. . . .

. . . Watts-Dunton leaned forward and 'Well, Algernon,' he roared, 'how was it on the Heath to-day?' Swinburne, who had meekly inclined his ear to the question, now threw back his head, uttering a sound that was like the cooing of a dove, and forthwith, rapidly, ever so musically, he spoke to us of his walk; spoke not in the strain of a man who had been taking his daily exercise on Putney Heath, but rather in that of a Peri who had at long last been suffered to pass through Paradise.

MAX BEERBOHM, 'No. 2. The Pines' in *And Even Now*, 1920,
originally written for Edmund Gosse in 1914

After dinner by water, the day being mighty pleasant and the tide serving finely – I up (reading in Boyles book of Colours) as high as Barne Elmes; and there took one turn alone, and then back to Putney Church, where I saw the girls of the schools, few of which pretty. . . . Here was a good sermon and much company, but I sleepy and a little out of order for my hat falling down through a hole underneath the pulpit; which however, after sermon, by a stick and the help of the clerk, I got up again.

SAMUEL PEPYS, *Diary, 28 April 1667*

Parsons Green

In a Village where I've been
They keep their Parson on a Green.
They tie him to a Juniper Tree
And bring him Currant Bread for tea.
A jollier man I've never seen
Than the one on Parson's Green.

ELEANOR FARJEON, *Nursery Rhymes of London Town*, 1916

Fulham Broadway

Our house was about equidistant from two big football grounds: Chelsea at Stamford Bridge and Fulham at Craven Cottage, whose teams were known respectively as the Pensioners and the Cottagers. Both grounds were and are in Fulham . . . it was thus that Roland and I observed from the front parlour window, on innumerable Saturday afternoons, the steady tramp of thousands and thousands of single-minded men along Gowan Avenue towards Walham Green if the important match of the week was at Chelsea's ground, or the other way towards Craven Cottage if it was at Fulham's. And on those days, and those only, there was an unbroken flow of one-way motor traffic, mainly taxicabs, hooting the trampers off the road and on to the footways.

. . . In the Fulham Road near the Fire Station a shop had been converted into a tiny cinema. . . . It was called the Parsons Green Moving Picture Theatre. . . . [It] seated an audience of thirty at the most, the front three rows of chairs being very small ones of the kind seen in nursery schools, and behind those (for the grown-ups) there were padded forms with no backs to them. Saturday performances started at 3 p.m. and the price of admission was twopence-halfpenny.

The music was provided by an old horn-type gramophone, operated by the ticket cashier, its horn protruding through a hole cut in the wall of the box-office. The films were all very short, and no doubt very old – they broke down many times in each performance. And at each breakdown a stout lady who always sat on a cushioned stool near the Exit . . . tugged at a little chain hanging from the gas-lamp near the door and, it seemed to our startled eyes, flooded the room with dazzling light.

C.H. ROLPH, *London Particulars*, 1980

West Brompton

It shone, pale amber, bluey-gray, and tenderly spacious and fine under clear autumnal skies, a London of hugely handsome buildings and vistas and distances, a London of gardens and labyrinthine tall museums, of old trees and remote palaces and artificial waters. I lodged near West Brompton at a house in a little square.

H.G. WELLS, *Tono-Bungay*, 1909

My walk to town to-day . . . was prodigiously hot: . . . it is two good miles, and just five thousand seven hundred and forty-eight steps; . . . When I pass the Mall in the evening it is prodigious to see the number of ladies walking there; and I always cry shame at the ladies of Ireland, who never walk at all, as if their legs were of no use, but to be laid aside. . . . Do you know that about our town we are mowing already and making hay, and it smells so sweet as we walk through the flowery meads; but the hay-making nymphs are perfect drabs, nothing so clean and pretty as further in the country. There is a mighty increase of dirty wenches in straw hats since I knew London.

JONATHAN SWIFT, from letter xxiii, 15–19 May 1711,
The Journal to Stella, 1768

Earl's Court

Change for Piccadilly line, other parts of the District line
and Kensington (Olympia) station

On 4 October 1911 Earl's Court received the first public escalators, or 'moving stairs', on the Underground. They linked the District platforms to the Piccadilly, but the public were wary of them and a man with a wooden leg, who was known as 'Bumper' Harris, was employed to ride up and down all day demonstrating how safe it was. Some old ladies were not encouraged in the slightest, because they had a suspicion about how Mr Harris had lost his other leg!

LAURENCE MENEAR, *London's Underground Stations*, 1983

The *Star* reported that the escalator was the greatest attraction in London: 'It opened yesterday, when it went like fun, and today even more so. The Underground officials were well pleased. They have got the moving staircase smile . . . but the greatest asset in the way of advertisement is a porter who acts as a "barker". As each Tube train runs into Earl's Court his showman's voice is heard announcing: "This way to the moving staircase! The only one of its kind in London! NOW running!" The lifts are also running, but they are practically deserted. Everybody wants to "stair" it.'

HUGH DOUGLAS, *The Underground Story*, 1963

High Street Kensington

The Albert Memorial, therefore, will not only be very beautiful, but also the most remarkable and interesting object in England, if not in Europe. . . . It stands in an elegant garden, and, with the Albert Hall, will make two magnificent objects, and still further ornament the already fine approach to Kensington.

ISABELLA BURT, *Historical Notices of Chelsea, Kensington, Fulham, and Hammersmith*, 1871

A service at St. Mary Abbots, Kensington. The red plumes and ribbon in two stylish girls' hats in the foreground match the red robes of the persons round Christ on the Cross in the east window. The pale crucified figure rises up from a parterre of London bonnets and artificial hair-coils, as viewed from the back where I am. The sky over Jerusalem seems to have some connection with the cornflowers in a fashionable hat that bobs about in front of the city of David. . . . When the congregation rises there is a rustling of silks like that of the Devils' wings in Paradise Lost. Every woman then, even if she had forgotten it before, has a single thought to the folds of her clothes. They pray in the litany as if under enchantment. Their real life is spinning on beneath this apparent one of calm, like the District Railway-trains underground just by – throbbing, rushing, hot, concerned with next week, last week.

THOMAS HARDY from his diary for 8 July 1888 quoted in *The Early Life of Thomas Hardy* by Florence E. Hardy

The Gardens are bounded on one side by a never-ending line of omnibuses. . . . There are more gates to the Gardens than one gate, but that is the one you go in at, and before you go in you speak to the lady with the balloons, who sits just outside. This is as near to being inside as she may venture, because, if she were to let go her hold of the rail ings for one moment, the balloons would lift her up, and she would be flown away. She sits very squat, for the balloons are always tugging at her, and the strain has given her quite a red face. . . . Returning up the Broad Walk we have on our right the Baby Walk, which is so full of perambulators that you could cross from side to side stepping on babies, but the nurses won't let you do it. . . .

. . . Well, Peter Pan got out by the window, which had no bars. Standing on the ledge he could see trees far away, which were doubtless the Kensington Gardens, and the moment he saw them he entirely forgot that he was now a little boy in a nightgown, and away he flew, right over the houses to the Gardens.

J.M. BARRIE, *The Little White Bird*, 1902

Notting Hill Gate
Change for Central line

. . . the Gaumont Cinema at Notting Hill Gate has a ghost, which the staff nicknamed 'Flora'. The cinema was originally the Coronet Theatre and the ghost is said to be the spirit of a cashier who was caught fiddling the box-office receipts in the 1900s. When confronted with the evidence of her misdemeanour by the Manager she ran from his office, climbed the stairs to the 'Gods', and threw herself to her death from the balcony. A report in the *Kensington Post* in 1969 tells how staff meetings were so disturbed by the ghost when they were held in a room in the upper, disused, part of the building, that they had to be transferred to an office in a more frequented part. Footsteps came from the stairs leading to the sealed-off Gods, and occasionally a pair of small brown shoes were seen, climbing the stairs by themselves. The haunting usually occurs during Christmas week.

J.A. BROOKS, *Ghosts of London*, 1982

Wyndham Lewis remarked to me that he, at any rate, as an author had 'never found it safe to live more than ten minutes away from Notting Hill Gate'.

GEOFFREY GRIGSON in *Coming to London*
edited by John Lehmann, 1957

Yet here fashionable people buy little pastel-coloured terraced houses, and the bell-bottomed and caftaned crew of flat-dwellers talk about the place in affectionate diminutives. It is, simply, 'The Gate', as Ladbroke Grove is 'The Grove' – as if they were living in some model village in Wiltshire with retired brigadiers behind every elmed drive. Notting Hill Gate incorporates a central paradox of city life, in that its nature is as prolific and untameable as anywhere in London, yet for some at least of its inhabitants it has been accommodated to an order so benign as to be cosy.

JONATHAN RABAN, 'The Magical City', *The Times*, 26 January 1974

Bayswater

He [James Forsyte] took the slanting path from the Bayswater side of the Row to Knightsbridge Gate, across a pasture of short, burnt grass, dotted with blackened sheep, strewn with seated couples and strange waifs lying prone on their faces, like corpses on a field over which the wave of battle has rolled.

J. GALSWORTHY, *The Man of Property*, 1906

Just after you have crossed the [Serpentine] bridge (whose very banisters, old and ornamental, of yellowish-brown stone, I am particularly fond of), you enjoy on your left, through the gate of Kensington Gardens as you go towards Bayswater, an altogether enchanting vista – a footpath over the grass, which loses itself beneath the scattered oaks and elms exactly as if the place were a 'chase'. There could be nothing less like London in general than this particular morsel, and yet it takes London, of all cities, to give you such an impresssion of the country.

HENRY JAMES, *English Hours*, 1905

Paddington
Change for Bakerloo and Hammersmith & City lines

And yet, and yet . . . tomorrow I am going to London, and there is the old excitement, the prospect of so many pleasures, as the train noses its way under the Victorian roof of Paddington. Perhaps I have always been happy there, after all.

SUSAN HILL in *Living in London* edited by Alan Ross, 1974

This day, according to annual custom, bread and cheese were thrown from Paddington steeple to the populace, agreeable to the will of two women who were relieved there with bread and cheese when they were almost starved; and providence afterwards favouring them, they left an estate in that parish to continue the custom for ever on that day.

The London Magazine, 18 December 1737, quoted in *London in the News Through Three Centuries* by William Kent, 1954

Edgware Road
Change for Circle line

This was Haydon's* neighbourhood. His house was in Burwood Place a little street running from the Edgware Road (then still called Connaught Terrace at its southern end) to Norfolk Crescent. The house, which has also vanished now, was four-storied with iron railings round the area and pretty little balconies at each of the tall first-floor windows. It was on the south side of the street on the corner of the Edgware Road, overlooking a stream of traffic, which sometimes included Queen Victoria on her way from Buckingham Palace to Paddington Station. It was one of the noisiest situations in London, but when Haydon was painting he became so absorbed in his work that nothing penetrated to his consciousness of all the uproar of carts, carriages, barking dogs, street cries, banging door knockers.

* Benjamin Robert Haydon, the painter, in the month of his death in 1846.

ALETHEA HAYTER, *A Sultry Month: Scenes of London Literary Life in 1846*, 1965

RICHMOND BRANCH

Richmond

We [Estella and Pip] came to Richmond all too soon, and our destination there was a house by the Green; a staid old house, where hoops and powder and patches, embroidered coats, rolled stockings, ruffles, and swords, had had their court days many a time.

CHARLES DICKENS, *Great Expectations*, 1860–1

About noon he [Jolyon Forsyte] set out on foot across Richmond Park, and as he went along, he thought: 'Richmond Park! By Jove, it suits us Forsytes!' Not that Forsytes lived there – nobody lived there save royalty, rangers, and the deer – but in Richmond Park Nature was allowed to go so far and no further. . . .

JOHN GALSWORTHY, *In Chancery*, 1920

Kew Gardens

Come down to Kew in lilac-time, in lilac-time, in lilac-time;
  Come down to Kew in lilac-time (it isn't far from London!)
And you shall wander hand in hand with love in summer's wonderland;
  Come down to Kew in lilac-time (it isn't far from London!)

ALFRED NOYES, 'The Barrel-Organ', *Poems*, 1904

Unprecedented was the tale of cabs and carriages that streamed across the bridges of the shining river, bearing the upper-middle class in thousands to the green glories of Bushey, Richmond, Kew and Hampton Court. Almost every family with any pretensions to be of the carriage-class paid one visit that year to the horse-chestnuts at Bushey, or took one drive amongst the Spanish chestnuts of Richmond Park.

JOHN GALSWORTHY, *The Man of Property*, 1906

I am his Highness' Dog at *Kew*;
Pray tell me Sir, whose Dog are you?

ALEXANDER POPE, Epigrams, 'Engraved on the Collar of a Dog which I gave
to his Royal Highness [Frederick, Prince of Wales]', 1737

There was a young curate of Kew,
Who kept a tom cat in a pew;
He taught it to speak
Alphabetical Greek,
But it never got farther than μû.

ANON., *Penguin Book of Limericks* edited by E.O. Parrott, 1983

Gunnersbury

Turn to page 90 for Turnham Green

Some cry up, Gunnersbury,
For Sion some declare;
And some say that with Chiswick-house
No villa can compare.
But ask the beaux of Middlesex,
If Strawb'ry-Hill, if Strawb'ry Hill
Don't bear away the bell? . . .

WILLIAM PULTENEY, Earl of Bath, 1674–1764

EALING BRANCH

Ealing Broadway

There was an Old Person of Ealing,
Who was wholly devoid of good feeling;
He drove a small Gig,
With three Owls and a Pig,
Which distressed all the People of Ealing.

EDWARD LEAR, *More Nonsense, Pictures, Rhymes, Botany, etc.*, 1872

In May 1754, after a terrible trying winter, much broken in health, [Henry] Fielding 'moved to Fordhook, a "little house" belonging to him at Ealing, the air of which then enjoyed considerable reputation, being reckoned the best in Middlesex', writes Mr. Austin Dobson. . . . Full of exquisite pathos is the scene on the morning of Fielding's departure from Fordhook.

EDITH JACKSON, *Annals of Ealing*, 1898

On this day, the most melancholy sun I had ever beheld arose, and found me awake at my house at Fordhook. By the light of this sun, I was, in my own opinion, last to behold and take leave of some of those creatures on whom I doated with a mother-like fondness, guided by nature and passion, and uncured and unhardened by all the doctrine of that philosophical school where I had learnt to bear pains and to despise death. . . . At twelve precisely my coach was at the door, which was no sooner told me than I kiss'd my children round, and went into it with some little resolution. My wife, who behaved more like a heroine and philosopher, tho' at the same time the tenderest mother in the world, and my eldest daughter, followed me; some friends went with us, and others here took their leave; and I heard my behaviour applauded, with many murmurs and praises to which I well knew I had no title.*

*Fielding died in Lisbon on 8 October following.

HENRY FIELDING, describing his departure for Lisbon on 26 June 1754
in *The Journal of a Voyage to Lisbon*, 1755

Ealing Common
Change for Piccadilly line

Ealing Fair
Commences *Thursday June 24*, 1813.
The following PRIZES to be Play'd for, on the GREEN:
FIRST DAY.
A WATCH, Value £2 to be Play'd for at Single-stick
A SHIFT, to be Run for by Young Women.
SECOND DAY.
JUMPING IN SACKS, for **10.6d**
GRINNING through a **HORSE COLLAR**,
For a Large Leg of Mutton.
THIRD DAY.
Old Women Drinking Tea, for a Pound of Tea.
A PIG, to be Run for.
The first that catches the Pig and holds it to be entitled to the Prize.
A WATCH, Value £3, to be Play'd for at Single-stick.
A POUND of TOBACCO, to be Smoaked for.
To begin at FOUR o'Clock each Day.

From lantern slides in the collection of the Ealing Photographic Society,
illustrated in *Ealing* by Charles Jones, 1903

The troglodyte in a crowded tunnel under central London, watching District Line trains crackle past in procession to Ealing and Wimbledon, and waiting for the Circle Line train that never comes, can look at the map on the wall and daydream of far away places called Ickenham and Boston Manor.

PHILIP HOWARD, *The Times*

Acton Town
Change for Piccadilly line

By 1900 there were 180 laundries in South Acton, which was colloquially known as 'Soapsuds Island'.

The London Encyclopaedia edited by Ben Weinreb and Christopher Hibbert, 1983

Chiswick Park

Sir Walter Scott, in his 'Diary', May 17th, 1828, tells us that . . . he drove to Chiswick, where he had never been before. 'A numerous and gay party,' he adds, 'were assembled to walk and enjoy the beauties of that Palladian dome. The place and highly ornamental gardens belonging to it resemble a picture of Watteau. There is some affectation in the picture, but in the *ensemble* the original looked very well. The Duke of Devonshire received every one with the best possible manners. The scene was dignified by the presence of an immense elephant, who, under the charge of a groom, wandered up and down, giving an air of Asiatic pageantry to the entertainment.'

W. THORNBURY AND E. WALFORD, *Old and New London*, 1873–8

Chiswick has witnessed the death of more than one political celebrity. At the end of August, 1806, the great statesman, Charles James Fox, was in his last illness removed to the Duke of Devonshire's villa, where he died a fortnight later. . . . The following anecdotes rest upon the authority of Samuel Rogers: 'Lady Holland announced the death of Fox in her own odd manner to those relatives and intimate friends of his who were sitting in a room near his bed-chamber, and waiting to hear that he had breathed his last; she walked through the room with her apron over her head. . . .'

W. THORNBURY AND E. WALFORD, *Old and New London*, 1873–8

Sir Stephen Fox's House at Chiswick, now possessed by the Earl of Wilmington, is a very fine and convenient Building; King William was so well pleased with it, that when he had seen the House and Garden, he said to the Earl of Portland, *This Place is perfectly fine, I could live here for five Days.*

DANIEL DEFOE, *A Tour thro' the Whole Island of Great Britain,* 1738

. . . as they wandered through the lighted streets with all their strange and variegated show, with glittering windows and glittering lamps, with the ebb and flow of faces, the voices and the laughter, the surging crowds about the theatre doors, the flashing hansoms and the omnibuses lumbering heavily along to strange regions, such as Turnham Green and Castelnau, Cricklewood and Stoke Newington – why they were as unknown as cities in Cathay! . . .

ARTHUR MACHEN, *The Secret Glory,* 1922

Turnham Green

All the angels at Turnham Green
Survey a gentle, idyllic scene –
Wide-winged, blue-eyed, English ones,
With their hair tied up in buns.
How lucidly they look – behold
Privet hedges green and gold
Round tiny gardens prettified
With stocks and pinks and London Pride,
Of houses built on a modest plan,
Semi-detached Victorian,
With freshly painted doors that shine
All along the District Line.
By Supermarket and Odeon
Celestial guardians march on. . . .

JOHN HEATH-STUBBS, *Satires and Epigrams,* 1968

Stamford Brook

From Wormwood Scrubs, Stamford Brook runs to Old Oak Common, touching the south-west corner of the Common, in the garden of the old Acton Wells Assembly Rooms, famous in the days of Queen Anne –

when Wormwood Scrubs was infinitely more fashionable than it is today – for their purging waters.

The story of Acton Wells typifies what happened to so many of London's wells. They were fashionable until the days of the American Revolution. An advertisement on 3 July 1771 stated: By the recommendation of Physicians and the encouragement of the nobility and gentry Acton Wells are newly opened for the benefit of the public. Every Monday, Wednesday and Friday from Lady Day to Michaelmas are public days for drinking the waters and breakfasting.

RICHARD TRENCH AND ELLIS HILLMAN,
London Under London, 1984, revised 1993

Ravenscourt Park

O men of Kensington! . . . sword in hand, you drove the Empire of Hammersmith back mile by mile, swept it past its own Broadway, and broke it at last in a battle so long and bloody that the birds of prey have left their name upon it. Men have called it, with austere irony, the Ravenscourt.

G.K. CHESTERTON, *The Napoleon of Notting Hill*, 1904

Ravenscourt, though not large (32 acres), is very beautiful. With Waterlow, Clissold, and Brockwell Parks it shares the distinction of being a real park, centuries old; and despite the new features, the gravelled paths, garden-beds, iron railings, etc., which had to be introduced when it was opened to the public, it retains much of its original park-like character. Its venerable elms, hornbeams, beeches, cedars, and hawthorns are a very noble possession. To my mind this indeed is the most beautiful park in London.

W.H. HUDSON, *Birds in London*, 1898

Hammersmith
Change for Hammersmith & City line station and Piccadilly line

One of the things I have always disliked about William Morris is that he is rude [at the start of *News from Nowhere*] about Hammersmith Bridge. For those unlucky enough not to know it, Hammersmith Bridge is a dignified Victorian structure, crowned with small but ornate pinnacles, which joins Middlesex to Surrey. When I was a child it was a source of intense and unmitigated delight. For one thing, being a suspension bridge it wobbled when buses went across. There you would be, clutching a parental hand high over the Thames, when suddenly the pavement would shiver and dance beneath your feet as a double-decker rumbled by. . . . Then there were the gulls. At Hammersmith, of course, the river is still tidal. On a good day you can smell the sea. At the ebb, wide mud-flats appear, and these would be covered, especially in stormy weather, with huge gulls. When you crossed the bridge, gulls would bank and glide under you and back and over your head. If you held a piece of bread over the rail, they would swoop and snatch it from your fingers . . . a safer idea was to take a bag of crusts and toss them in handfuls over the water. Instantly you would be the centre of a screaming, fighting white tornado. . . .

JOHN CAREY, *Original Copy*, 1987

Barons Court
Change for Piccadilly line

Earls Court
  With knee bent low,
Barons Court
  With a kiss and a blow.
I dropped a curtsey to the Earl,
  I'm the Baron's lady – O!

ELEANOR FARJEON, *Nursery Rhymes of London Town*, 1916

West Kensington

London moved me greatly because of the walks by the side of the Thames towards *Little Chelsea*. There were little houses there set off with rose trees that I found truly elegiac. It was the first time I was affected by the sentimental mode.

STENDHAL (M.H. Beyle), *Souvenirs d'Egotisme*, 1832

I am strongly biased about the London Underground, because it was the first thing in London which, in sporadic visits from a provincial youth, I fell in love with; it is still for me the most romantic and mysterious part of London.

DAVID PIPER, *The Companion Guide to London*, 1964

Earl's Court
Change for Kensington (Olympia)

And what has Earls Court got? . . .
A station (Metropolitan and Underground)
Known to commuters as a terminal . . .
What Earls Court has is this:
A sense of free and easy. There are no Joneses
For anybody to keep up with here.
The negroes in the snow are beautiful,
And you can wear what clothes you damn well please.
No debs. No escorts. No tycoons. But life
In great variety.

GAVIN EWART, *Londoners*, 1964

Kensington (Olympia)

During the last spring and the most beautiful summer that has succeeded it, I have, with the exception of a mere gallop into Somerset-
shire and back, been constantly at Kensington*, occupied chiefly in
sowing and rearing American trees and shrubs, of which I have now, I
think, a *million* of various sorts, including about ten thousand apple-
trees. 28 July 1825.

WILLIAM COBBETT, *Rural Rides*, 1830

*Cobbett's farm was on the south side of the present High Street. In 1831, he said of it that
it contained 'two cows, a bull-calf, two old sows, five male pigs, and seven females, all
these about three months old, two cocks, ten hens, and about seventeen pigeons'.

Gloucester Road
Change for Piccadilly line

When they finally threw us out of Pommeroy's, and after we had con-
sidered the possibility of buying the Bishop brandy in the Cock Tavern,
and even beer in the Devereux, I let my instinct, like an aged horse,
carry me on to the Underground and home to Gloucester Road, and
there discovered the rissoles, like some traces of a vanished civilization,
fossilized in the oven. She Who Must Be Obeyed was already in bed,
feigning sleep. When I climbed in beside her she opened a hostile eye.

'You're drunk, Rumpole!' she said. 'What on earth have you been doing?'

'I've been having a legal discussion,' I told her, 'on the subject of the admissibility of certain evidence. Vital, from my client's point of view. And, just for a change, Hilda, I think I've won.'

'Well, you'd better try and get some sleep.' And she added with a sort of satisfaction, 'I'm sure you'll be feeling quite terrible in the morning.'

JOHN MORTIMER, 'Rumpole and the Spirit of Christmas', *Regina for the Defence*, 1981

South Kensington
Change for Piccadilly line

It would not be true to say she was doing nothing:
She visited several bookshops, spent an hour
In the Victoria and Albert Museum (Indian section),
And walked carefully through the streets of Kensington
Carrying five mushrooms in a paper bag,
A tin of black pepper, a literary magazine,
And enough money to pay the rent for two weeks.
The sky was cloudy, leaves lay on the pavements.

Nor did she lack human contacts: she spoke
To three shop-assistants and a newsvendor,
And returned the 'Good-night' of a museum attendant.
Arriving home, she wrote a letter to someone
In Canada, as it might be, or in New Zealand,
Listening to the news as she cooked her meal,
And conversed for five minutes with the landlady.
The air was damp with the mist of late autumn.

A full day, and not unrewarding.
Night fell at the usual seasonal hour.
She drew the curtains, switched on the electric fire,
Washed her hair and read until it was dry,
Then went to bed; where, for the hours of darkness,
She lay pierced by thirty black spears
And felt her limbs numb, her eyes burning,
And dark rust carried along her blood.

FLEUR ADCOCK, 'Miss Hamilton in London', *Tigers*, 1967

Sloane Square

And you're giving a treat (penny ice and cold meat) to a party of
    friends and relations –
They're a ravenous horde – and they all came on board at Sloane
    Square and South Kensington stations.

W.S. GILBERT, *Iolanthe*, 1882

Now that we are wedged together,
Sweet stranger,
Closer than man and wife,
Why not make the best of this indignity?
Let our blood rioting together,
Murmur stories of our life's adventures,
Just as a river in its course
Brings emblems from its source.

Swing! Swing!
We are shamed, abashed:
Thrown breast to breast.
You dare not look in my eyes
Nor I in yours.

And yet in spite of this
I feel strange sympathies
Bearing my heart back
Along some time-tunnelling track
Which I do not recognize
Which I never trod before.

Swing! Swing!
The crowd is wheat
Before the scythe.
You are swept off your feet,
Thrown against me, a wave,
Dashed on a rock.
But we survive the shock.

RICHARD CHURCH, 'Strap-hanging',
Mood without Measure, 1928

Victoria
Change for Victoria line

. . . and it seemed to Jim you weren't necessarily any happier whichever side of Victoria Station you were born on. What a lot of miserable objects he carried luggage for – sleek, soft-voiced young men trailing behind old aunts bored to death because they were travelling abroad. Why, the very labels excited him: Paris, Milan, Rome, Geneva, Vienna, Bucharest, Athens, Cairo, Baghdad. If his bag ever had one of those labels on it he'd run all the way down the platform instead of drawling – 'Aw portah!' or 'How frightfully crowded!' or 'Really, my dear, it's preposterous!'

Lots of things were preposterous, but not having your luggage carried down the platform, with a Venice label on it, and a first-class seat to lounge in, and a first-class restaurant to eat in, and nothing to do but sit and glide away out of smoke into sunshine.

CECIL ROBERTS, *Victoria Four-Thirty,* 1937

I love to return to London from the country, relieved on the terminus platform by the metropolitan excitement of so many people hurrying in so many ways – though in fact I will probably go straight home and not leave the house for a week. It is simply a feeling that one is in some sort of important swim; just as the availability of so many theatre and night amusements is comforting, though we very seldom use them. But if we lived in the country, there would, I am sure be a sense of deprivation.

WILLIAM SANSOM in *Living in London* edited by Alan Ross, 1974

St. James's Park

Julian felt his heart beat uncommonly thick, as if conscious of approaching someone of the highest consequence [King Charles II]. The person whom he looked upon was past the middle age of life, of a dark complexion, corresponding with the long, black, full-bottomed periwig, which he wore instead of his own hair. His dress was plain black velvet, with a diamond star, however, on his cloak, which hung carelessly over one shoulder. His features, strongly lined, even to harshness, had yet an expresssion of dignified good-humour; he was well and strongly built, walked upright and yet easily, and had upon the whole the air of a person of the highest consideration. He kept rather in advance of his companions, but turned and spoke to them, from time to time, with much affability, and probably with some liveliness, judging by the smiles, and sometimes the scarce restrained laughter, by which some of his sallies were received by his attendants. . . . They shared the attention of their principal in common with seven or eight little black curl-haired spaniels . . . whose gambols, which seemed to afford him much amusement, he sometimes regulated, and sometimes encouraged. In addition to this pastime, a lacquey, or groom, was also in attendance, with one or two little baskets and bags, from which the gentleman we have described took, from time to time, a handful of seeds, and amused himself with throwing them to the water-fowl.

SIR WALTER SCOTT, *Peveril of the Peak*, 1822,
describing Charles II in St James's Park

In a Tube train, for instance, Ben could sit with his eyes shut for the whole journey, and if anyone noticed, no one commented. He felt especially safe if he could allow himself to be caught by the rush-hour, and in the Inner Circle Tube. The other passengers, sitting or strap-hanging or simply wedged upright by the pressure of the crowd, endured their journey with their eyes shut – you see them so, travelling home at the end of any working-day in London. Like them, Ben kept his eyes shut, but he was not tired. . . . No one ever saw what he was seeing: a fawn-coloured dog of incredible minuteness.

If Ben was sitting, he saw the dog on his knee. If he stood, he looked down with his shut eyes and saw it at his feet. The dog was always with him, only dashing ahead or lingering behind in order to play tricks of agility and daring. When Ben finally left the Tube train, for instance, the Chihuahua would play that dangerous game of being last through the closing doors. When Ben rode up the Up escalator with his eyes shut, the Chihuahua chose to run up the Down one, and always arrived at the top first. . . .

PHILIPPA PEARCE, *A Dog So Small*, 1962

Westminster

Mortality, behold and feare
What a change of flesh is here!
Thinke how many royall bones
Sleep within these heap of stones;
Here they lie, had realmes and lands,
Who now want strength to stir their hands;
Where from their pulpits seal'd with dust
They preach, 'In greatness is no trust.'
Here's an acre sown indeed,
With the richest, royallst seed,
That the earth did e'er suck in,
Since the first man dy'd for sin.

FRANCIS BEAUMONT, 'On the Tombes in Westminster',
printed anonymously in 1619

He, like to a high strecht lute string squeakt, 'O Sir,
'Tis sweet to talke of Kings.' 'At Westminster,'
Said I, 'The man that keepes the Abbey tombes,
And for his price doth with who ever comes,

Of all our Harries, and our Edwards talke,
From King to King and all their kin can walke:
Your eares shall heare nought, but Kings; your eyes meet
Kings only.'

JOHN DONNE, 'Satyre IIII', 1633

Sir Joshua Reynolds (1723–92) commented of Westminster Abbey as long as 200 years ago: 'Westminster is already so stuffed with statuary it would be a deadly sin against taste to increase the squeeze of tombs there.'

London is literally new to me; new in its streets, houses, and even in its situation; as the Irishman said, 'London is now gone out of town.' What I left open fields, producing hay and corn, I now find covered with streets, and squares, and palaces, and churches. I am credibly informed, that in the space of seven years, eleven thousand new houses have been built in one quarter of Westminster, exclusive of what is daily added to other parts of this unwieldy metropolis. Pimlico and Knightsbridge are now almost joined to Chelsea and Kensington; and if this infatuation continues for half a century, I suppose the whole county of Middlesex will be covered with brick.

TOBIAS SMOLLETT, *The Expedition of Humphry Clinker*, 1771

Embankment
Change for Bakerloo and Northern lines

The Great Frost was, historians tell us, the most severe that has ever visited these islands. Birds froze in mid-air and fell like stones to the ground. . . .

But while the country people suffered the extremity of want, and the trade of the country was at a standstill, London enjoyed a carnival of the utmost brilliancy. The Court was at Greenwich, and the new King seized the opportunity that his coronation gave him to curry favour with the citizens. He directed that the river, which was frozen to a depth of twenty feet and more for six or seven miles on either side, should be swept, decorated and given all the semblance of a park or pleasure ground, with arbours, mazes, alleys, drinking booths, etc., at his expense. . . . Coloured balloons hovered motionless in the air. Here and there burnt vast bonfires of cedar and oak wood, lavishly salted, so that the flames were of green, orange, and purple fire. But however fiercely they burnt, the heat was not enough to melt the ice which, though of singular transparency, was yet of the hardness of steel. So clear indeed was it that there could be seen, congealed at a depth of several feet, here a porpoise, there a flounder. Shoals of eels lay motionless in a trance, but whether their state was one of death or merely of suspended animation which the warmth would revive puzzled the philosophers. Near London Bridge, where the river had frozen to a depth of some twenty fathoms, a wrecked wherry boat was plainly visible, lying on the bed of the river where it had sunk last autumn, overladen with apples. The old bumboat woman, who was carrying her fruit to market on the Surrey side, sat there in her plaids and farthingales with her lap full of apples, for all the world as if she were about to serve a customer, though a certain blueness about the lips hinted the truth. . . . But it was at night that the carnival was at its merriest. For the frost continued unbroken; the nights were of perfect stillness; the moon and stars blazed with the hard fixity of diamonds, and to the fine music of flute and trumpet the courtiers danced.

VIRGINIA WOOLF, Orlando, 1928

Just as important to me . . . is all the furniture of my world; eye-pampering. . . . Streets, streets, streets, markets, theatres, churches, Covent Gardens, shops sparkling with pretty faces of industrious mill-iners, neat semp-stresses . . . authors in street with spectacles . . . lamps lit at night, pastry-cook and silversmith shops . . . noise of coaches, drowsy cry of mechanic watchmen at night, with Bucks reeling home drunk; if you happen to work at midnight, cries of 'Fire!' and 'Stop thief!' Inns of court (with their learned air and halls and butteries), just like Cambridge colleges; old book stalls. . . . These are thy plea-sures, O London!

CHARLES LAMB, letter to Thomas Manning, 28 November 1800,
Letters of Charles Lamb, 1905

Temple

There are, still, worse places than the Temple, on a sultry day, for basking in the sun, or resting idly in the shade. There is yet a drowsiness in its courts, and a dreamy dullness in its streets and gardens; those who pace its lanes and squares may yet hear the echoes of their footsteps on the sounding stones, and read upon its gates, in passing from the tumult of the Strand or Fleet Street, 'Who enters here leaves noise behind.' There is still the plash of falling water in fair Fountain Court. . . . There is yet, in the Temple, something of a clerkly monkish atmosphere.

CHARLES DICKENS, *Barnaby Rudge*, 1841

Gray's Inn for Walks,
Lincoln's Inn for a Wall,
Inner Temple for a Garden,
And the Middle for a Hall.

Old rhyme quoted by James Bone in *The London Perambulator*, 1925

Blackfriars

Seven Black Friars sitting back to back
Fished from the bridge for a pike or a jack.
The first caught a tiddler, the second caught a crab,
The third caught a winkle, the fourth caught a dab,
The fifth caught a tadpole, the sixth caught an eel,
And the seventh one caught an old cart-wheel.

ELEANOR FARJEON, *Nursery Rhymes of London Town*, 1916

I have known a man, dying a long way from London, sigh queerly for a sight of the gush of smoke that, on the platform of the Underground, one may see, escaping in great woolly clots up a circular opening, by a grimy, rusted iron shield, into the dim upper light. He wanted to see it again as others have wished to see once more the Bay of Naples, the olive groves of Catania. But – alas perhaps – no man will ever see that sight again, for the Underground itself has been 'electrified,' . . . and there is one of our glamours gone.

FORD MADOX HUEFFER, *England and the English: An Interpretation,* 1907

Mansion House

The Lord Mayor, in the stronghold of the mighty Mansion House, gave orders to his fifty cooks and butlers to keep Christmas as a Lord Mayor's household should.

CHARLES DICKENS, *A Christmas Carol,* 1843

Cannon Street

Every morning, trains disgorge thousands of city workers at Cannon Street station, a few yards east of the hidden mouth of the Walbrook, where the men of Rouen landed their cargoes a thousand years ago. The passengers step out into a street known by the 1180s as Candlewick Street, the home of the candle-wick makers. Many go straight along Walbrook, keeping some fifty yards east of the stream, which flows more than thirty feet underground; the name itself means 'stream of the Britons' and is London's sole reminder of the old population, whom the English called Weales and who are now commemorated in Wales.

TIMOTHY BAKER, *Mediaeval London,* 1970

CADE: Now is Mortimer lord of this city. And here, sitting upon London-stone*, I charge and command that, of the city's cost, the pissing-conduit run nothing but claret wine this first year of our reign.

WILLIAM SHAKESPEARE, *Henry VI Part II,* 1591

*London Stone, the old Roman milestone, is now rounded with age, and set in a stone case built into the outer southern wall of the church of St Swithin, Cannon Street – the very stone that the arch-rebel Jack Cade struck with his bloody sword after storming London Bridge.

Monument
Change for escalator to Bank station for Central and Northern lines

. . . one and sixpence. When I was your age, I had never seen so much money, in a heap. A shilling of it is in case of accidents – the mare casting a shoe, or the like of that. The other sixpence is to spend in the diversions of London; and the diversion I recommend is to go to the top of the Monument, and sitting there. There's no temptation there, sir – no drink – no young women – no bad characters of any sort – nothing but imagination. That's the way I enjoyed myself when I was your age, sir.

CHARLES DICKENS, *Barnaby Rudge,* 1841

. . . two people came to see the Monument. They were a gentleman and a lady; and the gentleman said, 'How much a-piece?'

The Man in the Monument replied, 'A Tanner.'

It seemed a low expression, compared with the Monument.

The gentleman put a shilling into his hand, and the Man in the Monument opened the dark little door. When the gentleman and lady had passed out of view, he shut it again, and came slowly back to his chair.

He sat down and laughed.

'They don't know what a many steps there is!' he said, 'It's worth twice the money to stop here. Oh, my eye!'

CHARLES DICKENS, *Martin Chuzzlewit,* 1843–4

Tower Hill
Change for Circle line

Baroness Orczy conceived the idea of *The Scarlet Pimpernel* in the booking hall of Tower Hill station.

. . . we all went to the next house upon Tower hill, to see the coming by of the Russia Embassador – for whose reception all the City trained bands do attend in the streets, and the King's Lifeguards, and most of the wealthy citizens in their black velvet coats and gold chains. . . . I could not see the Embassador in his coach – but his attendants in their habbits and fur caps very handsome comely men, and most of them with Hawkes upon their fists to present to the King. But Lord, to see the absurd nature of Englishmen, that cannot forbear laughing and jeering at everything that looks strange.

SAMUEL PEPYS, *Diary, 27 November 1662*

Aldgate East
Change for Hammersmith & City line

Gates in the wall of this City of old Time were Four; to wit, Aldgate for the East; Aldersgate for the North; Ludgate for the West; and the Bridge-gate, over the River of Thames for the South.

JOHN STOW, *Survey of London and Westminster,* 1598

Nature, or anything that reminds me of nature, disturbs me; it is too large, too complicated, above all too utterly pointless and incomprehensible. I am at home with the works of man; if I choose to set my mind to it, I can understand anything that any man has made or thought. That is why I always travel by Tube, never by bus if I can possibly help it. For, travelling by bus one can't avoid seeing, even in London, a few stray works of God – the sky, for example, an occasional tree, the flowers in the window-boxes. But travel by Tube and you see nothing but the works of man – iron riveted into geometrical forms, straight lines of concrete, patterned expanses of tiles. All is human and the product of friendly and comprehensible minds. All philosophies and all religions – what are they but spiritual Tubes bored through the universe! Through these narrow tunnels, where all is recognizably human, one travels comfortable and secure, contriving to forget that all round and below and above them stretches the blind mass of earth, endless and unexplored. Yes, give me the Tube and Cubismus every time; give me ideas, so snug and neat and simple and well made. And preserve me from nature.

ALDOUS HUXLEY, *Crome Yellow*, 1921

Whitechapel
Change for East London line

Gay go up and gay go down,
To ring the bells of London Town.

Nursery Rhyme quoted in *Gammer Gurton's Garland*, 1810

Two Sticks and Apple
Ring ye Bells at Whitechapple

Tommy Thumb's Pretty Song Book, 1774

I spent a most interesting afternoon with Mary in Whitechapel. Lizzie and I went by underground and walked along Whitechapel Road to Mayfield House. How curious those streets are! There were booths all along the edge of the pavement, it looked like a great fair right down the road. The people were fascinating to watch. I should have liked to walk up and down the street for hours. . . . I think I shall buy all my clothes in Whitechapel – I saw some splendid hats loaded with ostrich feathers for 5/11; and cloaks at the same price! March 6, 1891.

GERTRUDE BELL, *The Earlier Letters of Gertrude Bell*
collected and edited by Elsa Richmond, 1937

Stepney Green

I think Stepney is a very smokey place
But I like it
People in Stepney do things wrong
But I like them
Everything in Stepney has its disadvantages
But I like it.

It does not have clean air like the country
But I like it
The buildings are old and cold
But I like them
The summer is not very hot
But I like it.

ROSEMARIE DALE, 'Stepney', *Stepney Words I and II*, 1973

Mile End
Change for Central line

By this time they had reached the turnpike at Mile End; a profound silence prevailed, until they had got two or three miles further on, when Mr. Weller senior turning suddenly to Mr. Pickwick, said –

'Wery queer life is a pike-keeper's, Sir.'

'A what?' said Mr. Pickwick.

'A pike-keeper.'

'What do you mean by a pike-keeper?' enquired Mr. Peter Magnus.

'The old 'un means a turnpike keeper, gen'l'm'n,' observed Mr. Weller, in explanation.

'Oh,' said Mr. Pickwick, 'I see. Yes; very curious life. Very uncomfortable.'

'They're all on 'em, men as has met vith some disappointment in life,' said Mr. Weller senior.

'Ay, ay?' said Mr. Pickwick.

'Yes. Consequence of vich, they retires from the world, and shuts themselves up in pikes; partly vith the view of being solitary, and partly to rewenge themselves on mankind, by takin' tolls.'

'Dear me,' said Mr. Pickwick, 'I never knew that before.'

'Fact, Sir,' said Mr. Weller; 'if they was gen'l'm'n you'd call 'em misanthropes, but as it is they only takes to pike-keepin'.'

With such conversation, possessing the inestimable charm of blending amusement with instruction, did Mr. Weller beguile the tediousness of the journey, during the greater part of the day.

CHARLES DICKENS, *The Pickwick Papers*, 1836–7

Bow Road

There was an Old Person of Bow,
Whom nobody happened to know;
So they gave him some Soap,
And said coldly, 'We hope
You will go back directly to Bow!'

EDWARD LEAR, *More Nonsense, Pictures, Rhymes, Botany, etc.*, 1872

You owe me five farthings,
Say the bells of St Martin's.

When will you pay me?
Say the bells of Old Bailey.

I'm sure I don't know,
Says the great bell at Bow.

Tommy Thumb's Pretty Song Book, 1774

Bromley-by-Bow

Adjoining Bow in the south-east, in the parish of Bromley . . . a short
distance northwards of the church, a large brick-built mansion – one of
the former glories of the place – is still standing. . . . It is commonly
known as the Old Palace* . . .

Before quitting Bromley we must not omit to mention the bowling-
green, the village stocks, the whipping-post, the pond and ducking-
stool, and the parish pound, all of which remained in full operation
down to the latter part of the last century.

E. WALFORD, *Greater London*, 1882–4

* remembered in the lines:

Outside there's nothing now to show
The house was built so long ago:
But inside you will see,
The pendant ceiling, pannel'd wall,
Rich chimnies, Royal arms and all
Just as it used to be.
Then all was country around,
The forest near – then open ground
With Stebonheath close by.
And hunting was the favourite sport,
Of James the first, and all his court:
To make the hours fly.

West Ham

The story of West Ham's Football Club begins over fifty years ago. Not with the founding of a professional club but with the formation of a works team. Which is as it should be, for ever since these earliest days the West Ham club has found its supporters among the people of London's busiest, most hard-worked area. The Club belongs to the crowded streets, the docksides, the manufacturies, the print shops and transport depots of East London. West Ham United is truly of the place and the people. . . . A crowd that urges on the home side with shouts of 'Come on, the Hammers!' and cries of 'Up the Irons!' will clearly have no time for showy stuff on the field. The club has always got most of its players 'over the wall' from the back streets of East London and from the playing fields of Essex.

REG GROVES, *Official History of West Ham United*, 1947

Plaistow

Upon a fertile Spot of Land,
Does *Plaistow*, thriving *Plaistow*, stand:
The Sea, which whilom roll'd his Flood,
And hither brought the fat'ning Mud,
Has left a Richness in the Soil
That well rewards the Peasant's Toil.
One side the Level Marshes sees,
And all is interspers'd with Trees:
From hence the Silver *Thames* appears,
And the wing'd Vessels which she bears; . . .
A pleasing Sight, to see them ride
With Sails unfurl'd, with Wind and Tide.
From hence to our delighted Eyes,
Does Greenwich' Royal Spires arise; . . .

With wholsome Fare our Villa's stor'd;
Our Lands the best of Corn afford;
Nor Hertford Wheat, nor Derby Rye,
Nor Ipswich Pease, can our's outvye:
The largest Ox that *England* bred,
Was in our verdant Pastures fed.

Let *Irish* Wights no longer boast
The fam'd Potatoes of their Coast:
Potatoes now are *Plaistow's* Pride;
Whole Markets are from hence supply'd,
Nor finer Mutton can you spend,
Than what our fat'ning Marshes send,
And in our Farmers Yards you find,
Delicious Fowls of divers Kind;
Whose Cellars rarely ever fail,
To keep a Cask of Nappy Ale.

In Praise of Plaistow in the County of Essex. A Poem, 1753

Upton Park

Ham House and Park . . . was for many years the residence of Samuel Gurney, and the centre of the great philanthropic measures in which he and Mrs [Elizabeth] Fry (who lived in a house in Upton Lane close by) were the prime movers.

JAMES THORNE, *Handbook to the Environs of London*, 1876

East Ham

The [Tudor] mansion's popular name Boleyn Castle came from the erroneous tradition that Anne Boleyn lived here during Henry's courtship. . . . The immediate area is colloquially known as 'The Boleyn' and modern roads to the east are named after Henry VIII's wives and Anne's brother Lord Rochford.

The London Encyclopaedia edited by Ben Weinreb
and Christopher Hibbert, 1983

Barking

We saw passing from Barking to Dagenham, the famous Breach, made by an Inundation of the Thames, which was so great, that it laid near 5000 Acres of Land under Water, but which after near ten Years lying in that manner, and being several times blown up, has been at last effectually stopped by the application of Captain Perry; the Gentleman, who for several Years had been employed, in the Czar of Muscovy's Works, at Veronitza, on the river Don. This Breach appeared now effectually made up, and they assured us, that the new Work, where the Breach was, is by much esteemed the strongest of all the Sea Walls in that Level.

DANIEL DEFOE, *A Tour thro' the Whole Island of Great Britain*, 1738

In early times the vicar of Barking drew his income from the abbey, with a hog, a goose, a cheese and a lamb for diet; but after many disputes it was settled in 1437, between Catherine de la Pole, the abbess, and Sir John Greening, the vicar, that in future the vicar should have provision every day in the convent, so long as he should not be of a litigious disposition, he sitting at the chaplain's table, his servant with the domestics; but if he should, without licence of the abbess, have any familiarity or discourse with any of the nuns, he should, for the first offence, lose his diet for a week; for the second, a month; and for the third be excluded from the convent for life.

JAMES THORNE, *Handbook to the Environs of London*, 1876

Upney

Upney simply means the *upper-stream* and this local natural feature gives the name to this district.

CYRIL M. HARRIS, *What's in a Name?*, 1977

Becontree

Becontree is named after the beacon that was lit at the approach of the Armada.

Night sank upon the dusky beach, and on the purple sea,
Such night in England ne'er had been, nor e'er again shall be.
From Eddystone to Berwick bounds, from Lynn to Milford Bay,
That time of slumber was as bright and busy as the day;
For swift to east and swift to west the ghastly war-flame spread,
High on St. Michael's Mount it shone: it shone on Beachy Head.

Far on the deep the Spaniard saw, along each southern shire,
Cape beyond cape, in endless range, those twinkling points of fire . . .
From all the batteries of the Tower peeled loud the voice of fear;
And all the thousand masts of Thames sent back a louder cheer . . .
And on and on, without a pause, untired they bounded still:
All night from tower to tower they sprang; they sprang from hill to hill.

THOMAS BABINGTON, LORD MACAULAY,
from 'The Armada', *Lays of Ancient Rome*, 1842

Dagenham Heathway

A little beyond the Town, on the Road to Dagenham, stood a great
House, antient, and now almost fallen down, where Tradition says, the
Gunpowder-Treason Plot was at first contriv'd, and that all the first
Consultations about it were held there.

DANIEL DEFOE, *A Tour thro' the Whole Island of Great Britain*, 1724–6

Dagenham East

On the way to the coast for cockles they pass the Ford plant at
Dagenham, that Detroit moonscape where every man's car is processed
out; they inch past it choking each other to death with their fumes.
The dream of the bright young things, fast and furious whirling
through the countryside, twists round all our throats like Isadora
Duncan's scarf. The lady and the motoring veil: there's a dance
macabre for a brave choreographer.

MAUREEN DUFFY, *Capital*, 1975

Elm Park

Elm Park . . . takes its name from natural local woodland.

CYRIL M. HARRIS, *What's in a Name?*, 1977

Hornchurch

On Christmas-day, the following custom has been observed at
Hornchurch, in Essex, from time immemorial. The lessee of the tithes,

which belong to New College, Oxford, supplies a boar's head dressed, and garnished with bay-leaves etc. In the afternoon, it is carried in procession into the Mill Field, adjoining the church-yard, where it is wrestled for; and it is afterwards feasted upon, at one of the public-houses, by the rustic conqueror and his friends, with all the merriment peculiar to the season.

WILLIAM HONE, *The Every-Day Book and Table Book,* 1830,
entry for 25 December

Upminster Bridge

. . . there is a small iron road bridge, marked Upminster Bridge. Tradition has it that the Romans built a ford here over the River Ingrebourne during Caesar's invasion of England. It seeems that in *c.*1300 a wooden bridge was built to replace the ford.

CYRIL M. HARRIS, *What's in a Name?,* 1977

Upminster

Upminster Tithe Barn Hall Lane . . . dates from about the middle of the 15th century. It stands near the drive to Upminster Hall and was probably used by the monks of Waltham Abbey. . . . It has been made into a museum of agricultural and local history.

The London Encyclopaedia edited by Ben Weinreb
and Christopher Hibbert, 1983

EAST LONDON LINE

New Cross Gate

To-night the arc-lamps, poised from slender stems,
Will bloom like silvery fruits. Signals will gleam
With shifting specks of jade and crimson gems.

Then: music: hiss and gasp of throttled steam,
Staccato gamut of the shunted trains,
And murmurous diapason of the cranes.

PAUL SELVER (1888–?), 'New Cross. (Suburban Landscape)',
quoted in *London Between the Lines* compiled by
John Bishop and Virginia Broadbent, 1973

'Tis true, that the Suburbs of London *are larger then the Body of the City,
which make some compare her to a* Jesuites *Hat, whose brims are far larger
then the Block, which made Count* Gondamar *the* Spanish *Ambassador to
say, as the Queen of* Spain *was discoursing with him, upon his return from*
England, *of the City of* London, *Madam,* I believe there will be no City left
shortly, for all will run out at the Gates to the *Suburbs.*

J. HOWEL, *Londonopolis. An Historicall Discourse or Perlustration of the City of
London, The Imperial Chamber, and Chief Emporium of Great Britain,* 1657

New Cross

There was a young man of New Cross,
Who rode a most marvellous horse;
    As it couldn't be matched,
    All the others were scratched,
And he simply walked over the course.

A Lyttel Booke of Nonsense

Surrey Quays
[This station used to be called Surrey Docks]

One goes down the widening reaches through a monstrous variety of
shipping, great steamers, great sailing ships, trailing the flags of all the

world, a monstrous confusion of lighters, witches' conferences of brown-sailed barges, wallowing lugs, a tumultuous crowding and jostling of cranes and spars, and wharves and stores . . . and here and there beyond and amidst it all are church towers . . . riverside pubs.

H.G. WELLS, *Tono-Bungay,* 1909

Rotherhithe

Oh where's Ranelagh and Vauxhall Gardens, and perhaps most evocative of all the Cherry Garden in Rotherhithe now a warehouse, where you could wander till dawn, dancing and drinking or just being seen?

MAUREEN DUFFY, *Capital,* 1975

The Thames Tunnel, the world's first subaquaeous thoroughfare, was started in 1825 and took eighteen years to complete – a hundred and fifty-one years earlier than the Channel Tunnel, which opened in 1994. It was the great achievement of Sir Marc Isambard Brunel, father of the more famous Isambard Kingdom Brunel. The latter worked on the tunnel as a young assistant for only three years, but often mistakenly gets the full credit for it.

During its construction it attracted many visitors, who flocked to see the work in progress. Now it forms a section of the East London line between New Cross and Shoreditch.

Near to that part of the Thames on which the church at Rotherhithe abuts, . . . the strangest, the most extraordinary of the many localities that are hidden in London, wholly unknown, even by name, to the great mass of its inhabitants.

To reach this place, the visitor has to penetrate through a maze of close, narrow, and muddy streets, thronged by the roughest and poorest of water-side people, and devoted to the traffic they may be supposed to occasion. The cheapest and least delicate provisions are heaped in the shops; the coarsest and commonest articles of wearing apparel dangle at the salesman's door, and stream from the house-parapet and windows. Jostling with unemployed labourers of the lowest class, ballast-heavers, coal-whippers, brazen women, ragged children, and the raff and refuse of the river. . . . Arriving, at length, in streets remoter and less-frequented than those through which he has passed, he walks beneath tottering house-fronts projecting over the pavement, dismantled walls that seem to totter as he passes, chimneys half crushed, half hesitating to fall, windows guarded by rusty iron bars that time and dirt have almost eaten away, and every imaginable sign of desolation and neglect.

CHARLES DICKENS, *Oliver Twist*, 1837–8

. . . observation, an eye for detail, and memory. I was happily possessed, to a modest degree, of all three, due in the main, I feel sure, to an apparently witless game which my father made us play as children. In a shop window how many pots and pans, how many with lids, how many without? How many tea pots, plates with blue rims, jugs with pink roses? Make a mental list, look away for a moment or two, look back and check. In the Underground, look at the people opposite. Memorise the faces. Look at the feet. Look away. Who had the bunion, the toe-caps, the brogues, spats, lace-ups or buttons? . . .

I had no idea that this childhood game would one day prove to be the key to a life in a war. . . . I became a moderately accomplished specialist in an extremely complicated branch of Army Intelligence.

DIRK BOGARDE, *Snakes and Ladders*, 1978

Wapping

Wappineer, Wappinger: an inhabitant of Wapping. Old words going back to the 17th century.

PHILIP HOWARD, *The Times*

Your Molly has never been false, she declares,
Since last time we parted at Wapping Old Stairs,
When I swore that I still would continue the same,
And gave you the 'bacco box mark'd with your name;
When I pass'd a whole fortnight between decks with you,
Did I e'er give a kiss, Tom, to one of my crew?
To be useful and kind, with my Thomas I stay'd,
For his trousers I wash'd, and his grog, too, I made.

'ARLY', *The British Album*, 1790, quoted in
London in Song by W. Whitten, 1898

'Twas Landlady Meg that made such rare flip;
   Pull away, pull away, hearties!
At Wapping she lived, at the sign of the ship,
   Where tars meet in such jolly parties.
She'd shine at the play, and she'd jig at the ball,
   All rigg'd out so gay and so topping,
For she married six husbands, and buried them all;
   Pull away, pull away, pull away!

CHARLES DIBDIN, 'Meg of Wapping',
The Songs of Charles Dibdin, 1837

Wapping, being situated on the Pool, close to the original docks and the head of navigation, has always been the waterman's abode. . . . [It] is mentioned by Stow as Wapping in the Woze (or ooze). . . . It was originally a great waste watered by the Thames, and first recovered in the reign of Queen Elizabeth. . . .

. . . The riverside by Wapping and Shadwell and Limehouse has a bad name. Murders, theft, and all kinds of vice, dwell there; yet there are also streets and streets of 'mean houses' in which there live people who work honestly, men and women who live uprightly, whose children go to school. There are churches doing missionary work and proving themselves centres of civilisation. Gone, it is true, are the poplars and the open country in which King Charles could hunt the stag, but gone also are the executions by stake at high-tide, the brutalizing influence of which must have been felt far and wide. No longer are men hanged on the foreshore to make a public holiday. The tendency upward may be slow, but it is sure.

SIR WALTER BESANT, *The Fascination of London: The Thames*, 1903

The tunnel which runs under the Thames from this station was the first tunnel for public traffic ever to be driven beneath a river.

It was designed by Sir Marc Isambard Brunel (1769–1849) and completed in 1843. His son Isambard Kingdom Brunel (1806–1859) was engineer-in-charge from 1825 to 1828.

Plaque at Wapping Station, erected 1959

Shadwell

Shadwell was not the ordinary, industrial slum which just grew up round a factory. It was a village long before it was engulfed by the early-Victorian urban sprawl. It was also on the river; we looked to the Thames and the seas beyond for our livelihood. It was also an escape for the adventurous. I could see the funnels and masts of ships from my bedroom window. At night, I used to lie in bed, listening to the sirens of ships as they dropped down the London river to all those wonderful places I read about in Conrad. I knew the world would be my oyster while I was still a snotty-nosed kid.

The river gave Shadwell an identity. Much of its life moved with the tides, and the world came to us on the rising tide. Some of the boys in the church choir were sons of seamen, many of them aboard tramp-steamers which rarely saw the London river. The last hymn at Evensong was often 'For those in peril on the sea', and a few of the boys always had wet eyes. I suppose, in some ways, Shadwell was rather like a mining village, its tribal loyalty sustained by danger. But it was not claustrophobic, because of the river and the beckoning sea.

LOUIS HEREN, 'Benefits of a Shadwell education', BBC 2 broadcast
'The Light of Experience', reprinted in *The Listener*, 24 March 1977

Whitechapel
Change for District and Hammersmith & City lines

Pumbedita, Cordova, Cracow, Amsterdam,
Vilna, Lublin, Berditchev and Volozhin,
Your names will always be sacred,
Places where Jews have been.

And sacred is Whitechapel,
It is numbered with our Jewish towns.
Holy, holy, holy
Are your bombed stones.

If we ever have to leave Whitechapel,
As other Jewish towns were left,
Its soul will remain a part of us,
Woven into us, woof and weft.

AVRAM STENCL, *c*.1940, quoted in *London Lines*
edited by Kenneth Baker, 1982

Shoreditch

Peak hours only

When will you pay me?
Say the bells of Old Bailey.
When I grow rich,
Say the bells of Shoreditch.

Tommy Thumb's Pretty Song Book, 1774

Said Emma Black to William Bloggs, 'How could you ask a fee
For all that pretty gardening you did of late for me?
You came as friend, you worked as friend, with heart and right good will
And ne'er I thought, dear heart, you'd send that wicked little bill.

You know you brought your wife each day. I gave you tea and jam;
I gave you shrimps and muffins, too; for generous I am.
With feast and toil each dulcet eve passed gloriously away.
Then, William Bloggs, I'd ne'er believe I'd see this bill-black day.'

'Twas at the Shoreditch County Court her sobbing tale was told,
And though she was a widow lone the judge's heart was cold.
For all her teas and all her tears, she *must* pay William Bloggs.
O world! these unromantic years, You're going to the dogs!

W.P. RYAN, *Literary London*, 1898

HAMMERSMITH & CITY LINE

A dark purplish-red, or burgundy, is the colour of the Metropolitan, green of the District, yellow of the Circle, scarlet of the Central, brown of the Bakerloo, dark blue of the Piccadilly and black of the Northern. These are the colours of lines on Beck's map and also sometimes of station trims and new station bucket seats.

On the map the Victoria Line became light blue. When the Jubilee Line was nearly finished there was some speculation as to what colour would be used for it. Possibilities remaining were pink, lime green, orange and mauve.

London Transport Underground chose grey.

Pink has been given, unexpectedly and without precedent, to the Hammersmith branch of the Metropolitan [now the Hammersmith & City Line].

BARBARA VINE, *King Solomon's Carpet,* 1991

Hammersmith
Change for District line and Piccadilly line station

Saturday night! Saturday night!
I want to make Hammersmith hum.

A.P. HERBERT, 'Saturday Night', *Plain Jane,* 1927

The river flows before my door,
Sad with sea-gulls, mute with mud
Past Hammersmith and Castelnau,
And strung with barges at the flood.
Pink rowing girls by eight and four
Gently stroke the tide of blood.

A railway runs from side to side
And trains clank over on the hour.

GAVIN EWART, 'Tennysonian Reflections at Barnes Bridge',
Londoners, 1964

Goldhawk Road

Goldhawk Road was the original site of the Queen Charlotte's Maternity Hospital, which was founded in 1739 and was the earliest lying-in hospital in the British Isles.

Shepherd's Bush
Change for Central line station

The philanthropic interest which brought Dickens so often to Hammersmith was a home for the rehabilitation of prostitutes, founded and maintained by Angela Burdett Coutts (1814–1906) at Shepherd's Bush. Dickens, who was a life-long friend and adviser of the wealthy and philanthropic Miss Coutts, not only planned the organisation of the Home, but also chose the house where it was to be lodged . . . on the Acton Road. . . . The name of the house was Urania Cottage. . . .

For many years after its establishment in 1847 Dickens took the closest interest in the Home, advising Miss Coutts on every aspect of the venture, from the choosing of the girls, staff and educational syllabus, down to the minutest detail of the daily running of the Home: all of which is reflected in his many letters to Miss Coutts. . . .

The customary drab workhouse clothes were not acceptable to Dickens. . . . 'Colour' he said 'is what these people always want, and colour (as allied to fancy), I would always give them. . . . Derry [a kind of cotton cloth] might just as well break out into stripe, or put forth a bud, or even burst into a full blown flower. Who is Derry that he is to make quakers of us all, whether we will or no!'

MOLLY TATCHELL, *Leigh Hunt and His Family in Hammersmith*, 1969

Latimer Road

The road is named after Edward Latymer [1557–1626/7] who bequeathed most of his lands to the parishes [in Hammersmith and Edmonton] to the end that the deserving boys should be put to school 'to keep them from vagrant courses' and where, as Latymer specified in his will, the boys should be taught to read English and receive instruction in some part of God's true religion.'*

* The Latymer School was originally housed in Fulham and moved to Hammersmith in 1648. This was to become the Latymer Upper School.

W. WHEATLEY, *The History of Edward Latymer and His Foundations*, 1936, revised 1953

The district to the north [of the town of Kensington] was very rural, and until the beginning of the nineteenth century had undergone little change for ages. Although it was scarcely three miles from London, the traveller could imagine himself in the most remote part of the country. The main road passing through this locality is now represented by Latimer Road. At the end of Pottery Lane was a colony of pig-keepers, and every house had a collection of pigs in its yard. A number of carts filled with tubs passed daily to London gathering refuse from hotels and mansions to provide food for the large families of pigs gathered here.

HAROLD CLUNN, *The Face of London*, 1932

Ladbroke Grove

Notting Hill, you may not know it, derives its distinctive street plan from the racecourse which finally bankrupted its developer . . . he had come to live in Notting Hill totally in ignorance of the fact that a ghostly imprint of a racecourse lay over its streets.

He did not hear the thunder of two-year-olds down Lansdowne Road. He did not see mud fly in the right turn on Stanley Crescent. He saw the name of Ladbroke, of course. You cannot miss a Ladbroke in Notting Hill. It is there on Square and Road and Terrace. But Ladbroke's was not yet a famous firm of London bookmakers and if the street names were coded messages from the future, Oscar did not know how to read them.

PETER CAREY, *Oscar and Lucinda*, 1988

Westbourne Park

One vivid contrast hung in his mind symbolical. On the one hand were the coalies of the Westbourne Park yards, on strike and gaunt and

hungry, children begging in the black slush, and starving loungers outside a soup kitchen; and on the other, Westbourne Grove, two streets
further, a blazing array of crowded shops, a stirring traffic of cabs and
carriages, and such a spate of spending that a tired student in leaky
boots and graceless clothes hurrying home was continually impeded in
the whirl of skirts and parcels and sweetly pretty womanliness.

H.G. WELLS, *Love and Mr Lewisham*, 1900

Royal Oak

. . . the name of an old rural tavern, the entrance to which was by way
of a wooden plank over the Westbourne River.

CYRIL M. HARRIS, *What's in a Name?*, 1977

Sometimes Jass thought it might be just as well that she never saw the
places with names she liked. Royal Oak sounded like something out of
Shakespeare, though probably it was nothing but a pub.

CATHERINE STORR, *The Underground Conspiracy*, 1987

Paddington
Change for Bakerloo, Circle and District lines

Amongst the last of the departing guests the fourth and fifth brothers
[Forsyte], Nicholas and Roger, walked away together, directing their
steps alongside Hyde Park towards the Praed Street [Paddington]
Station of the Underground. . . .

They entered the station.

'What class are you going? I go second.'

'No second for me,' said Nicholas; 'you never know what you may
catch.'

He took a first-class ticket to Notting Hill Gate; Roger a second
to South Kensington. The train coming in a minute later, the two
brothers parted and entered their respective compartments. Each felt
aggrieved that the other had not modified his habits to secure his society a little longer; but as Roger voiced it in his thoughts:

'Always a stubborn beggar, Nick!'

And as Nicholas expressed it to himself:

'Cantankerous chap Roger always was!'

JOHN GALSWORTHY, *The Man of Property*, 1906

The Mole found himself placed next to Mr Badger, and, as the other two were still deep in river-gossip from which nothing could divert them, he took the opportunity to tell Badger how comfortable and home-like it all felt to him. 'Once well underground,' he said, 'you know exactly where you are. Nothing can happen to you, and nothing can get at you. You're entirely your own master, and you don't have to consult anybody or mind what they say. Things go on all the same overhead, and you let 'em, and don't bother about 'em. When you want to, up you go, and there the things are, waiting for you.'

The Badger simply beamed on him. 'That's exactly what I say,' he replied. 'There's no security, or peace and tranquillity, except underground. And then, if your ideas get larger and you wanted to expand – why, a dig and a scrape and there you are! If you feel your house is a bit too big, you stop up a hole or two, and there you are again! No builders, no tradesmen, no remarks passed on you by fellows looking over your wall, and, above all, no weather.'

KENNETH GRAHAME, *The Wind in the Willows*, 1908

Edgware Road
Change for District line

Mr. Sponge had gone along Oxford Street at a somewhat improved pace to his usual wont – had paused for a shorter period in the ''bus' perplexed 'Circus', and pulled up seldomer than usual between the Circus and the limits of his stroll. Behold him now at the Edgware Road end, eyeing the 'busses with a wanting-a-ride like air, instead of the contemptuous sneer he generally adopts towards those uncouth productions. Red, green, blue, drab, cinnamon-colour, passed and crossed, and jostled, and stopped, and blocked, and the cads telegraphed, and winked, and nodded, and smiled, and slanged, but Mr. Sponge regarded them not. He had a sort of ''bus' panorama in his head, knew the run of them all, whence they started, where they stopped, where they watered, where they changed, and wonderful to relate, had never been entrapped into a sixpenny fare when he meant to take a threepenny one. In cab and ''bus' geography there is not a more learned man in London.

R.S. SURTEES, *Mr Sponge's Sporting Tour*, 1853

Baker Street

Change for Bakerloo, Jubilee and Metropolitan lines

One night – it was on the 20th of March, 1888 – I was returning from a journey to a patient (for I had now returned to civil practice), when my way led me through Baker-street. As I passed the well-remembered door, which must always be associated in my mind with my wooing, and with the dark incidents of the Study in Scarlet, I was seized with a keen desire to see Holmes again, and to know how he was employing his extraordinary powers. His rooms were brilliantly lit, and, even as I looked up, I saw his tall spare figure pass twice in a dark silhouette against the blind. He was pacing the room swiftly, eagerly, with his head sunk upon his chest, and his hands clasped behind him. To me, who knew his every mood and habit, his attitude and manner told their own story. He was at work again. He had arisen out of his drug-created dreams, and was hot upon the scent of some new problem. I rang the bell, and was shown up to the chamber which had formerly been in part my own.

SIR ARTHUR CONAN DOYLE, 'A Scandal in Bohemia',
The Adventures of Sherlock Holmes, 1892

Great Portland Street

James Boswell died in a house on the site of No. 122 in 1795 and Carl Maria von Weber at No. 91 in 1826. Leigh Hunt lived at No. 98 in 1812, and David Wilkie at No. 117 in 1808–9.

The London Encyclopaedia edited by Ben Weinreb
and Christopher Hibbert, 1983

Euston Square

'We must be running late,' the passengers had been saying from time to time, uncertainly glancing at one another as though the feeling of lateness might be subjective, then at the blinded windows of the carriage. 'Whereabouts would we be now? – how far are we along?' Now and then somebody in a corner prised at a blind's edge, put an eye to the crack – but it was useless; Midland canals and hedges were long gone from view; not a hill or tower showed through the drape of night; every main-line landmark was blotted out. Only a loud catastrophic roar told them, even, when they were in a tunnel. But by now speed had begun to slacken; from the sound of the train, more and more often constricted deep in cuttings between and under walls, they must be entering London: no other city's built-up density could be so strongly felt. . . . Euston. All the way down the train doors burst open while the inky ribbon of platform still slipped by. Nobody could wait for the train to stop; everybody was hurling themselves on London.

ELIZABETH BOWEN, *The Heat of the Day*, 1949

King's Cross St. Pancras
Change for Northern, Piccadilly and Victoria lines

June 10, 1769. Advertisement [placed by John Armstrong].

St. Pancras Wells Waters are in the greatest perfection, and highly recommended by the most eminent physicians in the kingdom. To prevent mistakes, St. Pancras Wells is on that side the churchyard towards London; the house and gardens of which are as genteel and rural as any round this metropolis; the best of tea, coffee, and hot loaves, every day, may always be depended on, with neat wines, curious punch, Dorchester, Marlborough and Ringwood beers; Burton, Yorkshire, and other fine ales and cyder; and also cows kept to accommodate ladies and gentlemen with new milk and cream, and syllabubs in the greatest perfection.

W. THORNBURY AND E. WALFORD, *Old and New London*, 1873–8

Farringdon

Once on a stall in Farringdon Road I found
An atlas folio of great lithographs,
Views of Ionian Isles, flyleaf inscribed
By Edward Lear – and bought it for a bob.
Perhaps one day I'll find a 'first' of Keats,
Wedged between Goldsmith and *The Law of Torts;*
Perhaps – but that was not the reason why
Untidy bookshops gave me such delight.
It was the smell of books, the plates in them,
Tooled leather, marbled paper, gilded edge . . .

JOHN BETJEMAN, *Summoned by Bells*, 1960

Barbican

[John Milton] was buried in the same grave as his father at St Giles
Without Cripplegate, a much damaged and much restored medieval
church in the modern Barbican.

IAN OUSBY, *Literary Britain and Ireland*, 1990

Moorgate
Change for Northern Line

June 23rd 1887. I had my first experience of Hades to-day, and if the
real thing is to be like that I shall never again do anything wrong. I got
into the Underground railway at Baker Street. I wanted to go to
Moorgate Street in the City. . . . The compartment in which I sat was
filled with passengers who were smoking pipes, as is the British habit,
and as the smoke and sulphur from the engine fill the tunnel, all the
windows have to be closed. The atmosphere was a mixture of sulphur,
coal dust and foul fumes from the oil lamp above; so that by the time
we reached Moorgate Street I was near dead of asphyxiation and heat.
I should think these Underground railways must soon be discontinued,
for they are a menace to health. A few minutes earlier can be no consideration, since hansom cabs and omnibuses, carried by the swiftest
horses I have seen anywhere, do the work most satisfactorily.

R.D. BLUMENFELD, *R.D.B.'s Diary, 1887–1914*, 1930

Liverpool Street
Change for Central, Circle and Metropolitan lines

Ben did not go straight home from Liverpool Street Station. This was the last day of the boys' summer holidays, when Mrs Blewitt always gave them a treat. That was why she had brought Frankie and Paul to meet Ben. They all went straight to have baked beans on toast in the station Help-Yourself that overlooks the comings and goings of the trains.

PHILIPPA PEARCE, *A Dog So Small*, 1962

Aldgate East
Change for District line

The Saxons called it Ealdgate, old gate. It was rebuilt at some time between 1108 and 1147. In 1215, the year of Magna Carta, the Barons came through it on their way to lay siege to the Tower.

The London Encyclopaedia edited by Ben Weinreb
and Christopher Hibbert, 1983

Whitechapel
Change for District line

And away went the coach up Whitechapel, to the admiration of the whole population of that pretty densely-populated quarter.

'Not a wery nice neighbourhood this, Sir,' said Sam, with the touch of the hat which always preceded his entering into conversation with his master.

'It is not indeed, Sam,' replied Mr Pickwick, surveying the crowded and filthy street through which they were passing.

'It's a wery remarkable circumstance, Sir,' said Sam, 'that poverty and oysters always seems to go together.'

'I don't understand you, Sam,' said Mr Pickwick.

'What I mean, Sir,' said Sam, 'is, that the poorer a place is, the greater call there seems to be for oysters. Look here, Sir; here's a oyster stall to every half-dozen houses – the street's lined with 'em. Blessed if I don't think that ven a man's wery poor, he rushes out of his lodgings, and eats oysters in reg'lar desperation.'

'To be sure he does,' said Mr Weller senior, 'and it's just the same vith pickled salmon!'

'Those are two very remarkable facts, which never occurred to me before,' said Mr Pickwick. 'The very first place we stop at, I'll make a note of them.'

CHARLES DICKENS, *The Pickwick Papers*, 1836–7

All day I loafed in the streets, east as far as Wapping, west as far as Whitechapel. It was queer after Paris; everything was so much cleaner and quieter and drearier. . . . The crowds were better dressed and the faces comelier and milder and more alike, without that fierce individuality of the French. . . . It was the land of the tea urn and the Labour Exchange, as Paris is the land of the bistro and the sweatshop.

GEORGE ORWELL, *Down and Out in Paris and London*, 1933

In peak hours this line continues up to Barking.

JUBILEE LINE

Charing Cross
Change for Bakerloo and Northern lines

Undone, undone the lawyers are,
  They wander about the towne,
Nor can find the way to Westminster,
  Now Charing-cross is downe:
At the end of the Strand they make a stand,
  Swearing they are at a loss,
And chaffing say, that's not the way,
  They must go by Charing-cross.

'The Downfall of Charing-Cross', T. Percy's
Reliques of Ancient English Poetry, 1765

. . . the great railway station of which a bygone poet sang:
  'The terminus of Charing Cross
    Is haunted, when it rains,
  By Nymphs, who there a shelter seek,
    And wait for mythic trains.'

ARTHUR M. BINSTEAD, *Pitcher in Paradise*, 1903

. . . Trafalgar Square
(The fountains volleying golden glaze)
Gleams like an angel-market. High aloft
Over his couchant Lions in a haze
Shimmering and bland and soft,
A dust of chrysoprase,
Our Sailor takes the golden gaze
Of the slanting sun, and flames superb
As once he flamed it on his ocean round.

W.E. HENLEY, 'London Voluntaries',
London Voluntaries . . . and Other Verses, 1893

Green Park
Change for Piccadilly and Victoria lines

I have a weakness for the convenient, familiar, treeless, or almost tree-less, expanse of the Green Park, and the friendly part it plays as a kind of encouragement to Piccadilly. I am so fond of Piccadilly that I am grateful to any one or anything that does it a service.

HENRY JAMES, 'London', *English Hours*, 1905

Bond Street
Change for Central line

All Sublunary things of Death partake;
What Alteration does a Cent'ry make?
Kings and Comedians all are mortal found,
Caesar and *Pinkethman* are under Ground.
What's not destroy'd by Time's devouring Hand?
Where's *Troy*, and where's the *May-pole* in the *Strand*?
Pease, Cabbages, and Turnips once grew, where
Now stand new *Bond-Street*, and a newer Square;
Such Piles of Buildings now rise up and down,
London itself seems going out of *Town*.

JAMES BRAMSTON, *The Art of Politicks, In Imitation of Horace's Art of Poetry*,
1729 (published anonymously)

Old Bond street where, 'at the silk bag shop' in 1768, Laurence Sterne breathed his last. He murmured: 'Now it is come,' and then 'put up his hand as if to stop a blow, and died in a minute'. His servants rifled his possessions and made off with everything they could carry. It is said that even his body was stolen. It was dug up by the Resurrection men, at dead of night, and sold to an anatomist. While it was in the process of being dissected, the anatomist was joined by a colleague. As luck would have it, he was one of Sterne's life-long friends. He glanced at the corpse and fainted.

PETER BUSHELL, *London's Secret History*, 1983

Bond Street fascinated her; Bond Street early in the morning in the season; its flags flying; its shops; no splash; no glitter; one roll of tweed in the shop where her father had bought his suits for fifty years; a few pearls; salmon on an iceblock.

VIRGINIA WOOLF, *Mrs Dalloway*, 1925

I like to walk down Bond street, thinking of all the things I don't desire.

LOGAN PEARSALL SMITH, *Afterthoughts*, 1931

At Bond Street a lot of people get out, and the train stays still long enough to read comfortably the poem provided by the Keepers of the Underground, inserted into a row of advertisements.

DORIS LESSING, 'In Defence of the Underground', *London Observed*, 1992

Baker Street
Change for Bakerloo, Circle, Hammersmith & City
and Metropolitan lines

Ladies, are you aware that the great Pitt lived in Baker Street?

WILLIAM MAKEPEACE THACKERAY, *Vanity Fair*, 1847–8

St. John's Wood

The fields from Islington to Marybone,
To Primrose Hill and Saint John's Wood,
Were builded over with pillars of gold,
And there Jerusalem's pillars stood.

WILLIAM BLAKE, *Jerusalem: The Emanation of the Giant Albion,* 1804–20

. . . this was a district which no Forsyte entered without open disapproval and secret curiosity.

JOHN GALSWORTHY, *The Man of Property,* 1906

I had entered the precincts of St. John's Wood; and as I went past its villas of coquettish aspect, with gay Swiss gables, with frivolously Gothic or Italian or almost Oriental faces, their lighter outlook on existence, the air they have of not taking life too seriously, began to exert an influence.

St. John's Wood is the home in fiction of adventuresses and profligacy and outrageous supper-parties.

LOGAN PEARSALL SMITH, *More Trivia,* 1921

They had gone to live in St. John's Wood, that airy uphill neighbourhood where the white and buff-coloured houses, pilastered or gothic, seem to have been built in a grove. A fragrant, faint impropriety, orris-dust of a century, still hangs over part of this neighbourhood; glass passages lead in from high green gates, garden walls are mysterious, laburnums falling between the windows and walls have their own secrets. Acacias whisper at nights round airy, ornate little houses in which pretty women lived singly but were not always alone. In the unreal late moonlight you might hear a ghostly hansom click up the empty road, or see on a pale wall the shadow of an opera cloak.

ELIZABETH BOWEN, *To the North,* 1932

Swiss Cottage

Bulletin No. 1
GREETINGS to our nightly companions, our temporary cave dwellers, our sleeping companions, somnambulists, snorers, chatterers and all

who inhabit the Swiss Cottage station of the Bakerloo nightly from dusk to dawn.

This is the first in a series of announcements, issued in the name of co-operation, so that we may find what comfort and amenities there may be in this our nightly place of refuge.

Bulletin No. 2

EXPERT ADVICE: Vibration due to heavy gunfire or other causes will be felt much less if you do not lie with your head against the wall.

Bulletin No. 3

WITHOUT COMMENT: Our sleeping companions last night were a boy of six and his sister of nine. When the All Clear was sounded at 6.30 they said, 'We are going home now to a nice breakfast.' 'Not to sleep?' 'Oh yes! We go to sleep then, until twelve or half-past. Then about two o'clock we come back and wait until they let us into the station at four o'clock.'

WARBLING NOTE OF VARYING PITCH: One thousand five hundred and three people slept in this station-shelter the other evening. 1,503! 1,650 of whom seemed to be snoring. And the Government is distributing *ear*-plugs!

THE SWISS COTTAGER, *De Profundis*, Organ of the Air Raid Shelterers at
Swiss Cottage Station, London NW3, September 1940

Finchley Road
Change for Metropolitan line

I am a lucky Londoner, born in the Finchley Road, where Hampstead meets St. John's Wood; the old boundary stone still stood in our garden. For 20 years I lived in Kensington (naturally), and am now to be found in an area known to its residents as Bedford Park, Chiswick, Turnham Green or Acton, according to mood or political affiliation.

MICHAEL FLANDERS in Foreword to *London Between the Lines*
compiled by John Bishop and Virginia Broadbent, 1973

West Hampstead

I am in the little roads [in West Hampstead] full of houses. . . . The streets here are classically inclined. Agamemnon, Achilles, Ulysses, and there is Orestes Mews . . . one may postulate an army man, classically educated, who was given the job of naming these streets. In fact, this was not so far wrong. The story was this. . . . An ex-army man, minor gentry, had a wife in the country with many children, and a mistress in town, with many more. To educate all these he went in for property, bought farmland that spread attractively over a hill with views of London, and built what must have been one of the first northern commuter suburbs . . . for remember in the valley just down from this hill, towards London, were the streams, the cows and the green fields my old friend took a penny bus ride to visit every Sunday. The commuters went in by horse-bus or by train to the City.

DORIS LESSING, 'In Defence of the Underground', *London Observed*, 1992

Going home next day, he noticed as he waited on the platform for the tube to Baker Street, that the track sings as the train comes into West Hampstead, long before you can see it, and the silver lines shiver as it approaches.

BARBARA VINE, *King Solomon's Carpet*, 1991

Kilburn

The grittiness, stench and obscurity of Kilburn suddenly seemed a spiritual force – the immense force of poverty which had produced the narrow, yet intense, visions of Cockneys living in other times, with their home-made poetic philosophies – William Blake at Lambeth, Keats and Leigh Hunt at Hampstead, all the cockney characters of Dickens, dancing in the roads.

STEPHEN SPENDER, *World Within World*, 1951,
after a bad air raid in 1944

Walk a few hundred yards [from St John's Wood] and you are in Kilburn, that is to say, Ireland. Some of the pubs even have posters up for the next Irish horse-race.

WILLIAM SANSOM in *Living in London* edited by Alan Ross, 1974

Willesden Green

What a contrast did the lovely scene she [Mrs Sheppard] now gazed upon present to the squalid neighbourhood she had recently quitted!

On all sides, expanded prospects of country the most exquisite and most varied. Immediately beneath her lay Willesden, – the most charming and secluded village in the neighbourhood of the metropolis – with its scattered farm-houses, its noble granges, and its old grey church tower just peeping above a grove of rook-haunted trees.

W. HARRISON AINSWORTH, *Jack Sheppard*, 1839

Dollis Hill

Jack Sheppard and his companion left Willesden, and taking – as a blind – the direction of Harrow, returned at nightfall by a bye-lane to Neasdon, and put up at a little public-house, called the Spotted Dog. Here they remained till midnight, when, calling for their reckoning and their steeds, they left the house. It was a night well fitted to their enterprise, calm, still, and profoundly dark. As they passed beneath the thick trees that shade the road to Dollis Hill, the gloom was almost impenetrable.

W. HARRISON AINSWORTH, *Jack Sheppard*, 1839

I like travelling by Underground. This is a defiant admission. . . . This is the Jubilee line and I use it all the time. Fifteen minutes at the most to get in to the centre. The carriages are bright and new – well, almost. There are efficient indicators, Charing Cross: five minutes, three minutes, one minute. The platforms are no more littered than the streets, often less, or not at all.

DORIS LESSING, 'In Defence of the Underground',
London Observed, 1992

Neasden

Neasden! You won't be sorry that you breezed in
The traffic lights and yellow lines, the illuminated signs,
All so welcome to the borough that everybody's pleased in.
Neasden! where the birds sing in the trees-den
You can hear the blackbirds coo, so why not take the Bakerloo.
It will work out that much cheaper if you buy a seasdon.

JOHN BETJEMAN, song in 'Metroland'
(TV programme), 1973

Wembley Park
Change for Metropolitan line

The road to Harrow is dominated by one of London's most famous inter-war monuments, Wembley Stadium. Built in 1923 by the firm of Simpson and Ayrton, its four domed towers and scruffy concrete detailing have become the nostalgic symbol of the great days of English soccer – of a world of Brylcreem, shin pads and goalies in flat caps. The stadium was joined by the British Empire Exhibition of 1924, laid out on land to its north and intended as a permanent memorial to imperial achievement. It never attained permanence, but a number of its pavilions remain as gaunt shells along the Empire Way, sprouting occasional Egyptian doorways, classical pediments and even imperial lions. On the hillside above it, the Metroland suburb of Wembley Park looks down in disdain.

SIMON JENKINS, *The Companion Guide to Outer London*, 1981

Kingsbury

[In] Church Lane Kingsbury [there are] two churches in one church-yard, the old one very small, the new one all the prouder and in fact of more historic associations than the old building. The latter is some-times supposed to incorporate pre-Conquest work . . . the walls are more probably Norman than Saxon. Were they Saxon, they would be the only stone remains in Middlesex of so early a period. . . . The new church originally stood in Wells Street W1, and was re-erected at Kingsbury in 1933. It was a famous monument of Early Victorian Anglo-Catholicism, built in 1847. . . . Its Perp[endicular] front with NW tower and spire is big and earnest (and the spire succeeds in giving Kingsbury a genuine, not suburban look, when seen above the trees of the churchyard from across the Welsh Harp).

NIKOLAUS PEVSNER, *The Buildings of England: Middlesex*, 1951

Queensbury

When the new Metropolitan line to Stanmore was opened on 10 December 1932, one station was called Kingsbury. Two years later, a

further station was opened and the name *Queensbury* was invented for
it. Here then is a case of a district getting its name from a railway
station!

CYRIL M. HARRIS, *What's in a Name?*, 1977

Canons Park

Near this Town, the Duke of *Chandos*, has built one of the most magnificent Palaces in *England*, with a Profusion of Expence, and so well furnish'd within, that it has hardly its Equal in. *England*. The Plaistering
and Gilding are done by the famous *Pargotti*, an Italian. . . . The Pillars
supporting the Building are all of Marble: the great Stair-case is
extremely fine, and the Steps are all of marble. . . .

The Gardens are well designed, and have a vast Variety, and the
Canals are very large and noble. . . .

The Chapel is a Singularity, both in its Building and the Beauty of
its Workmanship.

DANIEL DEFOE, *A Tour thro' the Whole Island of Great Britain*, 1742

At Timon's Villa let us pass the day,
Where all cry out, 'What sums are thrown away!'
So proud, so grand, of that stupendous air,
Soft and Agreeable come never there. . . .

To compass this, his building is a Town,
His pond an Ocean, his parterre a Down:
Who but must laugh, the Master when he sees,
A puny insect, shiv'ring at a breeze! . . .

The suff'ring eye inverted Nature sees,
Trees cut to Statues, Statues thick as trees,
With here a Fountain, never to be play'd,
And there a Summer-house, that knows no shade.

ALEXANDER POPE, *Moral Essay Epistle IV: To Richard Boyle, Earl of Burlington*,
1731–5 [Pope had Canons in mind when he wrote this of Timon's Villa]

Whitchurch, alias Little Stanmore, was a place of great importance in
the last [eighteenth] century, during which time Canons, the palatial
residence of the Duke of Chandos, rose and vanished. The church, St.
Lawrence . . . now consists of a nave with a small chancel at its east

end, separated by richly carved oak pillars. . . . The roof of the Chancel is painted azure, and powdered with gilt stars. . . . The rich wood carving throughout the church is by Grinling Gibbons. The nave roof is coved, divided into compartments, and frescoed by the French artists Verrio and Laguerre.*

*Handel's Chandos Anthems were written and are kept in St Lawrence's Church.

REV. JOHN HANSON SPERLING,
Church Walks in Middlesex, 1849

Stanmore

Clement Atlee lived here for 14 years until 1945 [when he moved to 10 Downing Street]. The most picturesque part of the old village [Stanmore] is round the church of St. John in Church Road. Here is an eighteenth century rectory, a barn converted into cottages, and the old Church House. . . . I was looking for a tomb surmounted by a white angel – and there it was and on its base the word 'Mackintosh', the real inscription was on a horizontal slab – this was the grave of W.S. Gilbert.

BRUCE STEVENSON, *Middlesex*, 1972

METROPOLITAN LINE

Aldgate

The western approaches to the walled City of London were . . . magnificent, but to the east it was a very different story, for as the houses of the traders and shopkeepers grew larger and more dignified, the poor retreated to their own suburbs. Eastward, beyond the bars of Aldgate, Stow writes that '. . . in some places it scarce remaineth sufficient highway for the meeting of carriages and droves of cattle: much less is there any fair, pleasant, or wholesome way for people to walk on foot, which is no small blemish to so famous a city to have so unsavoury and unseemly an entrance or passage thereunto'.

MARY CATHCART BORER, *The City of London: A History*, 1977

Liverpool Street
Change for Central, Circle and Hammersmith & City lines

This is the most picturesque and interesting of the London Termini. It has the most varied users. Blond, blue-eyed and large . . . the Scandinavians and Dutch arrive from Harwich on the boat train. A few Belgians and French who come by air to Southend Airport get in at the nearest Essex station. . . . The county families, farmers, vicars, and agricultural manufacturers come in from Norfolk, East Suffolk and outer Essex, from the Gainsborough, Crome and Constable landscapes of flint church towers, deep red brick manor houses, willows, elms, malt houses and mills. . . . You find yourself on an elevated walk, a long and attractive one. . . . This high walk all under the roof of the station takes you past the original English yellow brick-and-stone Gothic of the Great Eastern's first effort into the really spendid vista of columns and iron roofs of what most people mean by Liverpool Street Station. The Great Eastern wanted their train shed to be Cathedral-like as the buildings. . . . Double columns support the two main aisles. Beyond these are yet further aisles. The eastward view is enlivened by a delightful verandah fret, outlined black against the grey east-London sky. . . . By some great good fortune a sister teashop to what is now the Stationmaster's office remains perched on our upland walk. I know no greater pleasure for elevenses in London than to sit in this tea place and watch the trains arrive and depart.

JOHN BETJEMAN, *London's Historic Railway Stations*, 1972

Moorgate
Change for Circle and Northern lines

When I was small I ran away
   And through the Moor-gate tried to stray
   To pick a bunch of heather;
But there a man paced to and fro
In garments that were white as snow,
   Though he was brown as leather.

His sword was like the sickle moon,
He stood up in his scarlet shoon
   Taller than any other!
He laid his finger on his breast,
And he looked East, so I ran West
   Crying for my Mother.

ELEANOR FARJEON, *Nursery Rhymes of London Town*, 1917

Barbican

When the great bell
BOOMS over the Portland stone urn, and
From the carved cedar wood
Rises the odour of incense,
I SIT DOWN
In St. Botolph Bishopsgate Churchyard
And wait for the spirit of my grandfather
Toddling along from the Barbican.

JOHN BETJEMAN, 'City', *Continual Dew*, 1937

Farringdon

I sallied out, down Holborn, and turned down Farringdon Street. . . .
There are in this street one or two places used as headquarters for the

stage waggons – the old six-horsed Saxon wains, with low broad wheels and hoop canopies. When laden and in motion they look like haystacks covered with tarpaulin, and rumbling on wheels. They have a tremendous difficulty to surmount on starting – to get up Holborn Hill. I have often watched them here – seen all the muscles of eight stout horses on the stretch for seven or eight minutes, to move one of these wains a distance of about thirty yards.

JOHN TOWNE DANSON, *Economic and Statistical Studies 1840-1890*, 1906

At FARRINGDON that lunch hour at a stall
He bought a dozen plants of London Pride;
While she, in arc-lit Oxford Street adrift,
Soared through the sales by safe hydraulic lift.

JOHN BETJEMAN, 'The Metropolitan Railway – Baker Street Station Buffet', *A Few Late Chrysanthemums*, 1954

King's Cross St. Pancras
Change for Circle, Hammersmith & City, Northern, Piccadilly and Victoria lines

Boadicea rallied her forces and sacked Colchester, London and St Albans, leaving in her wake seventy thousand Roman dead. . . . When the two armies met, the Iceni were overwhelmingly defeated, their dead outnumbering those of the Romans by two hundred to one. Boadicea and her daughters promptly swallowed poison. She lies buried somewhere under Platform 10 at King's Cross Station.

PETER BUSHELL, *London's Secret History*, 1983

Even when he had bought his ticket, a first-class that he could hardly afford, in the leisurely fashion demanded by such an act of self-indulgence, and had loitered at the kiosks buying papers and a tin of tobacco, Adam Stewart discovered that he had still some twenty minutes or so left. Not that it mattered; they would soon pass. He found himself repeating, with the solemn relish of one who achieves nonsense, 'Pancrastination is the thief of time.' St. Pancras, surely the most canonical of all our stations, seemed to rebuke his levity. Indignant puffs of smoke and steam, sudden red glares of anger, ascended to the great arched roof. The locomotives grunted and wheezed like outraged sacristans. The thin high voices of the newsboys ran together into a protesting chorus of virgins and elders. But no, that was Greek drama, Adam reminded himself, and nothing to do with cathedrals, and it is with cathedrals that large railway stations must always be compared.

J.B. PRIESTLEY, *Adam in Moonshine*, 1927

Dr Haldane sought out a pharmacist in Gower Street who had for many years dispensed his own 'Metropolitan Mixture' to ease the plight of persons emerging in distress from the nearby station. *

*A visit to this shop is described in a letter to *The Times*, 14 June 1879. The victim reported himself as instantly diagnosed: – 'Oh! I see – Metropolitan Railway!' As he gratefully downed the medicine, he was told by the pharmacist that he often treated up to twenty cases a day.

ALAN A. JACKSON, *London's Metropolitan Railway*, 1986

Euston Square

It was a railway passenger,
    And he leapt out jauntilie.
'Now up and bear, thou stout portèr,
    My two chattèls to me.

Bring hither, bring hither my bag so red,
    And portmanteau so brown:
(They lie in the van, for a trusty man
    He labelled them London town.)

And fetch me eke a cabman bold,
    That I may be his fare, his fare;
And he shall have a good shilling,
    If by two of the clock he do me bring
    To the Terminus, Euston Square.'

C.S. CALVERLEY, 'Striking', *Verses and Translations*, 1862

'The first Pullman cars in Europe to be hauled by electricity.'

'No, really? The first in Europe?' I was almost as interested as I pretended to be.

'The first in Europe. There's a lot of history in this line, you know. Heard of John Stuart Mill?'

'Yes.' (Of course not).

'Do you know what his last speech in the House was about?'

I think I must have shown that I didn't.

'The House of Commons. His last speech? It was about the Underground. Can you imagine that? The Railway Regulation Bill, 1868. An amendment was moved to the bill making it obligatory for all railways to attach a smoking carriage to their trains. Mill got the bill through. Made a great speech in favour of it. Carried the day.'

'Jolly good. It was jolly good wasn't it?'

'But – guess what – there was one railway, just one, that was exempted. That was the Metropolitan.'

'Why?'

'Ah. Because of the smoke in the tunnels. It's always been a bit special, you see.'

JULIAN BARNES, *Metroland*, 1980

Great Portland Street

I remember well, when I was in my eighth year [1774], Mr Nollekens calling at my father's house in Great Portland Street, to see the notorious Jack Rann, commonly called Sixteen-String Jack, go to Tyburn to be hanged. . . . The criminal was dressed in a pea-green coat with an immense nosegay in his button-hole, which had been presented to him at St Sepulchre's steps; and his nankeen small-clothes, we were told, were tied at each knee with sixteen strings. [Jack had boasted that his sixteen strings represented the sixteen times he had been tried and acquitted.]

J.T. SMITH, *A Book for a Rainy Day*, 1905 edition

November 6th 1863. To Hatton Garden by the Metropolitan Railway to get me a stronger pair of spectacles. Never saw the underground rail before; it gives one the idea of going into an immense, tidy coal cellar, did not strike cold but smelt rather sepulchral.

LOUISA BAIN quoted in *A Bookseller Looks Back*, 1940

Baker Street

Change for Bakerloo, Circle, Jubilee and Hammersmith & City lines

This plaque marks the restoration of Baker Street Station platforms 5 & 6. The two platforms were part of the world's first underground railway which opened in 1863 between Paddington and Farringdon. Unveiled by R.M. Robbins, April 1984

Plaque at Baker Street Station

As we came up at Baker Street,
Where tubes and trains and 'buses meet
There's a touch of fog and a touch of sleet;
And we go on up Hampstead way
Towards the closing of the day. . . .

But here we are in the Finchley Road
With a drizzling rain and a skidding 'bus
And the twilight settling down on us.

FORD MADOX HUEFFER, 'Finchley Road',
Songs from London, 1916

Finchley Road

Change for Jubilee line

I had now arrived at that particular point of my walk where four roads met – the road to Hampstead, along which I had returned, the road to Finchley, the road to West End, and the road back to London. I had mechanically turned in this latter direction, and was strolling along the lonely highroad – idly wondering, I remember, what the Cumberland young ladies would look like – when, in one moment, every drop of blood in my body was brought to a stop by the touch of a hand laid lightly and suddenly on my shoulder from behind me.

I turned on the instant, with my fingers tightening round the handle of my stick.

There, in the middle of the broad, bright highroad – there, as if it had that moment sprung out of the earth or dropped from the heaven – stood the figure of a solitary Woman, dressed from head to foot in white garments, her face bent in grave inquiry on mine, her hand pointing to the dark cloud over London, as I faced her.

I was far too seriously startled by the suddenness with which this extraordinary apparition stood before me, in the dead of night and in that lonely place, to ask what she wanted. The strange woman spoke first.

'Is that the road to London?' she said . . .

'Yes,' I replied, 'that is the way: it leads to St John's Wood and the Regent's Park.'

> WILKIE COLLINS, *The Woman in White*, 1860

Now in the evening, after work,
We race into the gathering murk
Together, on the Child's Hill bus,
While all the stars smile down on us –
I and my love, and London nights,
Sufficient for our naive delights!

> DOUGLAS GOLDRING, 'Finchley Road', *Streets*, 1912

Wembley Park
Change for Jubilee line

Wembley Park . . . originated as a private estate owned by Richard Page for whom it was landscaped by Humphrey Repton in 1793. The Metropolitan Railway passed through the park in 1880 and the whole estate was acquired by the Railway Company in 1889 for a leisure centre for north-west London.

> *The London Encyclopaedia* edited by Ben Weinreb and Christopher Hibbert, 1983

Preston Road

Smoothly from HARROW, passing PRESTON ROAD,
  They saw the last green fields and misty sky,
At NEASDEN watched a workmen's train unload,
  And, with the morning villas sliding by,
They felt so sure on their electric trip
That Youth and Progress were in partnership.

JOHN BETJEMAN, 'The Metropolitan Railway – Baker Street Station Buffet', *A Few Late Chrysanthemums*, 1954

Northwick Park

From then on, I was not only interested in my journey, but proud of it. The termitary of Kilburn; the grimy, lost stations between Baker Street and Finchley Road; the steppe-like playing-fields at Northwick Park; the depot at Neasden, full of idle, aged rolling-stock; the frozen faces of passengers glimpsed in the windows of fast Marylebone trains. They were all, in some way, relevant, fulfilling, sensibility-sharpening. And what was life about if not that?

JULIAN BARNES, Metroland, 1980

Harrow-on-the-Hill

Change for Amersham, Chesham and Watford branches

I wish to be buried in Harrow church: there is a spot in the church-yard, near the footpath, on the brow of the hill looking towards Windsor, and a tomb under a large tree (bearing the name of Peachie, or Peachey), where I used to sit for hours and hours when a boy: this was my favourite spot.

LORD BYRON, letter to John Murray, 26 May 1822,
from Montenero near Leghorn

> Ye scenes of my childhood, whose loved recollection
> Embitters the present, compared with the past;
> Where science first dawn'd on the powers of reflection,
> And friendships were form'd, too romantic to last. . . .
> Again, I behold where for hours I have ponder'd,
> As reclining, at eve, on yon tombstone I lay;
> Or round the steep brow of the churchyard I wander'd
> To catch the last gleam of the sun's setting ray.

LORD BYRON, 'On a distant view of the village and school of
Harrow on the Hill', Hours of Idleness, 1807

Harrow-on-the-Hill is in the middle of the suburbs: the tomb in the Parish churchyard where Byron once lay and composed poetry as he looked over rolling meadows now commands a fine view of the semis of Hillingdon and Pinner. It was only a few stops from Baker Street on the Metropolitan Line and we used to sit in the smoke-filled carriages to be jeered at as we went up to Lord's, dressed in top hat, pearl-grey waistcoat, morning coat and silver-topped stick with a dark-blue tassel. We weren't allowed to speak to the boys at the bottom of the hill, although a Prefect might occasionally give one of them sixpence to carry up his suitcase at the beginning of term.

JOHN MORTIMER, *Cng to the Wreckage*, 1982

UXBRIDGE BRANCH

West Harrow

Turn to page 151 for North Harrow

The parish church of Harrow, from its situation on the summit of a hill . . . is an object unusually conspicuous, and cannot fail to attract the notice of all who travel along the North Western Railway. It is recorded that when some divines were disputing with King Charles II about the *visible Church*, his Majesty said that he 'knew not where it was to be found, except, indeed, at Harrow'.

E. WALFORD, *Greater London*, 1882–4

'I love Harrow,' said Sir John Betjeman recently, 'first because it is not Eton and secondly because I believe I was at school there . . . in spirit if not in fact.'

I find no surprise that he should say so . . . and also for two reasons: first because it is one of the most complete, compact and unspoiled complexes of Victorian architecture in the country, and second because it is visibly, if not in fact, the capital city of Metroland – that strange Arcady that was the product, some fifty years ago, of a partnership between the Metropolitan Railway and the speculative builder.

HUGH CASSON, *Hugh Casson's London*, 1983

I have very early recollections of the various Underground railways – all electrified by 1902 – and of their biscuit-coloured basket-work seats, their swaying straps, the constant smell of hot metal from (I supposed) the 'live rail', and the shouts of the guards – one guard to every other carriage.

C.H. ROLPH, *London Particulars*, 1980

Rayners Lane
Change for Piccadilly line

It was at the lonely spot of Rayners Lane [1923] where the Metropolitan had a junction with the District Railway (so bleak in winter, that the windswept platforms were known as Pneumonia Junction) that the first large-scale housing development took place. . . . Another advertisement for three Nash houses claimed that 'living in Rayners Lane would be all peace and quiet, a place where the din and turmoil of the streets are exchanged for an aspect of spreading landscapes . . . of trees and green pastures where the only sounds are of birds . . .'. Growth was rapid: in 1930, Rayners Lane station was handling 22,000 passengers a year. By 1937 the total was a staggering four million!

DENNIS EDWARDS AND RON PIGRAM,
London's Underground Suburbs, 1986

Eastcote

The days of the great School Treat were still with us in the 1900s – a Victorian children's outing for a year of good attendance at Sunday School or day school – and went on well into the Thirties.

In west London children were taken on highly organised outings . . . to the countryside at Ruislip or Eastcote.

DENNIS EDWARDS AND RON PIGRAM,
London's Underground Suburbs, 1986

'Où habites-tu?' *they would ask year after year, drilling us for French orals; and always I would smirkingly reply,*

'J'habite Metroland.'

It sounded better than Eastwick, stranger than Middlesex; more like a concept in the mind than a place where you shopped. And so, of course, it was. As the Metropolitan Railway had pushed westward in the 1880s, a thin corridor of land was opened up with no geographical or ideological unity; you lived there because it was an area easy to get out of. The name Metroland – adopted during the First World War both by estate agents and the railway itself – gave the string of rural suburbs a spurious integrity.

JULIAN BARNES, *Metroland*, 1980

Ruislip Manor

And all that day in murky London Wall
The thought of RUISLIP kept him warm inside . . .

JOHN BETJEMAN, 'The Metropolitan Railway – Baker Street
Station Buffet', *A Few Late Chrysanthemums*, 1984

Ruislip

Even those who feel a preference for the delights of man-made civilisation invariably find that if their days are to be spent in the big city, they are happy to return, in the quiet dusk of the evenings, to nature's stronghold outside the town, enthused the Manor Homes brochure. At Ruislip each house was 'a palace in miniature' and prices started at £450 for a two-bedroomed home – with weekly repayments of 12s.6d. [62¹/₂p] after a £5 deposit.

DENNIS EDWARDS AND RON PIGRAM,
London's Underground Suburbs, 1986

The tricks of travel were learned early. How to fold a full-sized newspaper vertically so that you could turn over in the width of one page. How to pretend you hadn't seen the sort of women you were expected to stand up for. Where to stand in a full train to get the best chance of a seat when it began to empty. Where to get on a train so that you got off at just the right spot. How to use the no-exit tunnels for short cuts.

JULIAN BARNES, *Metroland*, 1980

Ickenham

So we together merrily to Swakely [Ickenham], Sir R. Viner's – a very pleasant place . . . He showed me a black boy that he had that died of a consumption; and being dead, he caused him to be dried in a Oven, and lies there entire in a box. By and by to dinner.

SAMUEL PEPYS, *Diary, 7 September 1665*

Hillingdon

The Red Lion entertained Charles I as an unwilling guest after his escape from Oxford, with Dr Michael Hudson, his chaplain, and Mr Ashburnham, one of his grooms of the bedchamber, in April 1646:

After we had passed Uxbridge at one Mr. Teasdale's house a taverne in Hillingdon, we alighted & stayed to refresh ourselves, betwixt 10 and 11 of the Clocke; & there stayed two or three hours: where the King was much perplexed what Course to resolve upon, London, or North-ward? The Considerations of the former Vote, & the apparent Danger of being discovered at London, moved him to resolve at last to go North-ward, & through Norfolke, where he was least knowne. . . . About 2 of the clocke we tooke a Guide towards Barnet, resolving to crosse the Roads into Essex. But, after we were passed Harrow upon the Hill, I told the King, if we were not knowne much in S. Albon's road, it was much the nearer Way to go thro' S. Albons, & thence towards Royston, which he approved of. And so we passed through S. Albons, where one old Man with an Halberd asked us, whence we came? I told him, from the Parliament; and threw him 6d & soe passed.

FRANCIS PECK, *Desiderata Curiosa*, vol. ii, lib. IX, 21, 1735

Uxbridge

It is supposed by some that, like Oxford, the town derived its name from the number of oxen continually passing through it from Bucking-hamshire and the western counties on their way up to London.

E. WALFORD, *Greater London*, 1882–4

On Thursday 30th June 1904 the Metropolitan laid on a lavish opening ceremony for its new line to Uxbridge. A special train, hauled by 0-0-4T no 1, gaily decorated with flags and evergreens, its coal painted white, was worked from Baker Street to South Harrow and Uxbridge. Luncheon was then served in a marquee in Uxbridge Station yard, where two of the new Metropolitan electric stock trailer cars were parked for inspection by the guests. It was evidently a very pleasant day, for a journey that would be unrecognisable to present residents of the area . . . bathed in glorious sunshine and scented with new mown hay, the countryside was at its best. Here stretches of meadowland, with herds of sleek cattle grazing lazily, there the clink and rattle of grass-cutting machines. Plump partridges raised their startled heads and a pheasant, with the glorious plumage shining like burnished gold, ran for cover.

Middlesex & Buckinghamshire Advertiser, 2 July 1904, quoted in *London's Metropolitan Railway* by Alan A. Jackson, 1986

AMERSHAM AND CHESHAM BRANCHES

North Harrow

By 1914, the western end of Harrow had reached out along the Pinner road mainly by the efforts of local builder Albert Cutler. . . .

Living at North Harrow was given an extra air of security by one of Cutler's advertisements: 'Many of our houses have been purchased by surveyors, bankers and architects.' No doubt they were attracted by the superb stained-glass windows in every hall and landing. There was a choice of designs: sailing ships; lighthouses and seagulls; windmills; and the inevitable sunrise. Surely, these rows of semi-detached houses in their narrow road overhung by flowering trees, the gardens full of rustic trellis and roses, capture the very essence of Metro-land.

DENNIS EDWARDS AND RON PIGRAM, *London's Underground Suburbs*, 1986

Pinner

There was an Old Person of Pinner,
As thin as a lath, if not thinner;
They dressed him in white,
And roll'd him up tight,
That elastic Old Person of Pinner.

EDWARD LEAR, *More Nonsense, Pictures, Rhymes, Botany, etc.*,1872

Early Electric! Sit you down and see,
  'Mid this fine woodwork and a smell of dinner,
A stained glass windmill and a pot of tea,
  And sepia views of leafy lanes in PINNER,
Then visualise far down the shining lines,
Your parents' homestead set in murmuring pines.

JOHN BETJEMAN, 'Metropolitan Railway – Baker Street Station Buffet',
  A Few Late Chrysanthemums, 1954

Pinner, a parish of a thousand souls,
'Til the railways gave it many thousand more.
Pinner is famous for its village Fair
Where once a year, St John the Baptist's Day,
Shows all the climbing High Street filled with stalls.
It is the Feast Day of the Parish Saint,
A medieval Fair in Metro-land.

JOHN BETJEMAN, 'Metro-land' (TV programme), 1973, quoted in
  The Best of Betjeman selected by John Guest, 1978

Northwood Hills

Oh, for the rolling Northwood Hills, the wild places of Ongar and the
savage ravines of Gants Hill. The names are as evocative and remote as
Persepolis and Samarkand.

PHILIP HOWARD, *The Times*

Northwood

. . . the most ambitious Metropolitan suburb along the 'Extension' Line
was between Pinner and Northwood. Here there were open fields until
1930, when two business men, H. Peachey and Harry Neal, produced
plans for a completely new suburb. A competition was held to find a
name through the local press. The winner of the £5 prize was a lady
from North Harrow with 'Northwood Hills'. . . .

Houses soon began creeping up muddy Porridge Pot Hill, which was
renamed Potter Street for suburban tastes . . . the first residents in the
chill of winter were not competely happy. . . . 'I arrived at a station,'
wrote one early Metro-land pioneer, 'and stepped into mud of the

most adhesive quality I had ever seen or felt yet I was to find that residing in a suburb adds a thrill and a zest to life. It is an experience in having no tradition to live up to.'

DENNIS EDWARDS AND RON PIGRAM,
London's Underground Suburbs, 1986

It is a comfort to those that never go farther out than the central warren of the London Underground that the roots of their system stretch out to the country where rabbits roam and stockbrokers play golf.

PHILIP HOWARD, *The Times*

Moor Park

Did ever Golf Club have a nineteenth hole
So sumptuous as this?
Did ever Golf Club have so fine a hall?
Venetian decor, 1732.

And yonder dome is not a dome at all
But painted in the semblance of a dome;
The sculptured figures all are done in paint
That lean towards us with so rapt a look.
How skilfully the artist takes us in.

What Georgian wit these classic Gods have heard,
Who now must listen to the golfer's tale
Of holes in one and how I missed that putt,
Hooked at the seventh, sliced across the tenth
But ended on the seventeenth all square.

Ye gods, ye gods, how comical we are!
Would Jove have been appointed Captain here?
See how exclusive thine Estate, Moor Park.

JOHN BETJEMAN, 'Metro-land' (TV programme), 1973, quoted in
The Best of Betjeman selected by John Guest, 1978

Rickmansworth

Rickmansworth was in the early Middle Ages Ryke-meres-wearth; that is, a rich moor-meadow; and indeed the characteristic features of the town are its rivers, lakes, and water-meadows.

NIKOLAUS PEVSNER, *The Buildings of England: Hertfordshire*, 1953

Chorleywood

Above the seats were sepia photographs of the line's beauty spots – Sandy Lodge Golf Course, Pinner Hill, Moor Park, Chorley Wood. Most of the original fittings remained: wide, loosely strung luggage racks with coat-hooks curving down from their support struts; broad leather window straps, and broad leather straps to stop the doors from swinging all the way back on their hinges; a chunky, gilded figure on the door, 1 or 3; a brass fingerplate backing the brass door handle; and, engraved on the plate, in a tone of either command or seductive invitation, the slogan 'Live in Metroland'.

Over the years I studied the rolling stock. From the platform I could tell at a glance a wide from an extra-wide compartment. I knew all the advertisements by heart, and all the varieties of decoration on the barrel-vaulted ceilings. I knew the range of imagination of the people who scraped the NO SMOKING transfers on the windows into new mottos: NO SNORING was the most popular piece of knife-work; NO SNOGGING a baffler for years; NO SNOWING the most whimsical. I stowed away in a first-class carriage one dark afternoon, and sat bolt upright in the soft seat, too frightened to look around me. I even penetrated, by mistake, the special single compartment at the front of each train, which was protected by a green transfer LADIES ONLY. Having only just caught my connection, I fell panting into the silent disapproval of three tweeded ladies; though my fear was cooled less by their silence than by my disappointment that the compartment contained no special appurtenances indicative, however obliquely, of just what it was that made women different.

JULIAN BARNES, *Metroland*, 1980

Chalfont & Latimer

John Milton came here [Chalfont St Giles] in 1665 to escape the Great Plague of London and complete *Paradise Lost.* . . .

Chalfont St Giles, in the Burnham Hundred, is part of the famous Chiltern Hundreds. Sir Robert Peel and Roy Jenkins are among the many Members of Parliament who have sought the now traditional appointment of 'Steward or Bailiff of Her Majesty's three Chiltern Hundreds of Stoke, Desborough and Burnham' so as to be able to relinquish membership of the House of Commons.

LEIGH HATTS, *Country Walks around London*, 1983

Amersham

Steam took us onwards, through the ripening fields,
Ripe for development. Where the landscape yields
Clay for warm brick, timber for post and rail,
Through Amersham to Aylesbury and the Vale.
In those wet fields the railway didn't pay,
The Metro stops at Amersham today.

JOHN BETJEMAN, 'Metro-land' (TV programme), 1973, quoted in
The Best of Betjeman selected by John Guest, 1978

* * *

Chesham

In the early 1960s, the Metropolitan Line (by which the purist naturally meant the Watford, Chesham and Amersham branches) still retained some of its original separateness. The rolling-stock, painted a distinctive mid-brown, had remained unchanged for sixty years; some of the bogeys my Ian Allen spotter's book informed me, had been running since the early 1890s. The carriages were high and square, with broad wooden running-boards; the compartments were luxuriously wide by modern standards, and the breadth of the seats made one marvel at Edwardian femural development. The backs of the seats were raked at an angle which implied that in the old days the trains had stopped for longer at the stations.

JULIAN BARNES, *Metroland*, 1980

WATFORD BRANCH

Croxley

In 1931 METROLAND described the area: 'Croxley bids fair to grow rapidly. Till lately it was somewhat difficult of access; its inhabitants are now offered almost a superabundance of transport facilities.' But the suburb was not built up very much before 1939 and even now is bordered by some attractive country.

DENNIS EDWARDS AND RON PIGRAM,
London's Underground Suburbs, 1986

Watford

Watford has . . . spread and sprawled. It is no longer a market town. The old High Street where at No. 288 my grandmother kept shop, is now the margin of the town. I went back to Watford a few years ago . . . the house where we spent our holidays, had been newly demolished. The two other houses in that little part of the street were still standing. For some reason on the site of the demolished building someone had planted a row of roses. They were young plants and looked as though they were freshly placed. It was mysterious to me to see those roses flourishing on the place where my grandparents flourished, kept shop, brought up their children and welcomed their granchildren. The flowers seemed to have been planted in their honour, but that was a fantasy – my grandparents were dead so long ago, and other tenants had taken their place. On that day I could almost hear my grandfather's voice again, as he mounted the creaky stairs with a cup of morning tea in his hand. 'Wake up . . .'

My grandparents' parlance often retained some flavour of the eighteenth century. Adelaide Uezzell didn't go for a walk, she 'went abroad'. As she kept a shop and had little time for household chores she sent the bed and table linen out to be washed. My grandfather, Tom, referred to this as 'the larndry'. I have heard elderly English people pronounce it so well into the 1940s.

MURIEL SPARK, *Curriculum Vitae*, 1992

NORTHERN LINE

For the Blewitt family were going to move house. . . .
'But I've to be within reach of my job, mind that,' said Mr. Blewitt. Mrs.
Blewitt pointed out that, for someone with Mr. Blewitt's kind of Underground
job, there wasn't much to choose between living towards the southern end of the
Northern Line, as they did at present, and living towards the northern end of
the same Line, as they would be doing. . . .
'And besides,' Mrs. Blewitt went on, 'the air – '
'I've heard enough about the flavour of that air,' her husband said with
finality. 'If we go,we go. That's all there is to it, Lil.'
'We go,' Mrs. Blewitt said happily. . . .

PHILIPPA PEARCE, *A Dog So Small*, 1962

Morden

The Northern Line . . . incorporates the longest continuous tunnel on
the London Underground of seventeen and a quarter miles from
Morden to East Finchley via the City; until recently this was the
longest railway tunnel in the world.

M.A.C. HORNE, *The Northern Line*, 1987

The Morden extension was opened [1926] by Col. J.T. Moore-Brabazon
MP, Parliamentary Secretary to the Minister of Transport. He drove the
special train from Clapham South to Morden. There was the usual official lunch – held in the car sheds, where the tables were decorated
with red and white carnations. . . . To encourage travel on the new line
15,000 free tickets were issued to people living near each station.

DENNIS EDWARDS AND RON PIGRAM,
London's Underground Suburbs, 1986

South Wimbledon

. . . actually, one bright morning, in full view of the ten-past-ten train
from Basingstoke, Monson's flying machine started on its journey.
They saw the carrier running swiftly along its rail, and the white

and gold screw spinning in the air. They heard the rapid rumble of wheels, and thud as the carrier reached the buffers at the end of its run. Then a whirr as the Flying-Machine was shot forward into the networks. All that the majority of them had seen and heard before. The thing went with a drooping flight through the framework and rose again, and then every beholder shouted, or screamed, or yelled, or shrieked after his kind. For instead of the customary concussion and stoppage, the Flying-Machine flew out of its five years' cage like a bolt from a crossbow, and drove slantingly upward into the air, curved round a little, so as to cross the line, and soared in the direction of Wimbledon Common. . . .

That was what the people in the train from Basingstoke saw. If you had drawn a line down the middle of that train, from engine to guard's van, you would not have found a living soul on the opposite side to the Flying-Machine. It was a mad rush from window to window as the thing crossed the line. And the engine-driver and stoker never took their eyes off the low hills about Wimbledon, and never noticed that they had run clean through Coombe and Malden and Raynes Park, until, with returning animation, they found themselves pelting, at the most indecent pace, into Wimbledon station.

H.G. WELLS, 'The Argonauts of the Air',
The Plattner Story, and Others, 1897

Colliers Wood

In 1881 [Willam Morris's] firm moved its works from Queen Square to Merton Abbey [near Colliers Wood]. The works at Merton had originally been a silk-weaving factory, started early in the eighteenth century by Huguenot refugees. . . . At Merton he had the advantage of the river Wandle, a clear and beautiful stream supplying water of the special quality required for madder dyeing. The river-side and the mill-pond were thickly set with willows and large poplars. . . . The whole thing was, in fact, the realization of a Ruskinian dream. . . .

To reach Merton from Hammersmith, Morris had to go by Underground railway to Farringdon Street, cross the City, and then get another train from Ludgate Hill, a journey which took about two hours.

The Letters of William Morris to His Family and Friends
edited by Philip Henderson, 1950

Tooting Broadway

Certainly [Thomas Hardy] advanced socially, elected to both the Savile
and the Rabelais Clubs, and meeting such leading figures as Tennyson,
Browning, Arnold and Henry James. But he would lie awake in his
Upper Tooting house, feeling the 'close proximity to a monster whose
body had four million heads and eight million eyes'.

EVELYN L. EVANS, *The Homes of Thomas Hardy*, 1968

Tooting Bec

Clapham we pass . . .

Tooting the next, sticks to its text,
    Travelly, gravelly, oh! oh!
Sutton a whet, thirsty we get,
    Palery, alery, take, take;
Smart four-in-hand comes to a stand,
    Legs of the longest ones ache, ache.

Drinkery, winkery, palery, alery, laughery,
    Chaffery, crash along, dash along –
        Down to the Derby as all of us go,
        These are the sights that all of us know;
        Yet off to the Downs as we often have been,
        Still every year is some novelty seen.

W.S.GILBERT, 'Down to the Derby, with Rhymes on the Road',
    Fun, 28 May 1864 (published anonymously)

Lavender Sweep is drowned in Wandsworth,
    Drowned in jessamine up to the neck,
Beetles sway upon bending grass leagues
    Shoulder-level to Tooting Bec.
Rich as Middlesex, rich in signboards,
    Lie the lover-trod lanes between,
Red Man, Green Man, Horse and Waggoner,
    Elms and sycamores round a green.

Burst, good June, with a rush this morning,
Bindweed weave me an emerald rope
Sun, shine bright on the blossoming trellises,
June and lavender, bring me hope.

JOHN BETJEMAN, 'South London Sketch, 1844',
New Bats in Old Belfries, 1945

Balham

Broad-bosomed, bold, becalmed, benign
Lies Bal-ham – four square on the Northern Line.

PETER SELLERS, 'Balham – Gateway to the South', 1958

On 18th April 1876 – a date which was to become known as 'the fatal Tuesday' – Charles Bravo, barrister-at-law, aged 30, caught the 4.7 p.m. train from Victoria Station to Balham. Balham was then still largely rural, and the Bedford Hill road along which he walked the three-quarters of a mile to his home on the edge of Tooting Common was a tree-embowered lane.

After greeting the beautiful and wealthy woman whom he had married only four months previously he rode out to exercise one of the pair of cobs they kept. . . .

Some three quarters of a mile from Balham station, at the point where the Bedford Hill Road emerges onto Tooting Common, there still stands The Priory where this tragedy was enacted. . . .

Until a few years ago a crimson rose which Florence had planted still clung to the wall, and nodded its blooms, below the window of the room wherein the tortured spirit of Charles Bravo left his stricken body, but the wisteria which was there in her day has managed to survive and still drapes the entrance front.

YSEULT BRIDGES, *How Charles Bravo Died*, 1956

In Balham you can buy Greek cheese; yams; Indian mirror cloth; dried fish; black-eyed peas; West African printed cotton sold in 12-yard lengths, sufficient to make a robe; olives in all sizes and colours; every kind of Pakistani sweetmeat; reggae records; hi-life records; canned bamboo shoots; goat; and once I went through the market and did not see a single banana which was neither green nor black. . . .

[My parents] came here in the 1920s because my father worked at nights and tubes run late on the Northern Line. For me, there is a certain inevitability about the place; whenever I've lived in London, it has always been here except for three weeks, once, in Earls Court, when I was running away from home. Nobody runs away from home to Balham because Balham is home.

ANGELA CARTER in *Living in London* edited by Alan Ross, 1974

Clapham South

[Henry] Cavendish, who has been styled 'the Newton of Chemistry', was distinguished as the founder of pneumatic chemistry, and for his successful researches on the composition of water, and his famous experiment, made at Clapham, for the determination of the earth's density. 'The man who weighed the world,' wrote his cousin, the late Duke of Devonshire, in his 'Handbook for Chatsworth', 'buried his science and his wealth in solitude and insignificance at Clapham.'

Almost the whole of his house here was occupied as workshops and laboratory. . . . 'The lawn was invaded by a wooden stage, from which access could be had to a large tree, to the top of which Cavendish, in the course of his astronomical, meteorological, electrical, or other researches, occasionally ascended.'

W. THORNBURY AND E. WALFORD, *Old and New London*, 1873–8

Clapham Common

23 September 1700. I went to visit Mr. Pepys at Clapham, where he has a very noble and wonderfully well-furnish'd house, especially with India and Chinese curiosities. The offices and gardens well accommodated for pleasure and retirement.

26 May 1703. This day died Mr. Sam. Pepys, a very worthy, industrious and curious person, none in England exceeding him in knowledge of the Navy. . . . When K[ing] James II went out of England, he laid down his office and would serve no more, but withdrawing himself from all public affaires, he liv'd at Clapham with his partner Mr. Hewer, formerly his clerk, in a very noble house and sweete place, where he enjoy'd the fruite of his labours in great prosperity. He was

universally belov'd, hospitable, generous, learned in many things, skill'd in music, a very greate cherisher of learned men of whom he had the conversation.

JOHN EVELYN, *Diary* quoted in *Memoirs, Illustrative of the Life and Writings of John Evelyn*, 1818

On November 13, 1895 I was brought down here from London. From two o'clock till half-past two on that day I had to stand on the centre platform of Clapham Junction in convict dress and handcuffed, for the world to look at. I had been taken out of the Hospital Ward without a moment's notice being given to me. Of all possible objects I was the most grotesque. When people saw me they laughed. Each train as it came up swelled the audience. Nothing could exceed their amusement. That was, of course, before they knew who I was. As soon as they had been informed, they laughed still more. For half an hour I stood there in the grey November rain surrounded by a jeering mob.

OSCAR WILDE, *De Profundis*, 1905

Clapham North

[Mrs Newcome's] mansion at Clapham was long the resort of the most favoured amongst the religious world. The most eloquent expounders, the most gifted missionaries, the most interesting converts from foreign islands, were to be found at her sumptuous table, spread with the produce of her magnificent gardens. Heaven indeed blessed those gardens with plenty, as many reverend gentlemen remarked; there were no finer grapes, peaches, or pineapples in all England.

WILLIAM MAKEPEACE THACKERAY, *The Newcomes*, 1853–5

What was later called 'The Clapham Sect' had come into being. Wherever she walked the child [Marianne Thornton] found herself surrounded by assorted Saints. It was not a closed sainthood, there were no entry tests, no esoteric hush-hush, but the members of it shared so many interests they hung together, and lived as near to each other as they could . . .

> E.M. FORSTER, *Marianne Thornton*, 1956

By the zeal, the munificence, the laborious activity, with which [the Clapham Sect] pursued their religious and semi-religious enterprises, they did more to teach the world how to get rid of existing institutions than by their votes and speeches at Westminster they contributed to preserve them. With their May meetings, and African Institutions, and Anti-Slavery Reporters, and their subscriptions of tens of thousands of pounds, and their petitions bristling with hundreds of thousands of signatures, and all the machinery for informing opinion and bringing it to bear on ministers and legislators which they did so much to perfect and even to invent, they can be regarded as nothing short of pioneers and fuglemen of that system of popular agitation which forms a leading feature in our internal history during the past half-century.

> G.O. TREVELYAN, *The Life and Letters of Lord Macaulay*, 1876

Stockwell

Change for Victoria line

In 1778 [Stockwell] was alarmed by an apparition, known to this day as 'the Stockwell Ghost', which spread such terror through the then retired village and neighbourhood. . . . This story is thus told by Charles Mackay in his *Extraordinary Popular Delusions* – 'Mrs Golding, an elderly lady, who resides alone with her servant, Anne Robinson, was sorely surprised, on the evening of the Twelfth Day, 1772, to observe an extraordinary commotion among the crockery. Cups and saucers rattled down the chimney, pots and pans were whirled downwards or through the windows; and hams, cheeses, and loaves of bread disported themselves upon the floor just as if the devil were in them. . . .

'It appears that Anne was anxious to have a clear house to carry on an intrigue with her lover, and she resorted to this trick in order to effect her purpose. She placed the china on the shelves in such a manner that it fell on the slightest motion; and she attached horse-hair to other articles, so that she could jerk them down from the adjoining room without being perceived by anyone.'

W. THORNBURY AND E. WALFORD, *Old and New London*, 1873–8

Oval

The Oval is green,
Flats, gnats,
And white-clothed figures move with grace,
The bat and ball!
These above all,
And the thrill, and the air of this place!

The sound of applause,
Lunch, crunch,
And the sudden dejected roar,
The light and the sight
Of Learie's old might,
The Pavilion's clamour for more!

More of this man!
Run! Run!
O run, Learie! run while you may!
A fight is in sight
And the play has a bite
It's a *wonderful* Oval day!

LESLIE FREWIN, 'On Seeing Sir Learie Constantine return (temporarily)
from Diplomacy to Cricket, September 1963', *The Poetry of Cricket*
edited by Leslie Frewin

At the Oval, men seem to have rushed away with some zest from their City offices. At Lord's, there is a *dilettante* look, as of men whose work, if ever, has yet to come.

JAMES PYCROFT, *Oxford Memories*, 1886

But whatever change has taken place in cricket – or in me – I swear there is no change in the jolly Oval crowd. It is, as it has always been, the liveliest, most intense, most good-humoured mob that ever shouted itself hoarse at cricket. It is as different from the Lord's crowd as a

country fair is from the Church Congress. At Lord's we take our cricket
solemnly as if we were at a prayer meeting.

'ALPHA OF THE PLOUGH' [A.G. Gardiner], *Many Furrows*, 1924

Kennington
Change for Bank branch
Turn to page 170 for Elephant & Castle

Mother, Sydney and I looked a crumpled sight as we ambled out
through the workhouse gates. It was early morning and we had
nowhere to go, so we walked to Kennington Park, which was about a
mile away. Sydney had ninepence tied up in a handkerchief, so we
bought half a pound of black cherries and spent the morning in
Kennington Park, sitting on a bench eating them. Sydney crumpled a
sheet of newspaper and wrapped some string around it and for a while
the three of us played catch-ball. At noon we went to a coffee-shop
and spent the rest of our money on a twopenny tea-cake, a penny
bloater and two halfpenny cups of tea, which we shared between us.
Afterwards we returned to the park where Sydney and I played again
while Mother sat crocheting.

In the afternoon we made our way back to the workhouse.

CHARLIE CHAPLIN, *My Autobiography*, 1964

CHARING CROSS BRANCH

Waterloo
Change for Bakerloo line

. . . on Waterloo Bridge. . . . The wind has blown up the waves. The
river races beneath us, and the men standing on the barges have to
lean all their weight on the tiller. A black tarpaulin is tied down over a
swelling load of gold. Avalanches of coal glitter blackly. As usual,
painters are slung on planks across the great riverside hotels, and the
hotel windows have already points of light in them. On the other side
the city is white as if with age; St. Paul's swells white above the fretted,
pointed, or oblong buildings beside it. The cross alone shines rosy-gilt.

VIRGINIA WOOLF, *Jacob's Room*, 1922

. . . exclaimed Sam [Weller] '. . . I had unfurnished lodgin's for a fortnight . . . the dry arches of Waterloo Bridge. Fine sleeping place –
within ten minutes' walk of all the public offices – only if there is any
objection to it, it is that the sitivation's *rayther* too airy. I see some
queer sights there.'

CHARLES DICKENS, *The Pickwick Papers*, 1836–7

Embankment
Change for Bakerloo, Circle and District lines

If you can put up with the thunderous noise of the trains close to your
backside, the sight of the Thames from the gangway across Hungerford
Bridge is one of the finest in London, especially when the wind lifts the
water into wavelets. It is Canaletto come alive.

JOHN HILLABY, *John Hillaby's London*, 1987

Charing Cross
Change for Bakerloo and Jubilee lines

1775. I talked of the cheerfulness of Fleet Street, owing to the constant
quick succession of people which we perceive passing through it.
JOHNSON. 'Why, Sir, Fleet Street has a very animated appearance;
but I think the full tide of human existence is at Charing Cross.'

1777. I had long complained to him that I felt myself discontented in
Scotland, as too narrow a sphere, and that I wished to make my chief
residence in London, the great scene of ambition, instruction, and
amusement; a scene which was to me, comparatively speaking, a
heaven upon earth. JOHNSON. 'Why, Sir, I never knew anyone who
had such a *gust* for London as you have; and I cannot blame you for
your wish to live there.'

I suggested a doubt, that if I were to reside in London, the exquisite zest with which I relished it in occasional visits might go off, and I might grow tired of it. JOHNSON. 'Why, Sir, you find no man, at all intellectual, who is willing to leave London. No, Sir, when a man is tired of London, he is tired of life; for there is in London all that life can afford.'

JAMES BOSWELL, *The Life of Samuel Johnson*, 1791

The Charing Cross trains rumbled through my dreams on one side, the boom of the Strand on the other, while before my windows, Father Thames under the Shot Tower walked up and down with his traffic.*

*Kipling was in lodgings in Villiers Street, off the Strand.

RUDYARD KIPLING, *Something of Myself*, 1889

Leicester Square
Change for Piccadilly line

Sir Joshua Reynolds 'At Home' at Leicester Square: It was no prim, fine table he set them down to. There was little order or arrangement; there was more abundance than elegance; and a happy freedom thrust conventionalism aside. Often was the dinner-board, prepared for seven or eight, required to accommodate itself to fifteen or sixteen; for often on the very eve of dinner, would Sir Joshua tempt afternoon visitors with intimation that Johnson, or Garrick, or Goldsmith was to dine there. Nor was the want of seats the only difficulty. A want of knives and forks, of plates and glasses, as often succeeded . . . it was easy to know the guests well acquainted with the house by their never failing to call instantly for beer, bread, or wine, that they might get them before the first course was over, and the worst confusion began.

JOHN FORSTER, *The Life and Adventures of Oliver Goldsmith*, 1848

His [Sir Joshua Reynolds's] study was octagonal. . . . His sitter's chair moved on castors, and stood above the floor a foot and a half. He held his palettes by a handle, and the sticks of his brushes were eighteen inches long. He wrought standing, and with great celerity. He rose early, breakfasted at nine, entered his study at ten, examined designs or touched unfinished portraits till eleven brought a sitter; painted till four; then dressed, and gave the evening to company.

ALLAN CUNNINGHAM, *The Lives of the Most Eminent British Painters, Sculptors and Architects,* 1829–33

. . . that curious region lying about the Haymarket and Leicester Square, which is a centre of attraction to indifferent foreign hotels and indifferent foreigners, racket-courts, fighting-men, swordsmen, footguards, old china, gaming houses, exhibitions, and a large medley of shabbiness and shrinking out of sight.

CHARLES DICKENS, *Bleak House,* 1852–3

We four kings of Leicester Square
Selling ladies' underwear:
How fantastic!
No elastic!
Only 15p per pair.

'Children's Rhymes' quoted in *London in Verse* edited by
Christopher Logue, 1982

And the underground railway itself turns into an object of superstition. People who live on the Northern Line I take to be sensitive citizens; it is a friendly communication route where one notices commuters reading proper books and, when they talk, finishing their sentences. But the Piccadilly Line is full of fly-by-nights and stripe-shirted young men who run dubious agencies, and I go to elaborate lengths to avoid travelling on it. It is an entirely irrational way of imposing order on the city, but it does give it a shape in the mind, takes whole chunks of experience out of the realm of choice, and deliberation, and places them in the less strenuous context of habit and prejudice.

JONATHAN RABAN, 'The Magical City', *The Times,* 26 January 1974

Tottenham Court Road
Change for Central line

John Forster quotes this comment by Charles Dickens on his boyhood experiences on the way to work from his home in Gower Street to the blacking factory at Hungerford-stairs: 'I could not resist the stale pastry put out at half-price on trays at the confectioners' doors in Tottenham-

court-road, and I often spent in that the money I should have kept for
my dinner.'

JOHN FORSTER, *The Life of Charles Dickens*, 1872–4

Some, by the bancks of *Thame* their pleasure taking;
Some, Sulli-bibs among the Milk-maids, making;
With musique, some upon the waters, rowing;
Some, to the next adjoyning Hamlets going;
And *Hogsdone, Islington,* and *Tothnam-Court,*
For Cakes and Creame, had then no small resort.

GEORGE WITHER, *Britain's Remembrancer*, 1628

Goodge Street

It appears . . . that the members of the [London Explorers'] Club take
coach trips all round London and are enthusiastic about everything
they see. . . . How much livelier a city London would be if charabanc-
loads of its citizens were constantly passing through its streets and if,
when they came, say, to Goodge Street, and somebody called out:
'Three cheers for Goodge Street!' and the company responded with a
shout! I doubt whether Goodge Street has ever been cheered in the
course of its history.

ROBERT LYND, *Searchlights and Nightingales*, 1939

It seemed a perpetual adventure to buy second-hand books in the
Charing Cross Road, or drink in the Swiss Pub or the York Minster or
stand outside Goodge Street Underground Station in that long silence,
filled with infinite possibilities, between the moment when the buzz-
bombs cut off and the thud as they fell somewhere else.

JOHN MORTIMER, *Clinging to the Wreckage*, 1982

Warren Street
Change for Victoria line
Turn to page 175 for Euston

Sunday, 20 October 1940. The most – what? – impressive, no, that's
not it – sight in London on Friday was the queue, mostly children with

suitcases, outside Warren St tube. This was about 11.30. We thought
they were evacuees, waiting for a bus. But there they were, in a much
longer line, with women, men, more bags & blankets, sitting still at 3.
Lining up for the shelter in the night's raid – which came of course.

VIRGINIA WOOLF, *Diary*, Vol. V, 1936–41

CITY BRANCH

Elephant & Castle
Change for Bakerloo line

By the cloisterly Temple, and by Whitefriars . . . and by Blackfriars-
bridge, and Blackfriars-road, Mr. George sedately marches to a street of
little shops lying somewhere in that ganglion of roads from Kent and
Surrey, and of streets from the bridges of London, centring in the far-
famed Elephant who has lost his Castle formed of a thousand four-
horse coaches, to a stronger iron monster than he, ready to chop him
into mince-meat any day he dares. To one of the little shops in this
street, which is a musician's shop, having a few fiddles in the window,
and some Pan's pipes and a tambourine, and a triangle, and certain
elongated scraps of music, Mr. George directs his massive tread. And
halting at a few paces from it, as he sees a soldierly looking woman,
with her outer skirts tucked up, come forth with a small wooden tub,
and in that tub commence a whisking and a splashing on the margin of
the pavement, Mr. George says to himself, 'She's as usual, washing
greens. I never saw her, except upon a baggage-wagon, when she
wasn't washing greens!'

CHARLES DICKENS, *Bleak House*, 1852–3

Borough

Once the main road to the south and the terminus for coaches when
London Bridge was too narrow to carry them into the city. In the 17th
century, according to Thomas Dekker, it was full of inns, 'a continued
ale house with not a shop to be seen between'.

The London Encyclopaedia edited by Ben Weinreb
and Christopher Hibbert, 1983

No. 85 High Street, Borough, stands on the site of the old Tabard Inn, where Chaucer's pilgrims assembled:

> Bifil that in that seson on a day,
> In Southwerk at the Tabard as I lay
> Redy to wenden on my pilgrymage
> To Caunterbury with ful devout corage,
> At nyght was come into that hostelrye
> Wel nyne and twenty in a compaignye,
> Of sondry folk, by aventure y-falle
> In felaweshipe, and pilgrimes were they alle,
> That toward Caunterbury wolden ryde.
> The chambres and the stables weren wyde,
> And wel we weren esed atte beste.

GEOFFREY CHAUCER, *The Canterbury Tales*, c.1387

Went to the Borough yesterday morning before going to Gadshill, to see if I could find any ruins of the Marshalsea. Found a great part of the original building – now 'Marshalsea Place'. Found the rooms that have been in my mind's eye in the story. Found, nursing a very big boy, a very small boy*, who, seeing me standing on the Marshalsea pavement, looking about, told me how it all used to be. God knows how he learned it (for he was a world too young to know anything about it), but he was right enough.

* In his Preface to the first edition of *Little Dorrit* in 1857, Dickens describes this same incident and says of this boy: 'the smallest boy I ever conversed with, carrying the largest baby I ever saw, offered a supernaturally intelligent explanation of the locality in its old uses, and was very nearly correct.'

CHARLES DICKENS, 1856, quoted in *The Life of Charles Dickens*
by John Forster, 1872–4

London Bridge

> London Bridge is broken down,
> Broken down, broken down,
> London Bridge is broken down,
> My fair lady.

Nursery Rhyme, c.1726

[William] Hogarth's studio [on London Bridge] resembled one of the alchemist's laboratories from the pencil of the elder Teniers. It was a complete, smoke-stained confusionary, with a German stove, crucibles, pipkins, and nests of drawers with rings of twine to pull them out; here a box of asphaltum, there glass-stoppered bottles, varnishes, dabbers, gravers, etching tools, walls of wax, obsolete copper-plates, many engraved on both sides, and poetry scribbled over the walls; a pallet hung up as an heir-loom, the colours dry upon it, hard as stone; all the multifarious *arcanalia* of engraving, and lastly, a Printing Press!

JOHN TIMBS, *Romance of London*, 1865

Beautiful it is to see
On London Bridge the bold-eyed seabirds wheel,
And hear them cry, and all for a light-flung crust
Fling us their wealth, their freedom, speed and gleam.

EDMUND BLUNDEN, 'Thames Gulls', *English Poems*, 1925

Bank
Change for Central line and for escalator to Monument station
for Circle and District lines

During the formidable riots of 1780 the Bank was in considerable danger. In one night there rose the flames of six-and-twenty fires. Newgate was sacked and burned. The mob, half thieves, at last decided to march upon the Bank, but precautions had been taken there. The courts and roof of the building were defended by armed clerks and volunteers, and there were soldiers ready outside. The old pewter inkstands had been melted into bullets. The rioters made two rushes; the first was checked by a volley from the soldiers; at the second, which was less violent, Wilkes rushed out, and with his own hand dragged in some of the ringleaders. Leaving several killed and many wounded, the discomfited mob at last retired.

W. THORNBURY AND E. WALFORD, *Old and New London*, 1873–8

...But that's all shove be'ind me – long ago an' fur away,
An' there ain' no 'buses runnin' from the Bank to Mandalay;
An' I'm learnin' 'ere in London wot the ten-year soldier tells:
'If you've 'eard the East a-callin', you won't never 'eed naught else.'
No! you won't 'eed nothin' else
But them spicy garlic smells,
An' the sunshine an' the palm-trees an' the tinkly temple-bells;
On the road to Mandalay . . .

RUDYARD KIPLING, 'Mandalay', *Barrack-Room Ballads I*, 1892

Moorgate
Change for Circle, Hammersmith & City and Metropolitan lines

A plaque at No. 85 Moorgate near its junction with London Wall in the City marks the site of [John Keats'] birthplace, a livery stable run by his father.

IAN OUSBY, *Literary Britain and Ireland*, 1990

Old Street

'The choicest fruits of the kingdom were reared in King James I's time by John Milton, in his Nursery in Old Street.'

Oldys on Trees [MS] quoted by H.B. Wheatley
in *London Past and Present*, 1891

Angel

[In the eighteenth century] a bell was rung periodically at the Angel, Islington, to announce the departure of a convoy of foot passengers across the fields to the City. They gathered at the end of St John Street and were escorted into the precincts of the City by an armed patrol.

CHRISTOPHER TRENT, *Greater London*, 1965

Most of all
I think my father loved me when we went
In early-morning pipe-smoke on the tram
Down to the Angel, visiting the Works.
'Fourth generation – yes, this is the boy.'
   The smell of sawdust still brings back to me
The rambling workshops high on Pentonville,
Built over gardens to White Lion Street,
Clicking with patents of the family firm
Founded in 1820.

JOHN BETJEMAN, *Summoned by Bells*, 1960

The City and South London was the first real 'tube' electric railway, and it still had, when I first knew it, the atmosphere of 1890, the year of its opening. Little orange engines carried rolling stock, with basket seats and cut glass electric lights. Many of the platforms, still to be seen at Angel, Kings Cross and south of the river, were central and narrow, with trains running either side of them. . . . The whole railway had a strong smell of wet feet or a changing room after games and the line was delightfully uneven, so that one could look down the length of the carriages and see them switchbacking up and down, behind or before one.

JOHN BETJEMAN, 'Coffee, Port and Cigars on the Inner Circle',
The Times, 24 May 1963

King's Cross St. Pancras
Change for Circle, Hammersmith & City, Metropolitan, Piccadilly
and Victoria lines

[The Midland Railway] tunnelled one line down to join the Metropolitan (steam) Underground Railway, which is now part of the Inner Circle. . . . Much of the trade of the line was beer from Burton-on-Trent, and the distance between the columns was measured by the length of beer barrels, which were carried down here from the station above by hydraulic lifts, and taken by drays out into London. . . . The hotel . . . was opened to the public in 1873. At the time it was easily the most magnificent of all London hotels. It was one of the first to have lifts, called 'ascending rooms' and worked by hydraulic power. It was also one of the first to have electric bells.

JOHN BETJEMAN, *London's Historic Railway Stations*, 1972

Euston
Change for Victoria line

How long ago Hector took off his plume,
Not wanting that his little son should cry,
Then kissed his sad Andromache goodbye –
And now we three in Euston waiting-room.

FRANCES CORNFORD, 'Parting in Wartime',
Travelling Home, 1948

Mornington Crescent
Temporarily closed

There was a few years ago a month of June which [Spencer Frederick]
Gore verily seems to have used as if he had known that it was to be for
him the last of its particularly fresh and sumptuous kind. He used to
look down on the garden of Mornington Crescent. The trained trees
rise and droop in fringes, like fountains, over the little well of green-
ness and shade where parties of young people are playing at tennis.
The backcloth is formed by the tops of the brown houses in the
Hampstead Road, and the liver-coloured tiles of the Tube station.

WALTER SICKERT, 'A Perfect Modern', *New Age*, 9 April 1914,
after Gore's death

Camden Town
Change for Mill Hill & Barnet branches of Northern line
Turn to page 184 for Kentish Town

From the geyser ventilators
    Autumn winds are blowing down
On a thousand business women
    Having baths in Camden Town.

Waste pipes chuckle into runnels,
    Steam's escaping here and there,
Morning trains through Camden cutting
    Shake the Crescent and the Square.

Early nip of changeful autumn,
  Dahlias glimpsed through garden doors,
At the back precarious bathrooms
  Jutting out from upper floors;

And behind their frail partitions
  Business women lie and soak,
Seeing through the draughty skylight
  Flying clouds and railway smoke.

Rest you there, poor unbelov'd ones,
  Lap your loneliness in heat.
All too soon the tiny breakfast,
  Trolley-bus and windy street!

JOHN BETJEMAN, 'Business Girls',
A Few Late Chrysanthemums, 1954

It cheers me that I live on the frontier of Camden Town and Regents Park.

V.S. PRITCHETT, 'As Old as the Century' from
The Turn of the Years, 1982

The first shock of a great earthquake had, just at that period, rent the whole neighbourhood. Houses were knocked down; streets broken through and stopped; deep pits and trenches dug in the ground; enormous heaps of earth and clay thrown up; buildings that were undermined and shaking, propped by great beams of wood. Here, a chaos of carts, overthrown and jumbled together, lay topsy-turvy at the bottom of a steep, unnatural hill; there, confused treasures of iron soaked and rusted in something that had accidentally become a pond. Everywhere were bridges that led nowhere; thoroughfares that were wholly impassable; Babel towers of chimneys, wanting half their height; temporary wooden houses and enclosures, in the most unlikely situations; carcases of ragged tenements, and fragments of unfinished walls and arches, and piles of scaffolding, and wildernesses of bricks, and giant forms of cranes, and tripods straddling above nothing. . . . In short, the yet unfinished and unopened Railroad was in progress.

CHARLES DICKENS, *Dombey and Son*, 1847–8

EDGWARE BRANCH

Haydon walked on to the village of Hampstead through the burning heat. North of Regent's Park the way to Golders Hill was almost all through open fields, with a few scattered farms and large houses, such as Belsize House in its great park. West across the fields ran the new Birmingham Railway from Euston. This was the area, beginning to be devastated by the railway and its accompanying streets and warehouses, that Dickens was just about to start describing so vividly in Dombey and Son, *the first words of which were written in Lausanne six days after this hot Sunday morning. The tentacles of Camden Town were stretching out along the railway into the fields . . . and the jangling Sunday church bells and the roar and rattle of the trains jarred the baking dusty fields as Haydon walked on to Hampstead. Sunday, 21 June 1846.*

ALETHEA HAYTER, *A Sultry Month: Scenes of London Literary Life in 1846*, 1965

Chalk Farm

Some farmers farm in fruit, some farm in grain,
　　Others farm in dairy-stuff, and many farm in vain,
But I know a place for a Sunday morning's walk
Where the Farmer and his Family only farm in chalk.
The Farmer and his Family before you walk back
Will bid you in to sit awhile and share their mid-day snack –
O they that live in Chalk Farm they live at their ease,
For the Farmer and his Family can't tell chalk from cheese.

ELEANOR FARJEON, *Nursery Rhymes of London Town*, 1916

Up to the year 1845, for fear of frightening the horses in the streets, the locomotive engines came no nearer to London than Chalk Farm, where the engine was detached from the train, and from thence to Euston Station the carriages were attached to an endless rope moved by a stationary engine at the Chalk Farm end of the line.

W. THORNBURY AND E. WALFORD,
Old and New London, 1873–8

Belsize Park

At the Foot of this Hill is an old Seat of the Earls of *Chesterfield*, called Bellsize . . . being taken by a certain *Projector*, who knew by what Handle to take the gay Part of the World, he made it a House of Pleasure and capital Entertainment. This brought a wonderful Concourse of People to the Place, and they were effectually gratified in all sorts of Diversion; but there being too great a License taken, it alarm'd the Magistrates, and now it is principally noted for Horseracing etc.

DANIEL DEFOE, *A Tour thro' the Whole Island of Great Britain*, 1738

BELLSIZE HOUSE

There is now the best Diversion in the Park that hath been yet; for the Proprietor hath actually got a great many Wild Deer, and will hunt one down every Thursday and Saturday, and kill it fairly before the Company. For that purpose he hath enlarged his Pack of Hounds, which will shew good Diversion for Two or Three Hours. The Hunting will begin exactly at Four of the Clock. And for the Conveniency of single Gentlemen, there will be a very good Ordinary, exactly at Two a Clock, and one of the Dishes will always be a Venison Pasty. And on the By-Days, every Evening, there will be good Sport shew'd in the Canals. And there will be a Scaffold erected there for the Musick to play, whilst the Gentlemen and Ladies are Walking there. The Walks round are made very commodious. And for the Safety of the Company, the Proprietor hath hired Twenty stout labouring Men, well known about Hampstead, to line the road betwixt Bellsize and London; so that they will be safe to pass as well by Night as Day.

Daily Post, 5 June 1722

One evening after dinner in a restaurant with some friends we returned home by Underground taking the Northern Line to Belsize Park. As a rule I went into town by car and I hadn't been by Tube for ages. For the first time that evening I saw people lying on the platforms at all the stations we stopped at. . . . I had never seen so many reclining figures and even the train tunnels seemed to be like the holes in my sculpture. And amid the grim tension, I noticed groups of strangers formed together in intimate groups and children asleep within feet of the passing trains. After this evening I travelled all over London by Underground. . . . I never made sketches in the Underground. It would have been like drawing in the hold of a slave ship. I would wander about sometimes passing a particular group that interested me half a dozen times. Sometimes, in a corner where I could not be seen, I would make notes on the back of an envelope so that I would be reminded when I sketched next day.

> HENRY MOORE, *Shelter Sketchbook*, 1940, quoted in *London Under London* by
> Richard Trench and Ellis Hillman, 1984, revised 1993

Hampstead

'Tis so near heaven, that I dare not say it can be a proper situation, for any but a race of mountaineers.

> DANIEL DEFOE, *A Tour thro' the Whole Island of Great Britain,* 1928 edition

> A steeple issuing from a leafy rise,
> With balmy fields in front and sloping green,
> Dear Hampstead, is thy southern face serene . . .
>
> A village, revelling in varieties. . . .
>
> LEIGH HUNT, *Rimini and Other Poems,* 1844

'You don't feel disposed, do you, to muffle yourself up, and start off with me for a good brisk walk over Hampstead-heath? I knows a good 'ous there where we can have a red hot chop for dinner and a glass of good wine': which led to our first experience of Jack Straw's-castle, memorable for many happy meetings in coming years.

> CHARLES DICKENS, letter, 1837, in *The Life of Charles Dickens*
> by John Forster, 1872–4

Hampstead . . . offers the perfect fusion of urban bustle and rural privacy, as if all the elements of English townscape had been tossed in the air and fallen on this hillside with hardly a piece out of place. The people of Hampstead – pump-room rowdies, 'Bohemian' commuters, left-wing intellectuals – are merely its passing phantoms. The lasting Hampstead is a maze of steps, alleyways, turnings and sudden views. It is sprays of clematis, wisteria, ivy and holly scattering sunlight on to red brick and white stucco. It is grand mansions, terraced cottages, Victorian extravagance and workhouse simplicity contained within a surprisingly intact eithteenth- and nineteenth-century hill town, defended on three sides by a rambling heath and on the fourth by the stern ramparts of Italianate Belsize Park. The twentieth century has lobbed an occasional grenade over these ramparts. But Hampstead's defenders have become increasingly adept at lobbing them back. For once, it is probable that the town we see today is the town we shall bequeath to our descendants.

SIMON JENKINS, *The Companion Guide to Outer London*, 1981

The station platforms at Hampstead [the deepest in London] are 192 feet under the surface – as far below ground as Nelson is above it in Trafalgar Square.

HUGH DOUGLAS, *The Underground Story*, 1963

It was something of an adventure for Lady Slane to go alone to Hampstead, and she felt happier after safely changing trains at Charing Cross.
. . . Yet, going up to Hampstead alone, she did not feel old; she felt younger than she had felt for years, and the proof of it was that she accepted eagerly this start of a new lap in life, even though it be the last. Nor did she look her age, as she sat, swaying slightly with the rocking of the Underground train, very upright, clasping her umbrella and her bag, her ticket carefully pushed into the opening of her glove. . . .

The train itself came to her assistance, for, after jerking over points, it ran into yet another white-tiled station, where a line of red tiles framed the name: Hampstead. Lady Slane rose unsteadily to her feet, reaching out her hand for a helpful bar; it was on these occasions and these alone, when she must compete with the rush of mechanical life, that she betrayed herself for an old lady. . . .

It was a wonder, arrived at Hampstead, that Lady Slane descended from the train in time, successfully clasping her umbrella, her bag, and her ticket inside her glove, but descend she did, and found herself standing in the warm summer air with the roofs of London beneath her. The passers-by ignored her, standing there, so well accustomed were they to the sight of old ladies in Hampstead. Setting out to walk, she wondered if she remembered the way; but Hampstead seemed scarcely a part of London, so sleepy and village-like, with its warm redbrick houses and vistas of trees and distance that reminded her pleasantly of Constable's paintings.

V. SACKVILLE-WEST, *All Passion Spent*, 1931

Golders Green

Thy verdant scenes, O Goulder's hill,
Once more I seek, a languid guest:
With throbbing temples and with burden'd breast
Once more I climb thy steep aerial way.
O faithful cure of oft-returning ill,
Now call thy sprightly breezes round,
Dissolve this rigid cough profound,
And bid the springs of life with gentler movement play.

MARK AKENSIDE*, 'An Ode on Recovery from a Fit of Sickness
in the Country, written in 1758'

* Mark Akenside frequently stayed at Golder's Hill, North End.

I was four years old when my father built his house in what was then
the village of North End, Hampstead. He was, in fact, the first of its
spoliators. When we settled there the tube reached no further than
Hampstead. Golders Green was a grassy cross-road with a sign pointing
to London, Finchley and Hendon; such a place as where 'the Woman
in White' was encountered. All round us lay dairy farms, market gardens and a few handsome old houses in brick or stucco standing in
twenty acres or more; not far off there survived woods where we
picked bluebells, and streams beside which we opened our picnic baskets. North End Road was a steep, dusty lane with white posts and rails
bordering its footways. North End, the reader may remember, was the
place where Bill Sikes spent the first night of his flight after the murder
of Nancy. . . .

. . . Eventually (I think soon after the first war) our postal address
was altered from Hampstead to Golders Green. My father deplored the
change, because Hampstead had historic associations, with Keats and
Blake and Constable, while Golders Green meant, to him, merely a
tube station.

EVELYN WAUGH, *A Little Learning*, 1964

Brent Cross

Gentle Brent, I used to know you
Wandering Wembley-wards at will,
Now what change your waters show you
In the meadowlands you fill!

181

Recollect the elm-trees misty
And the footpaths climbing twisty
Under cedar-shaded palings,
Low laburnum-leaned-on-railings
Out of Northolt on and upward to the heights of Harrow hill.

JOHN BETJEMAN, 'Middlesex', *A Few Late Chrysanthemums*, 1954

Brent Cross – a name which has come to symbolise the consumer society in car-owning, TV-watching, wine-drinking, mortgage-paying, credit card postwar Britain – is 10 years old tomorrow. Morris dancers, 'ethnic dancers', Tottenham Hotspurs, hot air balloons and a competition for the capital's worst-dressed man will celebrate its birthday in what foreigners will regard as inimitably Anglo-Saxon style.

The Times, third leader, 12 July 1986

Hendon Central

In the fourteenth century the manor of Hendon was in the gift of Westminster Abbey. During the Black Death the area became a haven. Cattle from other places were transported on the hoof, accompanied by one or two grangers, and were retained here till the worst of the plague was over.

The London Encyclopaedia edited by Ben Weinreb
and Christopher Hibbert, 1983

So obese is my cousin from Hendon,
She looks elephantine, seen end on;
    What preys most on her mind
    Is her efforts to find
A good deck-chair that she can depend on.

A.H. BAYNES, *Penguin Book of Limericks* edited by E.O. Parrott, 1983

Our Farnham which art in Hendon
Holloway Turnpike Lane
Thy Kingston come
Thy Wimbledon
In Erith as it is in Hendon . . .

Give us this day our Maidenhead
And lead us not into Penge station
But deliver us from Esher
For thine is the Kingston
The Tower and the Horley
For Iver and Iver
Crouch End.

Schoolboy apocryphal

Colindale

Near Colindale Station . . . is the British Museum newspaper repository. Within, the atmosphere is one of calm: one can obtain a temporary ticket for a day's research, with access to vast stocks of newspapers, extensive catalogues and elaborate indexes. In its reading rooms there is little sound save for the turning of yellowed leaves, and the occasional rumble of a trolley as the attendant delivers two or three elephant folios of newspapers, which are propped up on great reading stands.

BRUCE STEVENSON, *Middlesex*, 1972

In between the wars, Hendon Aerodrome became the centre for the famous RAF Pageants. (The RAF acquired the field in 1925.) Thousands flocked out by Underground to Colindale. . . . At the 1936 pageant, a certain aircraft designer called R.J. Mitchell displayed his Spitfire 'which will be on show for the first time'. No doubt most people thought that would be the last ever heard of it. The RAF last flew from Hendon in 1957. The magnificent RAF museum is now on part of the site.

DENNIS EDWARDS AND RON PIGRAM,
London's Underground Suburbs, 1986

Burnt Oak

Burnt Oak, Theydon Bois and Headstone Lane have names that whisper promises of wide open spaces and smiling, unsullied countryside. They are all stations on the London Underground system.

PHILIP HOWARD, *The Times*

The name probably derives from the Roman custom of burning a tree to mark a boundary. Until 1920 the area was mainly farmland, well-wooded and with the Silk Stream running through to Brent. . . . One of the area's principal public houses, the Bald Faced Stag, was a famous coaching inn patronised by generations of travellers from the north.

The London Encyclopaedia edited by Ben Weinreb
and Christopher Hibbert, 1983

Edgware

In this Road [Edgworth Road] lyes the Town of Edgworth, some will have it that it was built by King Edgar the Saxon Monarch, and called by his name, and so will have the town called Edgar, and that it was built as a garrison on the said Watling-Street, to preserve the high-way from thieves: But all this I take to be fabulous, and without authority.

DANIEL DEFOE, *A Tour thro' the Whole Island of Great Britain*, 1928 edition

Edgware. . . . The blacksmith's shop is that in which, according to tradition, worked the musical blacksmith, whose performance on the anvil whilst Handel took shelter from a shower, suggested to the great musician the well-known melody named after him.

JAMES THORNE, *Handbook to the Environs of London*, 1876

BARNET AND MILL HILL EAST BRANCHES

Kentish Town

There will soon be one street from London to Brentford; ay, and from London to every village ten miles round! Lord Camden has just let ground at Kentish Town for building fourteen hundred houses – nor do I wonder; London is, I am certain, much fuller than ever I saw it. I have twice this spring been going to stop my coach in Piccadilly, to inquire what was the matter, thinking there was a mob – not at all; it was only passengers.

HORACE WALPOLE, letter to the Miss Berrys, 8 June 1791

NORTHERN LINE

Pancras and Kentish Town repose
Among her golden pillars high,
Among her golden arches which
Shine upon the starry sky.

WILLIAM BLAKE, *Jerusalem: The Emanation of the Giant Albion*, 1804–20

The 'Mother Red Cap' at Kentish Town, was a house of no small terror
to travellers in former times. It has been stated that Mother Red Cap
was the 'Mother Damnable' of Kentish Town in the early days, and it
was at her house the notorious 'Moll Cutpurse', the highway-woman
of the time of Oliver Cromwell, dismounted and frequently lodged.

J.T. SMITH, *A Book for a Rainy Day*, 1845

One day in the early 1970s I was roaming through a particularly dis-
jointed and run-down area of Kentish Town, London NW5, and passed
a row of houses which were then occupied by squatters engaged in a
cold war with Camden Council. They were – and are – unremarkable
houses; a mid-Victorian terrace of the type that has been demolished
all over London in the past two decades, with none of the Georgian
cottage appeal that might commend them to preservationist forces. In
stock brick, three storeys, with a dank basement area below and a
parapet wall on top, they faced a busy road; the most quintessentially
ordinary houses, you would say, though of a uniquely English kind,
built by speculative builders for Philistines, unloved now for decades,
doomed soon, perhaps, to extinction.

Then I saw that over the lintel of one of them someone had carefully carved an inscription: the letters, cut through the sooty surface
into the fresh yellow brick below, stood out clearly –
    'The Fields Lie Sleeping Underneath.'
It is deeply satisfying to come unexpectedly face to face with your own
private vision in this way. For years, walking round London, I had
been aware of the actual land, lying concealed but not entirely
changed or destroyed, beneath the surface of the nineteenth- and
twentieth-century city.

GILLIAN TINDALL, *The Fields Beneath*, 1977

Rumbling under blackened girders, Midland, bound for Cricklewood,
Puffed its sulphur to the sunset where that Land of Laundries stood.
Rumble under, thunder over, train and tram alternate go,
Shake the floor and smudge the ledger, Charrington, Sells, Dale & Co.,
Nuts and nuggets in the window, trucks along the lines below.

. . .

Oh the after-tram-ride quiet, when we heard a mile beyond,
Silver music from the bandstand, barking dogs by Highgate Pond;
Up the hill where stucco houses in Virginia creeper drown –
And my childish wave of pity, seeing children carrying down
Sheaves of drooping dandelions to the courts of Kentish Town.

JOHN BETJEMAN, 'Parliament Hill Fields',
New Bats in Old Belfries, 1945

*Jenny Marx, wife of Karl, wrote of their move from Dean Street to Grafton
Terrace, Kentish Town, in 1856: '. . . a small house at the foot of romantic
Hampstead Heath, not far from lovely Primrose Hill. When we slept in our
own beds for the first time, sat on our own chairs and even had a parlour
with second-hand furniture, then we really thought we were living in a magic
castle.'*

ASA BRIGGS, *Marx in London*, 1982

*Liebknecht thus describes the Marx family outings of a Sunday, when they were
living in Kentish Town:*

*Once arrived on the Heath, we would first choose a place where we could spread
out tents, at the same time having due regard to the possibility of obtaining tea
and beer.*

*But after drinking and eating their fill, as Homer has it, the male and
female comrades looked for the most comfortable place of repose or seat; and
when this had been found he or she – provided they did not prefer a little nap –
produced the Sunday papers they had bought on the road, and now began the
reading and discussing of politics – while the children, who rapidly found comrades, played hide and seek behind the heather bushes.*

WILHELM LIEBKNECHT, *Karl Marx: Biographical Memoirs*, 1896,
translated into English by E. Untermann, 1901

Tufnell Park

According to tradition, Tufnell Park Road is an old Roman road: its straightness makes the story likely. The country atmosphere of the area remained undisturbed for many centuries and, as London extended, this northern part of Islington provided its share of the 'very extensive dairies for supplying the inhabitants of the metropolis with milk' . . . in the early 19th century, the painter J.M.W. Turner was still able to enjoy sketching a group of elms on the Old Roman Road.

The London Encyclopaedia edited by Ben Weinreb
and Christopher Hibbert, 1983

Archway

Work began on the [Archway] tunnel, however, and about 130 yards were completed. In the early hours of 13 April 1812 the tunnel collapsed. The *Sun* newspaper reported it thus: 'Between four and five o'clock yesterday morning, the Highgate tunnel fell in with a tremendous crash, and the labour of several months was, in a few moments, converted into a heap of ruins . . .'

. . . The collapse of the tunnel was a source of satisfaction to the residents of Highgate. Lloyd reprints a splendid travesty of a prospectus for rescuing the project. It is headed 'Proposals for removing Highgate Hill entirely, with the houses thereon'. It goes on to describe how the promoters planned to remove the whole village, chapel and all, and to form a salt-water lake where Highgate once stood from Kentish Town to Finchley.

JOHN RICHARDSON, *Highgate: Its History since the Fifteenth Century,* 1983

This was the old Hampstead and Highgate line (now at the heart of the Northern system) with carriages opening at the ends to swing gates and gatemen shouting the stations. What a clatter and what roaring gales through the tunnels! What strange smells from the dim red-and-white tiled platforms! How uncomfortable the shiny straw seats! My joy was to sit at the very back of the train and watch the bright circle of the station dwindle like a camera-lens stopped down.

G.W. STONIER, *Pictures on the Pavement,* 1955

Highgate

When we came upon Highgate hill and had a view of London, I was all
life and joy.

JAMES BOSWELL, *The London Journal*, 19 November 1762

The spot at Highgate Hill, whereon the legend states Whittington
stopped when he heard the sound of Bow bells, which he imagined
prophesied his becoming Lord Mayor, is believed to have been originally the site of a wayside cross, belonging to the formerly adjacent
lazar-house, or hospital, and Chapel of St. Anthony; this memorial was
removed, and Whittington is stated to have placed there an obelisk,
surmounted by a cross, which remained till 1795, when was erected
another stone, which has since been twice renewed.

JOHN TIMBS, *Romance of London*, 1865

As I came down the Highgate Hill,
The Highgate Hill, the Highgate Hill,
As I came down the Highgate Hill,
I met the sun's bravado,
And saw before me, fold on fold,
Grey to pearl and pearl to gold,
This London like a land of old,
The land of eldorado.

SIR HENRY BASHFORD, 'Romance', *Songs out of School*, 1916

Safe, in a world of trains and buttered toast
Where things inanimate could feel and think,
Deeply I loved thee, 31 West Hill!
At that hill's foot did London then begin,
With yellow horse-trams clopping past the planes
To grey-brick nonconformist Chetwynd Road
And on to Kentish Town and barking dogs
And costers' carts and crowded grocers' shops
And Daniels' store, the local Selfridge's,
The Bon Marché, the Electric Palace, slums
That thrilled me with their smells of poverty -
And buttered toast and 31 West Hill.

Here from my eyrie, as the sun went down,
I heard the old North London puff and shunt,
Glad that I did not live in Gospel Oak.

JOHN BETJEMAN, *Summoned by Bells*, 1960

East Finchley

Once a tongue of ice came as far as Finchley, bringing with it boulders of rock from far to the north, as well as clay and finely crushed rock from the lands over which it had travelled. When the ice melted the boulders embedded in clay were left behind in the deposit we know as boulder clay. So it is that we find large lumps of chalk from Lincolnshire in the tongue of boulder clay that today stretches from Whetstone to East Finchley Station.

R.S. FITTER, *London's Natural History*, 1945

The Eastern part of Finchley once consisted mainly of the notorious Finchley Common, crossed by the Great North Road, and a haunt of highwaymen until its enclosure in 1816.

The London Encyclopaedia edited by Ben Weinreb
and Christopher Hibbert, 1983

Eric Aumonier, who had provided a sculpture for 55 Broadway some ten years earlier, was commissioned to design another. . . . The powerful figure of the 'Archer' aiming in the direction of London symbolizes the rapid transit of modern electric trains and is the most distinctive feature of the station.

LAURENCE MENEAR, *London's Underground Stations*, 1983

Finchley Central

As late as 1790 Finchley Common was dangerous to traverse at night. In that year Sir Gilbert Elliot (by no means a timid man), writes to his wife [in *Life and Letters of Sir Gilbert Elliot*] when within a few stages of London, that instead of pushing on that night, as he easily could, he shall defer his arrival till the morning, for 'I shall not trust my throat on Finchley Common in the dark'.

JAMES THORNE, *Handbook to the Environs of London*, 1876

Finchley Central is two and sixpence
 From Golders Green on the Northern line,
And on the platform, by the kiosk,
 That's where you said you'd be mine.
There we made a date,
 For hours I waited,
 But I'm blowed,
 You never showed;
And Finchley Central ten long stations
 From Golders Green change at Camden Town,
I thought I'd made you, but I'm afraid you
 Only let me down.

GEOFF STEPHENS AND A. KLEIN (of the New Vaudeville Band), 1967

Mill Hill East

In the grounds [of Mill Hill school] . . . is a building known as the 'scriptorium' where James Augustus Henry Murray, a master there from 1870 to 1885, deposited three tons of paper slips, used in the preparation of the *Oxford English Dictionary*. That the 'greatest lexico-graphical project of the age' was prepared in this village is an inspiring thought.

BRUCE STEVENSON, *Middlesex*, 1972

West Finchley

Lord Finchley tried to mend the Electric Light
Himself. It struck him dead: And serve him right!
It is the business of the wealthy man
To give employment to the artisan.

HILAIRE BELLOC, *More Peers*, 1911

Woodside Park

Woodside Park was recorded as Fyncheley Wode in 1468 and was part of the great Middlesex woodland area, and named Woodside in 1686.

CYRIL M. HARRIS, *What's in a Name?*, 1977

Totteridge & Whetstone

Dick Turpin positively loved this highway and its associations, and his 'Knights of the Road' followed his taste. So great was the terror which they inspired among the wealthier classes, that many Scotch lords and squires preferred to make the journey from their native hills to the Parliament at Westminster by sea, rather than encounter the terrors of the Great North road within ten or twelve miles of London.

E. WALFORD, *Greater London*, 1882–4

At eleven o'clock in the morning of Saturday, 17th February [1849], I reached Carlton Terrace. . . . I announced myself to Lord Palmerston, one day sooner than I had promised to return; and then drove with my beloved ones to our favourite Totteridge.

BARON F. VON BUNSEN, Minister Plenipotentiary and envoy
extraordinary of his Majesty Frederic William IV at the Court
of St James's, *Memoirs*, 1868

High Barnet

April 14, 1471. The battle of Barnet was fought in the wars between the houses of York and Lancaster, and the Earl of Warwick, called 'the king-maker', was slain on the field.

WILLIAM HONE, *The Everyday Book*, 1830

The battlefield [of Barnet] lies direct north of the town. . . . Red Rose met White Rose, and a sorry chapter of our story closed that April morning of 1471, while still the sun was climbing high. . . . An obelisk, erected in 1740, marks the trraditional spot where Warwick the King-maker fell.

W.G. BELL, *Where London Sleeps*, 1926

Early on the seventh morning after he had left his native place, Oliver limped slowly into the little town of Barnet. The window-shutters were closed; the street was empty; not a soul had awakened to the business of the day. The sun was rising in all its splendid beauty; but the light only served to show the boy his own lonesomeness and deso-lation, as he sat, with bleeding feet and covered with dust, upon a cold door-step. . . .

. . . He had been crouching on the step for some time: wondering at the great number of public-houses (every other house in Barnet was a tavern, large or small), gazing listlessly at the coaches as they passed through, and thinking how strange it seemed that they could do, with ease, in a few hours, what it had taken him a whole week of courage and determination beyond his years to accomplish: when he was roused by observing that a boy, who had passed him carelessly some minutes before, had returned, and was now surveying him most earnestly from the opposite side of the way.

CHARLES DICKENS, *Oliver Twist*, 1837–8

PICCADILLY LINE

HEATHROW BRANCH

Heathrow Terminal 4

Last night in London Airport
I saw a wooden bin
labelled UNWANTED LITERATURE
IS TO BE PLACED HEREIN.
So I wrote a poem
and popped it in.

CHRISTOPHER LOGUE, 'Last Night in London Airport',
Ode to the Dodo: Poems 1953–1978, 1981

Heathrow Terminals 1, 2, 3

It never failed to surprise [Margaret] that in all the years we had been travelling . . . the control officers at Heathrow had never raised an eyebrow as they stamped her passport. Yet, as she had often remarked, 'I'll bet I'm the only person using this beastly airport that was actually born right here right underneath the control tower!'

Which was not strictly true. For when she was born there was no control tower, no airport – just the ancient farmhouse that was her home, lying at the core of its surrounding orchards and fields. . . .

Most of the land was given over to orchards – Morello cherries . . . apples and plums.

Most weekdays, long before dawn, some of the great shire horses were harnessed to the firm's massive canary-yellow carts to take the loads of fruit and flowers to the [family's] stall in Covent Garden.

MARGARET AND ALICK POTTER, *Everything is Possible*, 1984

Hatton Cross

On 16 December 1977 Her Majesty the Queen rode in the cab of a special train from Hatton Cross to Heathrow Central and unveiled a memorial plaque. The Heathrow extension was both officially open and open to the public. Air travellers began to 'Fly the Tube' the same day, the first of 12 million eventually expected to use the line every year.

JOHN R. DAY, *The Story of London's Underground*, 1963

Hounslow West

Return'd with my Lord by Hounslow Heath, where we saw the newly-rais'd army encamp'd, design'd against France, in pretence at least, but which gave umbrage to the Parliament. His Majesty and a world of company were in the field, and the whole army in battalia: a very glorious sight. Now were brought into service a new sort of Soldiers called Granadiers, who were dextrous in flinging hand granados, every one having a pouchfull; they had furr'd caps with coped crownes, like Janizaries, which made them look very fierce, and some had long hoods hanging down behind, as we picture fools. Their clothing being likewise pybald yellow and red.

JOHN EVELYN, *Diary, 29 June 1678*

As far back as about 1650 [Hounslow] was noted for its numerous inns and ale-houses. . . .

At the accession of Queen Victoria there were as many as five hundred stage-coaches and one thousand five hundred horses daily employed in transit through the town.

E. WALFORD, *Greater London*, 1882–4

Sir,
. . . In the early morning mist, in the early 1940s, six boys from a west London grammar school would assemble at Hounslow West Station – at that time the end of the Piccadilly line . . . and equipped with an Underground map and red pencil, we would 'travel the tracks'. . . . We could be back at Hownslow Central sufficiently early in the evening to avoid arousing parental suspicion.

Yours sincerely,
James Mogford

Letter to *The Times*, 19 February 1994

Hounslow Central

Hounslow Heath is a sample of all that is bad in soil, and villainous in look.

WILLIAM COBBETT, *Rural Rides*, 1830

Celebrated 'powder mills' at North Feltham . . . some of the first gunpowder made in England was manufactured here. It was chancy stuff: the explosions, which occurred every few months, terrified Middlesex residents for two centuries. Horace Walpole complained about one which in 1772, damaged parts of his house at Strawberry Hill.

BRUCE STEVENSON, *Middlesex*, 1972

Hounslow East

You have read of my calamity without knowing it, and will pity me when you do. I have been blown up; my castle is blown up; Guy Fawkes has been about my house; and the 5th of November has fallen on the 6th of January! In short, nine thousand powder-mills broke loose yesterday morning on Hounslow-heath; a whole squadron of them came hither, and have broken eight of my painted-glass windows; and the north side of the castle looks as if it had stood a siege. The two saints of the hall have suffered martyrdom! they have had their bodies cut off, and nothing remains but their heads. . . . As the storm came from the north-west, the china-closet was not touched, not a cup fell down. The bow-window of brave old coloured glass, at Mr. Hindley's, is massacred; and all the north sides of Twickenham and Brentford are shattered. At London, it was proclaimed an earthquake, and half the inhabitants ran into the street.

HORACE WALPOLE, letter to the Hon. H.S. Conway, 7 January 1772

Osterley

Osterley House is magnificent. . . . Gresham, its original owner, was ostentatious. When Elizabeth I visited him here in 1576 she criticised the proportions of the courtyard. So Sir Thomas, overnight, had a wall built down the middle of it: 'It was questionable,' wrote Thomas Fuller, 'whether the Queen was more contented with the conformity to her fancy, or more pleased with the surprise and the sudden performance thereof.'

BRUCE STEVENSON, *Middlesex*, 1972

On Friday we went to see – oh, the palace of palaces! [Osterley House] – and yet a palace *sans crown, sans coronet*, but such expense! such taste! such profusion! . . . The old house I have often seen, which was built by Sir Thomas Gresham; but it is so improved and enriched, that all the Percies and Seymours of Syon must die of envy . . . a drawing-room worthy of Eve before the Fall. Mrs. Child's dressing-room is full of pictures, gold filigree, china and japan. So is all the house; the chairs are taken from antique lyres, and make charming harmony. . . . Not to mention a kitchen-garden that costs 1400 l. a-year, a menagerie full of birds that come from a thousand islands . . . and then the Park is – the ugliest spot of ground in the universe – and so I returned comforted to Strawberry.

HORACE WALPOLE, letter to the Countess of Ossory, 21 June 1773

Boston Manor

Boston Manor House at Brentford is a fine Tudor/Jacobean building said to be haunted by a Lady Boston who was killed by her husband when he found her *in flagrante delicto* with another man. He was successful in keeping her death secret, burying her body in the park. Her ladyship glides shadow-like from the back of the house along a path leading to a great cypress tree, where she disappears. A lady in white, who drowned herself in the lake after an unhappy love-affair, also haunts the lawns at the back of the house.

J.A. BROOKS, *Ghosts of London*, 1982

Northfields

Charles Blondin the tightrope walker lived here; there is no plaque, but Niagara House, a block of flats in Northfield Avenue, may remind the passer-by of one of his exploits.

BRUCE STEVENSON, *Middlesex*, 1972

South Ealing
Turn to page 199 for Acton Town

The manor of Ealing [or as it was sometimes written Yealing, Yelling, or Yeling] has belonged to the See of London from the earliest times.

E. WALFORD, *Greater London*, 1882–4

While we were away in Yorkshire my sister was born. My brother Cyril and I were silenced by this incomprehensible piece of news. Were our parents not satisfied with us? No sooner are we in Ealing than there is another baby, my youngest brother. Another betrayal. Why clutter up the place? It happens on my birthday, too.

V.S. PRITCHETT, *A Cab at the Door*, 1968

UXBRIDGE BRANCH
In peak hours this branch starts at Uxbridge.

Rayners Lane

Early Electric! Maybe even here
   They met that evening at six-fifteen
Beneath the hearts of this electrolier
   And caught the first non-stop to WILLESDEN GREEN,
Then out and on, through rural RAYNER'S LANE
To autumn-scented Middlesex again.

JOHN BETJEMAN, 'The Metropolitan Railway – Baker Street Station Buffet',
A Few Late Chrysanthemums, 1954

South Harrow

There was an old lady of Harrow
Whose views were exceedingly narrow.
   At the end of her paths
   She built two bird baths
For the different sexes of sparrow.

ANON.

Sudbury Hill

Thomas Trollope, father of the novelist, came to Illots Farm Sudbury in 1813–15 and his son used it as a model for 'Orley Farm'.

The London Encyclopaedia edited by Ben Weinreb
and Christopher Hibbert, 1983

Sudbury Town

Sir William Perkin, the greatest organic chemist of his time . . . was experimenting in a rough laboratory in his home at Sudbury. Working with his brother on aniline compounds, he discovered the first completely fast mauve dye. It was enthusiastically received by Pullar's of Perth. Within a few months Perkin had opened a small factory at Greenford, and was making dyes in quantity. 'A rage for your colour has set in among that all-powerful class of the community – the ladies,' wrote Pullar; 'if they once take a mania for it and you can supply the demand, your fame and fortune are made.' Mauve was the favourite colour of Queen Victoria – and the fortune was made: Perkin retired at the age of 35 to The Chestnuts, Sudbury. There he devoted himself to research in pure chemistry, to good works and to chamber music.

BRUCE STEVENSON, *Middlesex*, 1972

Alperton

Besides the farmhouses, it comprises a few straggling cottages, with a 'public' [the Chequers] and two or three beershops, along the road by the Grand Junction Canal, and between the canal and little river Brent. It is a pretty summer evening stroll from Sudbury to Twyford and Hanger Hill, across the Alperton meadows, but the brickmaker and the builder threaten a descent upon them.

JAMES THORNE, *Handbook to the Environs of London*, 1876

Park Royal

I remember Park Royal as a little wooden platform, high above the football ground of the Queens Park Rangers and what a pleasant walk one could take by leafy lanes and elmy fields of Middlesex between Preston Road Station on the Metropolitan to the newly electrified Kenton Station on the extension beyond Queens Park of the Bakerloo.

JOHN BETJEMAN, 'Coffee, Port and Cigars on the Inner Circle', *The Times*, 24 May 1963

North Ealing

In the 1890s Ealing was known as 'Queen of the Suburbs'.

Ealing Common
Change for District line

Great Ealing School, second only to the great public schools of Eton and Harrow. . . . In the record of former scholars are men whose names have become household words in every department of English life . . . Thackeray, Newman, Captain Marryat. . . . Huxley's father was a teacher in the school, and undoubtedly Professor Huxley, at an early age, was a scholar, although not for long, as the Huxley family left Ealing when the embryo scientist was only eight years of age.

It is also a matter of note that Louis Philippe, King of the French, was, in the days of his exile, a teacher in the school.

CHARLES JONES, *Ealing*, 1903

Acton Town
Change for District line

Richard Baxter (the nonconformist divine) decided to leave London, which in any case he says he found deleterious to both health and study:

. . . all Publick Service being at an end, I betook my self to live in the Country (at Acton) that I might set myself to writing, and do what Service I could for Posterity, and live as possibly I could out of the World. Thither I came 1663, July 14. . . .

The Plague which began at *Acton*, July 29 1665 being ceased on March 1 following, I returned home; and found the Church-yard like a plow'd field with Graves, and many of my Neighbours dead; but my

House (near the Church-yard) uninfected, and that part of my Family, which I left there, all safe, thro' the great mercy of God, my merciful Protector.

Of the Great Fire which followed in September he laments especially 'the Loss of Books' as 'an exceeding great Detriment to the Interest of Piety and Learning' and records: 'I saw the half burnt Leaves of Books near my Dwelling at Acton six miles from London but others found them near Windsor, almost twenty miles distant.'

RICHARD BAXTER, *Reliquiae Baxterianae*, 1696

Turnham Green

By the morning of November 13th [1642] the King found his way barred by some 24,000 men drawn up on the broad common of Turnham Green.

W.G. BELL, *Where London Sleeps*, 1926

Great and Bloody News
from
Turnham-Green,
or a
Relation
Of a sharp Encounter
Between the Earl of Pembrook, and his Company,
with the Constable and Watch belonging to the
Parish of Chiswick on the 18 Instant [1680].
In which Conflict Mr Smeethe a Gentleman, and
one Mr Halfpenny a Constable of the said
Parish were mortally Wounded.

W.G. BELL, *Where London Sleeps*, 1926

The most significant suburb built in the last century, probably the most significant in the Western world is Bedford Park, Chiswick [served by Turnham Green Station], laid out in 1876 by Norman Shaw. It was designed specifically for 'artistic people of moderate incomes'. It stands in orchard land and the picturesque brick houses with their faintly Dutch look are late Victorian versions of the small parsonage houses which were built in the heyday of the Gothic revival a generation earlier. . . .

Bedford Park was the origin of many another garden suburb.

> JOHN BETJEMAN, 'The Most Significant Suburb – Bedford Park',
> *Daily Telegraph*, 22 August 1960, quoted in *Betjeman's London*
> edited by Pennie Denton

London Burning! I watched this event from my Chiswick flat last night with disgust and indignation, but with no intensity though the spectacle was superb, I thought. It is nothing like the burning of Troy. Yet the Surrey Docks were ablaze at the back with towers and spires outlined against them, greenish yellow searchlights swept the sky in futile agony, crimson shells burst behind the spire of Turnham Green church. This is all that a world catastrophe amounts to. Something which one is too sad or sullen to appreciate. Perhaps we are really behaving heroically. . . . Someone else will have to say. Now and then tracts of the horizon flashed a ghastly electric green. Or the fire ahead burst up as I hoped it was dying down. Oh! I cried once faintly then returned to my bed and read *Middlemarch*. God help us all. . . . In the morning a crimson valance of cloud hung above the fire itself.

> E.M. FORSTER, 8 September 1940*

*During the Second World War, E.M. Forster lived in No. 9 Arlington Park Mansions, Turnham Green. From his flat he watched the bombing of London's dockland.

Hammersmith
Change for District line and Hammersmith & City line station

So long as Hammersmith is called Hammersmith, its people will live in the shadow of that primal hero, the Blacksmith, who led the democracy of the Broadway into battle till he drove the chivalry of Kensington before him and overthrew them at the place which in honour of the best blood of the defeated aristocracy is still called Kensington Gore.

> G.K. CHESTERTON, *The Napoleon of Notting Hill*, 1904

In the Village of Hammersmith, which was formerly a long scattering Place, full of Gardeners Grounds, with here and there an old House of some Bulk: We see now great Numbers of fine Houses, and a continued Range of great Length, which makes the main Street. A handsome

Square was also begun, but it did not succeed, and the Place is turn'd in to Gardening.

DANIEL DEFOE, *A Tour thro' the Whole Island of Great Britain*, 1738

Barons Court

The Barons Court Estate. This estate was planned by the late Sir William Palliser. The title was devised in allusion to the Court Baron held by the Lord of the Manor, and was, perhaps, suggested to Sir William by the name of the neighbouring district, Earl's Court.

CHARLES JAMES FERET, *Fulham Old and New*, 1900

Earl's Court
Change for District line

The tube station is the soul of the place made visible. Around and about it Earl's Court anchors itself. Out of it is disgorged and into it is ingested a steady stream of humanity. A multi-hued, multi-lingual crowd is always gathered near its entrance. Earl's Court is nothing if not cosmopolitan. Long-haired students from the continent weighted under rucksacks studded with the flags of their countries pore over street maps. Bearded Australians study the poster that invites them to join the Zambesi Club – Rhodesians, South Africans, New Zealanders and Canadians also welcome.

SHIVA NAIPAUL in *Living in London* edited by Alan Ross, 1974

Gloucester Road
Change for Circle and District lines

James Barrie, novelist, lived at No. 133 Gloucester Road from 1896 to 1902.

South Kensington
Change for Circle and District lines

Towards five o'clock he [George Forsyte] went out, and took a train at South Kensington Station (for everyone to-day went Underground).

JOHN GALSWORTHY, *The Man of Property*, 1906

As one goes into the South Kensington Art Museum [now the Victoria & Albert] from the Brompton Road, the Gallery of Old Iron is overhead to the right. But the way thither is exceedingly devious and not to be revealed to everybody, since the young people who pursue science and art thereabouts set a peculiar value on its seclusion. The gallery is long and narrow and dark, and set with iron gates, iron-bound chests, locks, bolts, and bars, fantastic great keys, lamps, and the like, and over the balustrade one may lean and talk of one's finer feelings and regard Michael Angelo's horned Moses, or Trajan's Column (in plaster) rising gigantic out of the hall below and far above the level of the gallery.

H.G. WELLS, *Love and Mr Lewisham*, 1900

Knightsbridge

I'm eighteen actually, although
Most people take me for *much* more;
I'm *not* a debutante, you know.
I think it's *such* a bore to go
To parties until three or four.
My father was an aide-de-camp.
We've got an aubergine front door.
I'm *frightfully* keen on Terence Stamp.

I *wish* I had a bigger bust,
Though Mummy says it's frightfully smart
And any more would beckon lust.
She says I absolutely *must*
Stop trying to be keen on art
And dressing like a King's Road tramp.
I simply don't know where to start.
I'm *frightfully* keen on Terence Stamp.

I'm starting on a course quite soon,
It's sort of cookery and flowers.
My latest colour's deep maroon.
And sometimes in the afternoon
I simply lie for hours and hours
Beneath dear Mummy's sun-ray lamp
And contemplate the Carlton Towers.
I'm *frightfully* keen on Terence Stamp.

CANDIDA LYCETT GREEN, 'Knightsbridge Ballade', 1967

. . . the most respectable people have taken to living in neighbour-
hoods which, in my young days, were marshes and grazing meadows
for dairymen's cows, and were at night infested by highwaymen and
footpads. I should like to know where Pagoda Square, Kensington, was
thirty years ago. My dear, Brompton was in the country then, and you
had scarcely passed Hyde Park Corner before you were in the green
lanes. Knightsbridge Green meant something more, in those days, than
a street full of rubbishing little shops.

G.A. SALA, *Lady Chesterfield's Letters to Her Daughter*, 1860

Then, behind, all my hair is done up in a plait,
And so, like a cornet's, tuck'd under my hat,
Then I mount on my palfrey as gay as a lark,
And, follow'd by John, take the dust in Hyde Park.
In the way I am met by some smart macaroni,
Who rides by my side on a little bay pony –
No sturdy Hibernian, with shoulders so wide,
But as taper and slim as the ponies they ride;
Their legs are as slim, and their shoulders no wider,
Dear sweet little creatures, both pony and rider! . . .

In Kensington Gardens to stroll up and down,
You know was the fashion before you left town, . . .

Yet, though 'tis too rural – to come near the mark,
We all herd in *one* walk, and that, nearest the park;
There with ease we may see, as we pass by the wicket,
The chimneys of Knightsbridge, and footmen at cricket.

THOMAS TICKELL (1686–1740), 'On a Woman of Fashion'
quoted in *London Between the Lines* compiled by John Bishop
and Virginia Broadbent, 1973

Hyde Park Corner

Good Mirabell, don't let us be familiar or fond, nor kiss before folks,
like my Lady Fadler and Sir Francis: nor go to Hyde Park together the
first Sunday in a new chariot, to provoke eyes and whispers; and then
never be seen there together again; as if we were proud of one another
the first week, and ashamed of one another ever after. . . . Let us be

very strange and well-bred: let us be as strange as if we had been married a great while; and as well bred as if we were not married at all.

WILLIAM CONGREVE, *The Way of the World*, 1700

Hyde Park, everyone knows, is the promenade of London: nothing was so much in fashion, during the fine weather, as this promenade, which was the rendezvous of magnificence and beauty: every one, therefore, who had either sparkling eyes, or a splendid equipage, constantly repaired thither; and the king [Charles II] seemed pleased with the place.

COUNT ANTHONY HAMILTON, *Memoirs of Count Grammont*,
translated with notes by Horace Walpole, with additional notes
and biographical sketches by Sir Walter Scott and
Mrs Ann Jameson, 1888 (first published 1713)

I [Bridget Tisdall] would be wheeled daily into Hyde Park. . . . Here sat the Balloon Woman with her bunch of balloons and red and yellow windmills on sticks which the nannies bought for their charges. We would then cross Rotten Row . . . and turn right into The Daisy Walk where upper-crust Nannies with crested prams sat knitting, complaining, and generally comparing each other's situations. . . .

The Pryce-Jones Nanny had wheeled herself behind the [Albert] Memorial and sat down on an empty bench. After a while an older Nanny appeared, pushing a pram on which was painted a small gold coronet. She sat down too and they eyed one another. At length the older Nanny turned to the younger one, coughed, and said 'Excuse me, Nanny, is your mummy a titled mummy?' 'Actually, no,' said the Pryce-Jones Nanny.

'You will excuse my mentioning it, Nanny, but this bench is reserved for titled mummies' nannies, Nanny.'

J. GATHORNE-HARDY, *The Rise and Fall of the British Nanny*, 1972

Green Park

Change for Jubilee and Victoria lines

. . . it's dark now, and the long rows of lamps in Piccadilly after dark were beautiful. . . . On the right of that thorough-fare is a row of trees, the railing of the Green Park, and a fine broad eligible piece of pavement.

'Oh, my!' cried Henrietta presently. 'There's been an accident!' I looked to the left, and said, 'Where, Henrietta?'

'Not there, stupid!' said she. 'Over there by the Park railings. Where the crowd is. Oh no, it's not an accident, it's something else to look at! What's them lights?'

She referred to two lights twinkling low amongst the legs of the assemblage: two candles on the pavement.

'Oh, do come along!' cried Henrietta, skipping across the road with me. I hung back, but in vain. 'Do let's look!'

Again, designs upon the pavement. Centre compartment, Mount Vesuvius going it (in a circle), supported by four oval compartments, severally representing a ship in heavy weather, a shoulder of mutton attended by two cucumbers, a golden harvest with distant cottage of proprietor, and a knife and fork after nature; above the centre compartment a bunch of grapes, and over the whole a rainbow. The whole, as it appeared to me, exquisitely done.

CHARLES DICKENS, 'Somebody's Luggage', Christmas Number of *All the Year Round*, 1862, reprinted in *Christmas Stories*

. . . *we returned to the station [Green Park] to find that in one of the underground corridors with superb acoustics, Rachel, an attractive lass from St John's Wood, was already deep into the first movement* (Allegro ma non troppo) *of Beethoven's Violin Concerto in D Major with its superb octaval leaps and G-string twiddly bits* staccatissimo. . . . *She was accompanied by a taped orches-*

tral backing known to subterranean maestros as a 'one out', that is with the solo parts professionally erased.

JOHN HILLABY, *John Hillaby's London*, 1987

Piccadilly Circus
Change for Bakerloo line

A pickadil [is] that round hem, or the several divisions set together about the skirt of a Garment, or other thing; also a kinde of stiff collar, made in fashion of a Band. Hence, perhaps the famous Ordinary near St. James, called Pickadilly, took denomination; because it was then the outmost, or skirt house of the Suburbs, that way. Others say it took name from this, that one *Higgins* a Tailor, who built it, got most of his Estate by Pickadilles, which in the last age were much worn in England.

T. BLOUNT, *Glossographia*, 1656

London. I had the first time in my life, a feeling of health. . . . London was indescribably beautiful. The red and brown chimney-pots contrasted so sharply with the blue sky, and all the colours glowed, the gay shops gleamed and the blue air poured out of every cross street and enveloped the background. . . . How beautifully the roses in Piccadilly gleamed in the sunshine, and how full of vitality everything seemed. It gave me a strange but very comforting sensation and I felt the power of returning health. I shall bring away very dear memories of this town, and when I drive off on the stage-coach. . . . I shall look back many a time and think of the pleasure I have had here.

FELIX MENDELSSOHN, letter to his family, 6 November 1829

I remember an evening at the Café Royal (can we grey beards *never* set pen to paper without remembering some evening at the Café Royal?) when Oscar Wilde, who had for some time been talking in a vein of iridescent nonsense about some important matter, paused and said, with good reason and with genuine feeling, 'My dear Will [Rothenstein], don't look so serious!'

MAX BEERBOHM, *A Peep into the Past and Other Prose Pieces* collected by Rupert Hart-Davis, 1972

There, on that October evening – there, in that exuberant vista of gilding and crimson velvet set amidst all those opposing mirrors and
upholding caryatids, with fumes of tobacco ever rising to the painted
and pagan ceiling, and with the turn of presumably cynical conversation broken into so sharply now and again by a clatter of dominoes
shuffled on marble tables, I drew a deep breath and 'This indeed,' said I
to myself, 'is life'.

> MAX BEERBOHM, describing his first visit to the Café Royal,
> Piccadilly, with William Rothenstein

> It's a long way to Tipperary, it's a long way to go;
> It's a long way to Tipperary, to the sweetest girl I know!
> Goodbye Piccadilly, farewell Leicester Square;
> It's a long long way to Tipperary, but my heart's right there!

> HARRY WILLIAMS AND JACK JUDGE, 1908

Leicester Square
Change for Northern line

. . . in 1783 he [John Hunter, the founder of the Royal College of
Surgeons] took a house upon a much larger scale, in Leicester Square,
about the middle of the eastern side, which extended through, into
Castle-Street. This was fitted up in a very expensive manner; – and
here he established an expansive room for his Museum, – another for a
public medical levee, on every Sunday evening, another for a lyceum
for medical disputation, – another for his course of lectures; another
for dissection, – another for a printing warehouse and a press, – and
another for reading his medical works. . . .

   . . . Soon as he was settled in this new house, he sent out cards of
invitation to those of the faculty, his selection suggested, – to attend on
Sunday evenings, during the winter months, at his levee; and they

were regaled, with tea and coffee, and treated with medical occur-
rences.

JESSE FOOT, *The Life of John Hunter*, 1794

Covent Garden

1752. One night when Beauclerk and Langton had supped at a tavern
in London, and sat till about three in the morning, it came into their
heads to go and knock up Johnson, and see if they could prevail on
him to join them in a ramble. They rapped violently at the door of his
chambers in the Temple, till at last he appeared in his shirt, with his little black wig on the top of his head, instead of a nightcap, and a poker
in his hand, imagining, probably, that some ruffians were coming to
attack him. When he discovered who they were, and was told their
errand, he smiled, and with great good-humour agreed to their propo-
sal: 'What, is it you, you dogs! I'll have a frisk with you.' He was soon
drest, and they sallied forth together into Covent Garden . . .

JAMES BOSWELL, *The Life of Samuel Johnson*, 1791

I have been apprised several times during the night that this was a
market morning in Covent Garden. I have seen waggons surmounted
by enormous mountains of vegetable baskets wending their way
through the silent streets. I have been met by the early costermongers
in their donkey-carts, and chaffed by the costerboys on my forlorn
appearance. But I have reserved Covent Garden as a *bonne bouche* – a
wind-up to my pilgrimage; for I have heard and read how fertile is the
market in question in subjects of amusement and contemplation.

I confess that I am disappointed. Covent Garden seems to me to be
but one great accumulation of cabbages. I am pelted with these vegeta-
bles as they are thrown from the lofty summits of piled waggons to
costermongers standing at the base. I stumble among them as I walk;
in short, above, below, on either side, cabbages preponderate.

G.A. SALA, *Papers Humorous and Pathetic*, 1872

. . . a boy being born on St George's Day, 1775, began soon after to
take interest in the world of Covent Garden, and put to service such
spectacles of life as it afforded.

. . . Besides men and women, dusty sunbeams up or down the street
on summer mornings; deep furrowed cabbage-leaves at the green-

grocer's; magnificence of oranges . . . ; wheelbarrows round the corner;
and Thames' shore within three minutes' race. . . .

His foregrounds had always a succulent cluster or two of greengrocery at the corners. Enchanted oranges gleam in Covent Gardens of the Hesperides; and great ships go to pieces in order to scatter chests of them on the waves.

JOHN RUSKIN on J.M.W. Turner's boyhood,
Modern Painters, Part IX, 1860

Of ballet fans we are the cream,
    We never miss a night;
The ballet is our only theme,
Our Russian accent is a dream,
We say the name of every prim
    A *ballerina* right;
The ballet is our meat and drink,
    It is our staff of life,
Our prop, our safety valve, our link,
Our vice, our passion, foible, kink,
The ballet is,
We really think,
    Our mistress and our wife.

It's true that many lesser clans
    For ballet also thirst,
But they are merely *nouveau* fans,
    It's we who liked it first,
And we who know it best, becos,
    Ask any *connoisseur*,
The ballet isn't what it was
    When we were what we were.
        Oh, the urge
        To see Serge!
        What a thrill!
        What a pill!
        What a purge!
        So adept
        When he leapt,
        We were dumb,
        Overcome,
        Overswept!

H. FARJEON, 'When Bolonsky Danced Belushka',
Nine Sharp and Earlier, 1938

The phantom of William Terriss, a famous leading man of the 1890s, also prefers to haunt in winter. He visits Covent Garden Underground Station as well as the Adelphi Theatre where he was appearing at the time of his violent death. An account of an appearance of his ghost was printed in the *Sunday Dispatch* on 15 January 1956:

Who is the ghost of Covent Garden Underground Station? Some people believe the station is haunted by a Victorian actor.

A four-page report has been sent to the London Transport Executive divisional headquarters. And this question has been put to officials:

Is the statuesque figure wearing white gloves and seen by members of the station staff, the spectre of William Terriss, the actor stabbed to death at the Adelphi Theatre by a maniac 59 years ago? . . .

Just after midnight last November the last passenger had left the platform. Foreman Collector Jack Hayden saw a tall distinguished-looking man go into the exit.

'Catch that man coming up the emergency stairs, Bill,' he phoned the booking clerk. *But no one was there.*

J.A. BROOKS, *Ghosts of London*, 1982

Aldwych
Peak hours only

The Aldwych branch of the Piccadilly from Holborn was closed on 21 September 1940 and it stayed closed throughout the war, re-opening on 1 July 1946. Many British Museum treasures, including the Elgin Marbles, spent the war in the Aldwych branch tunnels.

JOHN R. DAY, *The Story of London's Underground*, 1963

Holborn

Change for Central line

GLOUCESTER:
> My Lord of Ely, when I was last in Holborn,
> I saw good strawberries in your garden there;
> I do beseech you send for some of them.

ELY:
> Marry, and will, my Lord, with all my heart.

WILLIAM SHAKESPEARE, *Richard III*, 1593

. . . a brook 'as clear as crystal' once ran right down Holborn, when Turnstile really was a turnstile leading slap away into the meadows.

CHARLES DICKENS, *Bleak House*, 1852–3

> When I am sad and weary
> When I think all hope is gone
> When I walk along High Holborn
> I think of you with nothing on.

ADRIAN MITCHELL, 'Celia Celia', *Adrian Mitchell: Greatest Hits*, 1991

Russell Square

. . . his bedroom window looked out on a south-west garden-wall, covered with flowering jessamine through June and July. There had been roses, too, in this London garden. Gray must always have flowers about him, and he trudged down to Covent Garden every day, for his sweet peas and pinks, scarlet martagon lilies, double stocks and flowering marjoram. His drawing-room looked over Bedford Gardens, and a fine stretch of upland fields, crowned at last against the sky by the villages of Highgate and Hampstead . . . he is working every day at the Museum, feasting upon literary plums and walnuts.

EDMUND GOSSE, *Gray*, 1882, describing Thomas Gray's (1716–71)
lodgings near Russell Square, where he had come to study in the
newly opened British Museum

He sat in the Underground train to Russell Square. Before anything

else he must get back his Reading Room ticket. That was his true identity card.

MAUREEN DUFFY, *Capital*, 1975

> What? Russell Square!
> There's lilac there!
> And Torrington
> And Woburn Square
> Intrepid don
> The season's wear.
> In Gordon Square and Euston Square –
> There's lilac, there's laburnum there!
> In green and gold and lavender
> Queen Square and Bedford Square,
> All Bloomsbury and all Soho
> With every sunbeam gayer grow,
> Greener grow and gayer.

JOHN DAVIDSON, 'Laburnum and Lilac',
Pall Mall Magazine, 1906

King's Cross St. Pancras
Change for Circle, Hammersmith & City, Metropolitan, Northern
and Victoria lines

> O Time, bring back those midnights and those friends,
> Those glittering moments that a spirit lends,
> That all may be imagined from the flash,
> The cloud-hit god-game through the lightning gash,
> Those hours of stricken sparks from which men took
> Light to send out to men in song or book;
> Those friends who heard St. Pancras's bells strike two,
> Yet stayed until the barber's cockerel crew,
> Talking of noble styles, the Frenchman's best,
> And thought beyond great poets not expressed,
> The glory of mood where human frailty failed,
> The forts of human light not yet assailed.

JOHN MASEFIELD, 'Biography', *Collected Poems*, 1923

Caledonian Road

A work-basket made of an old armadillo
  Lined with pink satin now rotten with age,
A novel entitled *The Ostracized Vicar*
  (A spider squashed flat on the title-page),
A faded album of nineteen-oh-seven
  Snapshots (now like very weak tea)
Showing high-collared knuts and girls expectant
  In big muslin hats at Bexhill-on-Sea,
A gasolier made of hand-beaten copper
  In the once modern style known as *art nouveau*
An assegai, and a china slipper,
  And *What a Young Scoutmaster Ought to Know.*

Who stood their umbrellas in elephants' feet?
  Who hung their hats on the horns of a moose?
Who crossed the ocean with amulets made
  To be hung round the neck of an ailing papoose?
Who paid her calls with a sandalwood card-case?
  From whose eighteen-inch waist hung that thin châtelaine?
Who smoked that meerschaum? Who won that medal?
  That extraordinary vase was evolved by what brain?
Who worked in wool the convolvulus bell-pull?
  Who smiled with those false teeth? Who wore that wig?
Who had that hair tidy hung by her mirror?
  Whose was the scent-bottle shaped like a pig? . . .

Laugh if you like at this monstrous detritus
  Of middle-class life in the liberal past,
The platypus stuffed, and the frightful épergne.
  You who are now overtaxed and declassed,
Laugh while you can, for the time may come round
  When the rubbish you treasure will lie in this place –
Your wireless set (bust), your ridiculous hats,
  And the photographs of your period face.
Your best-selling novels, your 'functional' chairs,
  Your primitive comforts and notions of style
Are just so much fodder for dealers in junk
  Let us hope that they'll make your grandchildren smile.

WILLIAM PLOMER, 'The Caledonian Market', *Selected Poems*, 1940

---

*The Cyclopean eye of the advancing train, the adventure of boarding, the fastid-
iousness in the choice of a neighbour, the sense of equality, the mysterious and
flattering reflection of oneself in the opposite windows, even of the colours of the
various stations – from the orange and lemon of Covent Garden to the bistre
melancholy of Caledonian Road or Camden Town, faint cerulean like an
autumnal sky.*

COMPTON MACKENZIE (?), 1933 (?)

Holloway Road

The new lumber of a London-going dray,
The still-new stucco on the London clay,
Hot summer silence over Holloway.

JOHN BETJEMAN quoted in Betjeman Country
by Frank Delaney, 1985

. . . Crane Grove Secondary, up past Highbury Corner, off the
Holloway Road. The five- and six-storey schools in this part stand
above the three-storey streets like chaotic castellations. Dead cinemas
and a music hall sadden corners, abandoned. Only Arsenal stadium,
older-looking in its outdated modernity than last century's houses,
competes in height with the dark red brick, stonedressed schools.
Swart sleek diesels shaped as functionally as otters pass and re-pass
solemnly between strips of houses at eaves-level pulling trains of rust-
stained waggons.

B.S. JOHNSON, Albert Angelo, 1964

Arsenal

The story of Islington's favourite football club in fact begins in
Woolwich in the days of the first soccer boom, when as yet there was
more enthusiasm for rugger than soccer in the south. The Scots then
working at Woolwich Arsenal wanted to redress the balance by setting
up a football team. David Danskin managed to get 15 signatures per 6d
a time but he had to add a further 10s.6d from his own pocket to buy a
soccer ball.

Originally the team, founded in the autumn of 1886, was known as
Dial Square after the particular set of workshops from which most of
the players were drawn. From the first the colours of the team were

215

scarlet. . . . Subsequently as the fame of the team spread and the rumour went around that the key to a job at the Arsenal was the ability to play football well the name was changed first to Woolwich Arsenal . . . and subsequently when the club moved its headquarters to Highbury in 1913 it became commonsense to drop the Woolwich part of the title.

SONIA ROBERTS, *The Story of Islington*, 1975

The thirties were a good decade for the team: they won their first FA Cup in 1930, and in the course of the decade were league champions five times. Their glory was celebrated in the renaming of Gillespie Road Underground station [to Arsenal]. They won their first League and FA Cup double in 1970/71.

ANN USBORNE, *A Portrait of Islington*, 1981

Finsbury Park
Change for Victoria line

The train, though it did not start for an hour, was already drawn up at the end of the platform, and he lay down in it and slept. With the first jolt he was in daylight; they had left the gateways of King's Cross, and were under blue sky. Tunnels followed, and after each the sky grew bluer, and from the embankment at Finsbury Park he had his first sight of the sun. It rolled along behind the eastern smokes – a wheel, whose fellow was the descending moon – and as yet it seemed the servant of the blue sky, not its lord.

E.M. FORSTER, *Howards End*, 1910

Not long ago, at the height of the rush hour, I was strap-hanging, and in that half of the carriage, that is, among fourteen people, three people read books among all the newspapers. In the morning, off to work, people betray their allegiances: The Times, *the* Independent, *the* Guardian, *the* Telegraph, *the* Mail. . . . *At night the* Evening Standard *adds itself to the display. Three people. At my right elbow a man was reading the* Iliad. *Across the aisle a woman read* Moby Dick. *As I pushed out, a girl held up* Wuthering Heights *over the head of a new baby asleep on her chest.*

The poem holding its own among the advertisements was:
INFANT JOY

DORIS LESSING, 'In Defence of the Underground', *London Observed*, 1992

Manor House

Manor House. Close by the station stands the Manor House public house. Known as the 'Manor Tavern' when it was built in *c.*1820 as a stopping place for travellers between London and Cambridge.

CYRIL M. HARRIS, *What's in a Name?*, 1977

Turnpike Lane

The Turnpike gate, which was erected in 1767, was removed in the 1870s.

For my part, now, I consider supper as a turnpike, through which one must pass in order to get to bed.' 17 April 1778.

J. BOSWELL, *The Life of Samuel Johnson*, 1791

Wood Green

Wood Green has a history as a rural hamlet originating in a small settlement at the foot of a wooded hill in the heart of which was a green. . . . Today it is best known for its shopping city, a complex designed by Richard, Sheppard, Robson and Partners which took seven years to build and was officially opened by the Queen on 13 May 1981.

The London Encyclopaedia edited by Ben Weinreb and Christopher Hibbert, 1983

Bounds Green

Bounds Green . . . name is derived from its association with the families of John le Bonde in 1294 and Walter le Bounde during the 13th century . . . recorded as Le boundes in 1365.

CYRIL M. HARRIS, *What's in a Name?*, 1977

Arnos Grove

The largest oak in this district [in Middlesex], known as the Minchenden oak, is at Arno's Grove, Southgate. It is said to have the widest spread of branches of any English oak. This oak, then termed the Chandos oak, is figured in Strutt's *Sylvia*, and also in Loudon's *Arboretum*. The latter gives the branch spread as having an overall diameter of 118 feet, and the girth, one foot from the ground, as 18 ft. 3 in.

The Victoria History of the County of Middlesex edited by William Page, 1911

DEVELOPMENT ACT 1929
PICCADILLY RAILWAY
Southgate Extension from Finsbury Park
STATION SITE
suggested names
ARNOS GROVE   ARNOS PARK   SOUTHGATE
Write and tell us what name you suggest.

Large notice outside the original Arnos Grove station

Southgate

. . . it is a pleasure to me to know that I was even born in so sweet a village as Southgate. I first saw the light there on the 19th of October 1784. It found me cradled, not only in the lap of the nature which I love, but in the midst of the truly English scenery which I love beyond all other. Middlesex in general . . . is a scene of trees and meadows, of 'greenery' and nestling cottages; and Southgate is a prime specimen of Middlesex. It is a place lying out of the way of innovation, therefore it has the pure, sweet air of antiquity about it.

LEIGH HUNT, *Autobiography*, 1850

Oakwood

Oakwood station is decorated with the coat of arms showing stags heads and a Latin motto alleging that oak trees grow from acorns. But as well as the rural fictions of heraldry there are proper country trees beside the track waving their branches wildly in the south-west wind.

PHILIP HOWARD, *The Times*

Cockfosters

. . . few except the natives ever take the golden road to Cockfosters and the other terminal stations of Underground lines.

PHILIP HOWARD, *The Times*

So she spent the next three hours doing what she always did when she was on her own in the holidays. She rode on the London Transport trains. Sitting on a Piccadilly Line train which she picked up at King's Cross, she travelled to Cockfosters, at the end of the line. She would have liked to get out of the station and see the place, but that wasn't possible. She had only her imagination to give her a picture of what Cockfosters might look like. Jass imagined the sort of country she liked best. Soft, grassy hills, folding into each other as far as you could see. Perhaps an old farmhouse, with yellow lichen on the roof.

CATHERINE STORR, *The Underground Conspiracy*, 1987

VICTORIA LINE

Brixton

Another cab conveyed her to Brixton and set her down before a block of recently built flats. She ascended to the second floor, pressed the button of a bell, and was speedily confronted by a girl of the natty parlour-maid species. This time she began by giving her name, and had only a moment to wait before she was admitted to a small drawing-room, furnished with semblance of luxury. A glowing fire and the light of an amber-shaded lamp showed as much fashionable upholstery and bric-à-brac as could be squeezed into the narrow space.

GEORGE GISSING, *In the Year of Jubilee*, 1894

Stockwell
Change for Northern line

Stockwell remained a rural village until well into the nineteenth century. A cockney on a September outing in 1825 described how he breakfasted at the Swan on the Green and pressed on to Blackheath by way of Brixton without 'meeting anything beyond yellow-hammers and sparrows'.

The London Encyclopaedia edited by Ben Weinreb and
Christopher Hibbert, 1983

Vauxhall

Image [Vauxhall Gardens] to yourself . . . a spacious garden, part laid out in delightful walks, bounded with high hedges and trees, and paved with gravel; part exhibiting a wonderful assemblage of the most picturesque and striking objects, pavilions, lodges, groves, grottoes, lawns, temples and cascades; porticoes, colonades, and rotundos; adorned with pillars, statues, and painting: the whole illuminated with an infinite number of lamps, disposed in different figures of suns, stars, and constellations; the place crowded with the gayest company, ranging through those blissful shades, or supping in different lodges on cold collations, enlivened with mirth, freedom, and good humour, and animated by an excellent band of music.

TOBIAS SMOLLETT, *The Expedition of Humphry Clinker*, 1771

> Come hither ye gallants, come hither ye maids,
> To the trim gravelled walks, to the shady arcades;
> Come hither, come hither, the nightingales call; –
> Sing *Tantarara*, – Vauxhall! Vauxhall! . . .
>
> Here Beauty may grant, and here Valour may ask!
> Here the plainest may pass for a Belle (in a mask)!
> Here a domino covers the short and the tall; –
> Sing *Tantarara*, – Vauxhall! Vauxhall!
>
> 'Tis a type of the world, with its drums and its din;
> 'Tis a type of the world, for when you come in
> You are loth to go out; like the world 'tis a ball; –
> Sing *Tantarara*, – Vauxhall! Vauxhall!

HENRY AUSTIN DOBSON, 'A New Song of the Spring Gardens',
Magazine of Art and *At the Sign of the Lyre*, 1885

Pimlico

> My Uncle Paul of Pimlico
> Has seven cats as white as snow,
> Who sit at his enormous feet
> And watch him, as a special treat,
> Play the piano upside-down
> In his delightful dressing-gown;
> The firelight leaps, the parlour glows,
> And, while the music ebbs and flows,
> They smile (while purring the refrains),
> At little thoughts that cross their brains.

MERVYN PEAKE, *Rhymes without Reason*, 1944

Coming out with your clutch of postcards
in a Tate Gallery bag and another clutch
of images packed into your head you pause
on the steps to look across the river

and there's a new one: light bright buildings,
a streak of brown water, and such a sky
you wonder who painted it – Constable? No:
too brilliant. Crome? No: too ecstatic –

a madly pure Pre-Raphaelite sky,
perhaps, sheer blue apart from the white plumes
rushing up it (today, that is,
April. Another day would be different

but it wouldn't matter.
All skies work.)
Cut to the lower right for a detail: seagulls pecking on mud, below
two office blocks and a Georgian terrace.

Now swing to the left, and take in plane-trees
bobbled with seeds, and that brick building,
and a red bus. . . . Cut it off just there,
by the lamp-post. Leave the scaffolding in.

That's your next one. Curious how
these outdoor pictures didn't exist
before you'd looked at the indoor pictures,
the ones on the walls. But here they are now,

marching out of their panorama
and queuing up for the viewfinder
your eye's become. You can isolate them
by holding your optic muscles still.

You can zoom in on figure studies
(that boy with the rucksack), or still lives,
abstracts, townscapes. No one made them.
The light painted them. You're in charge

of the hanging committee. Put what space
you like around the ones you fix on,
and gloat. Art multiples itself.
Art's whatever you choose to frame.

FLEUR ADCOCK, 'Leaving the Tate' from *The Incident Book*, 1986

Victoria

Change for Circle and District lines

The flashiest of all suburban travellers are those who travel daily from Victoria by first-class Pullman trains to Brighton. Indeed, Brighton so dominates Victoria Station that though continental trains depart from its South Eastern Section, though many of the inner London suburbs are served by puzzling loop lines which start here and end at London Bridge, Victoria is the station of what moneyed leisure is left in London. Though it is meant to be associated with the South Coast and summer holidays, the sea is not what one associates with those who use it regularly. They do not look as though they took a winter dip in the English Channel. Warm flats, television, cocktail cabinets and bridge seem to be more in their line.

JOHN BETJEMAN, 'London Railway Stations',
Flower of Cities: A Book of London, 1949

Green Park

Change for Jubilee and Piccadilly lines

So called because of its verdure of grass and trees. . . . It is said to have been the burial ground of the lepers from the hospital of St James's, which is supposedly why there are no flowers here as there are in the adjoining St James's Park.

It was enclosed by Henry VIII and made into a Royal Park by Charles II who laid out walks and built a snow house for cooling drinks in summer. The mound of this snow house can still be seen opposite No. 119 Piccadilly, surmounted by one of the park's fine plane trees.

In the 18th century the park was a favoured place for duels. . . . The park was also much frequented by highwaymen: Horace Walpole was but one of numerous gentlemen who were held up here. Many balloon ascents were made here and several firework displays given. There was a particularly fine display to celebrate the Peace of Aix-la-Chapelle of 1748 for which Handel composed the incidental music.

The London Encyclopaedia edited by Ben Weinreb
and Christopher Hibbert, 1983

Oxford Circus

Change for Bakerloo and Central lines

London was beginning to illuminate herself against the night. Electric lights sizzled and jagged in the main thoroughfares, gas-lamps in the side streets glimmered a canary gold or green. The sky was a crimson battlefield of spring, but London was not afraid. Her smoke mitigated the splendour, and the clouds down Oxford Street were a delicately painted ceiling, which adorned while it did not distract.

E.M. FORSTER, *Howards End*, 1910

Down in the docks one sees things in their crudity, their bulk, their enormity. Here in Oxford Street they have been refined and transformed. The huge barrels of damp tobacco have been rolled into innumerable neat cigarettes laid in silver paper. The corpulent bales of wool have been spun into thin vests and soft stockings. The grease of sheep's thick wool has become scented cream for delicate skins. And those who buy and those who sell have suffered the same city change. Tripping, mincing, in black coats, in satin dresses, the human form has adapted itself no less than the animal product. Instead of hauling and heaving, it deftly opens drawers, rolls out silk on counters, measures and snips with yard sticks and scissors.

VIRGINIA WOOLF, 'Oxford Street Tide',
The London Scene, first published 1975

. . . the joke – after the event, at any rate – was at Oxford Circus itself. The southbound station tunnel there had to support the weight of Peter Robinson's – hats, dresses, tights, undies and all. While the women were admiring themselves on top, feeling as safe as houses, they little knew that, theoretically, they were being held up on the shoulders of the miners underneath. A concrete raft

was built to hold up the store. In November 1965, the diggers on their way south skimmed safely underneath it.

> MACDONALD HASTINGS, 'Brave New Underworld', *The Listener,*
> 6 March 1969, on the opening of the Victoria line

Warren Street
Change for Northern line

No blue plaque marks the former home of the famous Dr William Kitchiner in Warren Street. . . . But many of the Warren Street houses remain much as they were in his day and it is easy to picture No. 43 with its windows lit-up and carriages drawn-up outside on a Tuesday evening, when Dr Kitchiner held his conversaziones. . . .

Dr Kitchiner is worthy of a place among great British Eccentrics, an amateur who dabbled in many subjects, and was professional in at least one: medicine. . . .

He entertained his friends with food cooked according to his own principles, although not (one imagines) by his own hands, and also with music. . . . 'Come at seven, go at eleven' was an admonition displayed on the mantlepiece and, at eleven sharp, his guests' hats, overcoats and umbrellas were brought, as an indication that their host wished to retire to rest.

Sometimes they were allowed to share another of his interests: astronomy. At the top of the house was an observatory with a telescope at least partly home-made. (He had written a book on optics.) . . . Charles Turner's portrait of Kichiner includes a telescope as well as a keyboard instrument and a stuffed tiger, as part of the background.

> MOLLIE SANDS, 'The Eccentric Dr Kitchiner, 1775–1827',
> *Camden History Review* issue 6

Like many others who have lived long in a great capital, she had strong feelings about the various railway termini. They are our gates to the glorious and the unknown. Through them we pass out into adventure and sunshine, to them, alas! we return. In Paddington all Cornwall is latent and the remoter west; down the inclines of Liverpool Street lie fenlands and the illimitable Broads; Scotland is through the pylons of Euston; Wessex behind the poised chaos of Waterloo.

> E.M. FORSTER, *Howards End,* 1910

Euston
Change for Northern line

Euston, including its dependency, Camden Station, is the greatest rail port in England, or indeed in the world. It is the principal gate through which flows and reflows the traffic of a line which has cost more than twenty-two millions sterling. . . .

What London is to the world, Euston is to Great Britain. . . . Grouse from Aberdeen, fat cattle from Norfolk, piece goods from Manchester, hardwares from Sheffield, race horses from Newmarket, coals from Leicestershire, and schoolboys from Yorkshire, are despatched and received, for the distance of a few hundred miles, with the most perfect regularity, as a matter of course. We take a ticket to dine with a friend in Chester or Liverpool, or to meet the hounds near Bletchley or Rugby, as calmly as we engage a cab to go a mile; we consider twenty miles an hour disgustingly slow, and grumble awfully at a delay of five minutes in a journey of a hundred miles.

SAMUEL SIDNEY, *Rides on Railways*, 1851

King's Cross St. Pancras
Change for Circle, Hammersmith & City, Metropolitan, Northern and Piccadilly lines

1777. I remember well that in an autumn evening of this year . . . going with [my father] and his pupils on a sketching party to what is now called Pancras Old Church . . . which was at that time so rural that it was only enclosed by a low and very old hand-railing, in some parts entirely covered with docks and nettles.

J.T. SMITH, *A Book for a Rainy Day*, 1845

Bringing the line [of the Midland Railway] to London . . . was difficult
enough. . . . In order to do this the very large and very crowded burial
ground of old St. Pancras would have to be levelled. When the work
started, skulls and bones were seen lying about; a passer-by saw an
open coffin staved in through which peeped a bright tress of hair.
Great scandal was caused and the company was forced to arrange for
reverent reburial. The architect in charge of the reburial was A.W.
Blomfield, and he sent one of his assistants to watch the carrying away
of the dead to see that it was reverently done. That assistant was
Thomas Hardy, and his poems 'The Levelled Churchyard' and 'In the
Cemetery' recall the fact . . .

> O Passenger, pray list and catch
> Our sighs and piteous groans,
> Half stifled in this jumbled patch
> Of wrenched memorial stones!
>
> We late-lamented, resting here,
> Are mixed to human jam,
> And each to each exclaims in fear,
> 'I know not which I am!'

Hardy never forgot the event.

JOHN BETJEMAN, *London's Historic Railway Stations*, 1972

Highbury & Islington

> At Islington
> A fair they hold,
> Where cakes and ale
> Are to be sold.

Poor Robin's Almanac, 1676, quoted in *London in Verse*
edited by Christopher Logue (1982)

Islington. A large Village, half a League from *London*, where you drink
Waters that do you neither Good nor Harm, provided you don't take
too much of them. There is Gaming, Walking, Dancing; and a Man
may spend an Hour there agreeably enough. It is not much flock'd to
by People of Quality.

HENRI MISSON, *Memoirs & Observations in His Travels Over England*,
1698 (English translation 1719)

These were the streets my parents knew . . .
                                        and I, by descent, belong
  To these tall neglected houses divided into flats.
Only the church remains, where carriages used to throng
  And my mother stepped out in flounces and my father stepped out
    in spats
To shadowy stained-glass matins or gas-lit evensong
  And back in a country quiet with doffing of chimney hats.

JOHN BETJEMAN, 'St. Saviour's, Aberdeen Park,
Highbury, London, N.' Selected Poems, 1948

Finsbury Park
Change for Piccadilly line

It was in much-loved Finsbury Park that the supporters of Thomas Woodstock, Duke of Gloucester, assembled to form a league against the favourites of Richard II.

C.H. ROLPH, London Particulars, 1980

MASTER STEPHEN: Because I dwell at Hoxton, I shall keep company with none but the archers of Finsbury? Or the citizens that come a-ducking to Islington ponds?

BEN JONSON, Every Man in His Humour, 1616

Finsbury Park, that is to say the open park itself, is a relic of the days when the London housewife had nowhere to dry a day's washing. There is an old ballad concerning the 'Life and Death of the Two Ladies of Finsbury [who] gave Moorfields to the City for the Maidens of London to Dry their Clothes'. It has this verse:

> Where lovingly both man and wife
> May take the evening air
> And London dames to dry their clothes
> May hither still repair.

Seven Sisters

The *Seven Sisters* . . . one of the memorabilia of Tottenham, were seven elm-trees growing in a circle by the roadside at Page Green. According to an obscure tradition they were planted by seven sisters when about to separate.

JAMES THORNE, *Handbook to the Environs of London*, 1876

> Seven Sisters in patchwork cloaks
> Sat in the shadow of Seven Oaks
> Stringing acorns on silken strings,
> Awaiting the coming of Seven Kings.
>
> Seven years they endured their trials
> And then they consulted their Seven Dials –
> 'O it's time, it's time, it's time,' they said,
> 'It's very high time that we were wed!'

ELEANOR FARJEON, *Nursery Rhymes of London Town*, 1916

Tottenham Hale

Tottenham Wood – a then existent fragment of the old Forest of Middlesex [inspired the following proverbs]:
  'You shall as easily remove Tottenham Wood.' [i.e. it's not likely to be accomplished]
  'Tottenham was turn'd French.' . . . 'about the beginning of the reign of King Henry VIII, French mechanics swarmed in England, to the great prejudice of English artizans, which caused the insurrection in London, on May-day, A.D. 1517.'

JAMES THORNE, *Handbook to the Environs of London*, 1876

> There was a young lady of Tottenham.
> Her manners – she'd completely forgotten 'em;
>   While at tea at the vicar's
>   She took off her knickers,
> Explaining she felt much too hot in 'em.

ANON., *Penguin Book of Limericks* edited by E.O. Parrott, 1983

Blackhorse Road

London Transport has used the black horse for decorating the station both on the platforms and on its outside wall.

Blackhorse Road was recorded as *Black House Lane* in 1848 which is the correct spelling, for the road takes its name from an old *Black House*. Changed to *Blackhorse Lane* (then road) at a later date.

CYRIL M. HARRIS, *What's in a Name?*, 1977

Walthamstow Central

. . . about 9 a'clock took horse with both the Sir Williams [Batten and Penn] for Walthamstow; and there we found my Lady and her daughters all. And a pleasant day it was and all things else, but that my Lady was in a bad moode, which we were troubled at; and had she been noble, she would not have been so with her servants when we came thither. . . . After dinner we all went to the Church stile – and there eate and drank. And I was as merry as I could counterfeit myself to be.

SAMUEL PEPYS, *Diary, 18 April 1661*

[The forest legends] tell of Henry [VIII] waiting in the Forest of Waltham for the sounds of gunfire from the Tower of London that would announce the execution of his second consort and thus make way for the third, Jane Seymour. . . . Henry is reputed to have ordered the day's hunting to begin as soon as the fateful signal was heard.

KENNETH NEALE, *Discovering Essex in London*, 1970

[In 1849 the Morris family] moved to Woodford Hall, a Palladian mansion standing within its own park of fifty acres with twice that amount of farmland. Only a fence separated the park from Epping Forest. . . . In *News from Nowhere*, Morris writes of 'the wide green sea of Essex marshland . . .'. It was the kind of landscape to which he was always most drawn.

PHILIP HENDERSON, *William Morris: His Life, Work and Friends*, 1967

Past the Docks eastward and landward it is all flat pasture, once marsh, except for a few gardens, and there are very few permanent dwellings there, scarcely anything but a few sheds and cots for the men who come to look after the great herds of cattle pasturing there. But, however, what with the beasts and the men, and the scattered red-tiled roofs and the big hay-ricks, it does not make a bad holiday to get a quiet pony and ride about there on a sunny afternoon of autumn, and look over the river and the craft passing up and down, and on Shooter's Hill and the Kentish uplands, and then turn round to the wide green sea of the Essex marsh-land, with the great domed line of the sky, and the sun shining down in one flood of peaceful light over the long distance.

WILLIAM MORRIS, *News from Nowhere; or An Epoch of Rest*, 1890

ACKNOWLEDGEMENTS

We would like to thank our families and friends who have helped us over the years during the preparation of this book, especially Sandy Marriage, Robin Ollington, Bryan Rooney, Suzanne St Albans, Anthony Sampson, Kathleen Tillotson, Malcolm Holmes of the Camden Local History Library and the staff of the North Reading Room, British Library.

The compilers and publishers gratefully acknowledge permission to reproduce the following copyright material in this book:

Fleur Adcock: 'Leaving the Tate' from *The Incident Book*, © Fleur Adcock 1986. 'Miss Hamilton in London' from *Selected Poems* (1983), © Oxford University Press 1967. Originally published in *Tigers*, 1967. Reprinted by permission of Oxford University Press.

J.S. Bain: *A Bookseller Looks Back*, © J.S. Bain 1940. Reprinted by permission of Macmillan London.

Timothy Baker: *Mediaeval London*, © Timothy Baker 1970. Reprinted by permission of Cassell.

Julian Barnes: *Metroland*, © Julian Barnes 1980. Reprinted by permission of Jonathan Cape.

Max Beerbohm: *And Even Now*, © Max Beerbohm 1920. *A Peep into the Past*. © Max Beerbohm 1972. Reprinted by permission of Mrs Reichmann.

Hilaire Belloc: 'Rebecca, who slammed doors for fun and perished miserably' from *Cautionary Tales for Children*, © Hilaire Belloc 1908. *More Peers*, © Hilaire Belloc 1911. Reprinted by permission of Peters, Fraser & Dunlop.

John Betjeman: 'City' (*Continual Dew* 1937), 'Business Girls', 'Harrow-on-the-Hill', 'The Metropolitan Railway – Baker Street Station Buffet', 'Middlesex' (*A Few Late Chrysanthemums* 1954), 'Monody on the Death of Aldersgate Street Station', 'Parliament Hill Fields', 'South London Sketch' (*New Bats in Old Belfries* 1945), and 'St Saviour's, Aberdeen Park, Highbury, London, N.' (*Selected Poems* 1948) from *Collected Poems*. © John Betjeman 1958. 'A Mind's Journey to Diss' from *A Nip in the Air*, © John Betjeman 1974. *Summoned by Bells*, © John Betjeman 1960. 'Civilized Woman' from *Uncollected Poems*, © John Betjeman 1982. Reprinted by permission of John Murray.

ACKNOWLEDGEMENTS

Edmund Blunden: 'Thames Gulls' from *English Poems*, © Edmund Blunden 1925. Reprinted by permission of Peters, Fraser and Dunlop on behalf of the Estate of Edmund Blunden.

Dirk Bogarde: *Snakes and Ladders*, © Dirk Bogarde 1978. Reprinted by permission of Chatto & Windus.

Michael Bond: *A Bear Called Paddington*, © Michael Bond 1958. Reprinted by permission of Lemon, Unna & Durbridge, published by HarperCollins.

Mary Cathcart Borer: *The City of London: A History*, © Mary Cathcart Borer 1977. Reprinted by permission of Constable. *London Walks and Legends*, © Mary Cathcart Borer 1981. Reprinted by permission of Mary Cathcart Borer.

Elizabeth Bowen: *The Heat of the Day*, © Elizabeth Bowen 1949. *To the North*, © Elizabeth Bowen 1932. Reprinted by permission of Jonathan Cape.

J.A. Brooks: *Ghosts of London*, © J.A. Brooks 1982. Reprinted by permission of Jarrold Publishing.

Peter Bushell: *London's Secret History*, © Peter Bushell 1983. Reprinted by permission of Constable.

John Carey: *Original Copy*, © John Carey 1987. Reprinted by permission of Faber & Faber.

Peter Carey: *Oscar and Lucinda*, © Peter Carey 1988. Reprinted by permission of Faber & Faber.

Angela Carter: in *Living in London* edited by Alan Ross, © Angela Carter 1974. Reprinted by permission of London Magazine.

Hugh Casson: *Hugh Casson's London*, © Hugh Casson 1983. Reprinted by permission of John Johnson.

Charlie Chaplin: *My Autobiography*, © Charlie Chaplin 1964. Reprinted by permission of The Bodley Head.

Richard Church: 'Strap-hanging' from *Mood without Measure*, © Richard Church 1928. Reprinted by permission of Faber & Faber.

Rosemarie Dale: 'Stepney' from *Stepney Words I and II*, © Rosemarie Dale 1973. Reprinted by permission of Centreprise Publications.

Frank Delaney: *Betjeman Country*, © Frank Delaney 1983. Reprinted by permission of Hodder & Stoughton.

ACKNOWLEDGEMENTS

Pennie Denton (ed.): *Betjeman's London,* © Pennie Denton 1988. Reprinted by permission of John Murray.

Maureen Duffy: *Capital,* © Maureen Duffy 1975. Reprinted by permission of Jonathan Cape.

Evelyn L. Evans: *The Homes of Thomas Hardy,* © J. Stevens-Cox 1968. Reprinted by permission of Toucan Press.

Gavin Ewart: 'Earl's Court' and 'Tennysonian Reflections at Barnes Bridge' from *Londoners,* © Gavin Ewart 1964. Reprinted by permission of William Heinemann.

H. Farjeon: 'When Bolonsky Danced Belushka' from *Nine Sharp and Earlier,* © H. Farjeon 1938. Reprinted by permission of David Higham Associates and the Estate of Herbert Farjeon.

R.S. Fitter: *London's Natural History,* © R.S. Fitter 1945. Reprinted by permission of HarperCollins.

E.M. Forster: *Howard's End,* © E.M. Forster 1910. *Marianne Thornton,* © E.M. Forster 1956. Reprinted by permission of King's College, Cambridge and The Society of Authors as the literary representatives of the E.M. Forster Estate.

A.G. Gardiner: *Many Furrows,* © A.G. Gardiner 1924. Reprinted by permission of J.M. Dent.

Robert Gray: *A History of London,* © Robert Gray 1978. Reprinted by permission of Hutchinson Books.

Candida Lycett Green: 'Knightsbridge Ballade', © Candida Lycett Green 1967. Reprinted by permission of Candida Lycett Green.

Leigh Hatts: *Country Walks around London,* © Leigh Hatts 1983. Reprinted by permission of David & Charles.

Alethea Hayter: *A Sultry Month: Scenes of London Literary Life in 1846,* © Alethea Hayter 1965. Reprinted by permission of Robin Clark.

John Heath-Stubbs: *Satires and Epigrams,* © John Heath-Stubbs 1968. Reprinted by permission of David Higham Associates.

Philip Henderson: *William Morris: His Life, Work and Friends,* © Philip Henderson 1967. Reprinted by permission of Thames & Hudson.

John Hillaby: *John Hillaby's London,* © John Hillaby 1987. Reprinted by permission of Constable.

ACKNOWLEDGEMENTS

Alan Hollinghurst: *The Swimming Pool Library*, © Alan Hollinghurst 1988. Reprinted by permission of Chatto & Windus.

Philip Howard: 'Wapping' and 'Philip Howard looks at London' from *The Times*, © Times Newspapers. Reprinted by permission of Times Newspapers.

H. Howson: *London's Underground*, © H. Howson 1951 (first edition). Reprinted by permission of Ian Allan.

Aldous Huxley: *Crome Yellow*, © Aldous Huxley 1921. Reprinted by permission of Chatto & Windus.

Alan A. Jackson: *London's Metropolitan Railway*, © Alan A. Jackson 1986. Reprinted by permission of David & Charles.

Simon Jenkins: *The Companion Guide to Outer London*, © Simon Jenkins 1987. Reprinted by permission of HarperCollins.

B.S. Johnson: *Albert Angelo*, © B.S. Johnson 1964. Reprinted by permission of Constable.

Doris Lessing: 'In Defence of the Underground' from *London Observed: Stories and Sketches*, © Doris Lessing 1992. Reprinted in an abridged form by permission of Jonathan Clowes on behalf of Doris Lessing, published by HarperCollins.

Christopher Logue: *London in Verse* (ed.), © Christopher Logue 1982. 'Last Night in London Airport' from *Ode to the Dodo: Poems 1953–1978*, © Christopher Logue 1981, published by Jonathan Cape. Reprinted by permission of Christopher Logue.

Robert Lynd: *Searchlights and Nightingales*, © Robert Lynd 1939. Reprinted by permission of J.M. Dent.

Rose Macaulay: *Told by an Idiot*, © Rose Macaulay 1923. Reprinted by permission of Peters, Fraser & Dunlop.

Arthur Machen: *The Secret Glory*, © Arthur Machen 1922. Reprinted by permission of Janet Pollock and A.M. Heath.

John Masefield: 'Biography' from *Collected Poems*, © John Masefield 1923. Reprinted by permission of The Society of Authors as literary representatives of the Estate of John Masefield.

A.A. Milne: 'Busy' from *Now We Are Six*, © A.A. Milne 1927. Reprinted by permission of Methuen Childrens Books.

Adrian Mitchell: 'Celia Celia' from *Adrian Mitchell: Greatest Hits*, © Adrian Mitchell 1991. Reprinted by permission of Bloodaxe Books.

ACKNOWLEDGEMENTS

John Mortimer: *Clinging to the Wreckage*, © John Mortimer 1982. Reprinted by permission of Weidenfeld & Nicolson. 'Rumpole and the Spirit of Christmas' from *Rumpole for the Defence*, © Ad van Press Ltd 1981. Reprinted by permission of Penguin Books. 'Rumpole and the Age of Retirement' from *The Trials of Rumpole*, © John Mortimer 1979. Reprinted by permission of Peters, Fraser & Dunlop.

H.V. Morton: *The Nights of London*, © H.V. Morton 1926. Reprinted by permission of Methuen London.

Iris Murdoch: *A Word Child*, © Iris Murdoch 1975. Reprinted by permission of Chatto & Windus.

Shiva Naipaul: in *Living in London* edited by Alan Ross, © Shiva Naipaul 1974. Reprinted by permission of London Magazine.

V.S. Naipaul: *The Mimic Men*, © V.S. Naipaul 1967. Reprinted by permission of Aitken, Stone & Wylie.

George Orwell: *Down and Out in Paris and London*, © George Orwell 1933. Reprinted by permission of A.M. Heath on behalf of the estate of Sonia Brownell Orwell, published by Martin Secker & Warburg.

Ian Ousby: *Literary Britain and Ireland*, © Ian Ousby 1990. Reprinted by permission of A. & C. Black.

Philippa Pearce: *A Dog So Small*, © Philippa Pearce 1962. Reprinted by permission of Constable.

Hesketh Pearson: *Conan Doyle: His Life and Art*, © Hesketh Pearson 1943. Reprinted by permission of A.P. Watt on behalf of Michael Holroyd.

Nikolaus Pevsner: *The Buildings of England: Hertfordshire* (second edition revised by Bridget Cherry 1977), © Nikolaus Pevsner 1953, and Nikolaus Pevsner and Bridget Cherry 1977. *The Buildings of England: Middlesex*, © Nikolaus Pevsner 1951. Reprinted by permission of Penguin Books.

David Piper: *The Companion Guide to London*, © David Piper 1964. Reprinted by permission of Peters, Fraser & Dunlop.

William Plomer: 'The Caledonian Market' from *Selected Poems*, © William Plomer 1940. Reprinted by permission of The Hogarth Press.

Margaret and Alick Potter: *Everything is Possible*, © M. and A. Potter 1984. Reprinted by permission of Margaret and Alick Potter, published by Alan Sutton.

ACKNOWLEDGEMENTS

J.B. Priestley: *Adam in the Moonshine*, © J.B. Priestley 1927. Reprinted by permission of Peters, Fraser & Dunlop. *Angel Pavement*, © J.B. Priestley 1930. Reprinted by permission of William Heinemann.

V.S. Pritchett: *A Cab at the Door*, © V.S. Pritchett 1968. *London Perceived*, © V.S. Pritchett 1962. Reprinted by permission of Chatto & Windus. *The Turn of the Years*, © V.S. Pritchett 1982. Reprinted by permission of Peters, Fraser and Dunlop on behalf of V.S. Pritchett.

Jonathan Raban: *Coasting*, © Jonathan Raban 1986. Reprinted by permission of HarperCollins.

W.G. Ramsey and R.L. Fowkes: *Epping Forest Then and Now*, © W.G. Ramsey and R.L. Fowkes 1986. Reprinted by permission of Battle of Britain Prints International.

Ruth Rendell: Live Flesh, © Ruth Rendell 1986. Reprinted by permission of Hutchinson Books.

John Richardson: *Highgate: Its History since the Fifteenth Century*, © John Richardson 1983. Reprinted by permission of Historical Publications.

Cecil Roberts: *Victoria Four-Thirty*, © Cecil Roberts 1937. Reprinted by permission of Hodder & Stoughton.

C.H. Rolph: *London Particulars*, © C.H. Rolph 1980. Published by Oxford University Press. Reprinted by permission of David Higham Associates.

Vita Sackville-West: *All Passion Spent*, © Vita Sackville-West 1931. Reprinted by permission of Curtis Brown.

William Sansom: in *Living in London* edited by Alan Ross, © William Sansom 1974. Reprinted by permission of London Magazine.

Ann Saunders: *The Art and Architecture of London*, © Ann Saunders 1984. Reprinted by permission of Phaidon Press.

Logan Pearsall Smith: *Afterthoughts*, © Logan Pearsall Smith 1931. *More Trivia*, © Logan Pearsall Smith 1921. Reprinted by permission of Constable.

Muriel Spark: *Curriculum Vitae*, © Muriel Spark 1992. Reprinted by permission of David Higham Associates.

Bruce Stevenson: *Middlesex*, © Bruce Stevenson 1972. Reprinted by permission of B.T. Batsford.

G.W. Stonier: *Pictures on the Pavement*, © G.W. Stonier 1955. Reprinted by permission of Michael Joseph.

ACKNOWLEDGEMENTS

Catherine Storr: *The Underground Conspiracy*, © Catherine Storr 1987. Reprinted by permission of Peters, Fraser & Dunlop.

The Times: 'Brent Cross', third leader from *The Times*, 12 July 1986, Times Newspapers Ltd 1986. Reprinted by permission of Times Newspapers.

Gillian Tindall: *The Fields Beneath*, © Gillian Tindall 1977. Reprinted by permission of Curtis Brown on behalf of Gillian Tindall.

Richard Trench and Ellis Hillman: *London Under London*, © Richard Trench and Ellis Hillman 1984, 1993. Reprinted by permission of John Murray.

Ann Usborne: *A Portrait of Islington*, © Ann Usborne 1981, 1989. Reprinted by permission of Damien Tunnacliffe.

Barbara Vine: *King Solomon's Carpet*, © Kingsmarkham Enterprises Ltd 1991. Reprinted by permission of Penguin Books.

Jill Paton Walsh: *The Fireweed*, © Jill Paton Walsh 1969. Reprinted by permission of Thomas Nelson.

Evelyn Waugh: *A Little Learning*, © Evelyn Waugh 1964. Reprinted by permission of Peters, Fraser & Dunlop.

Ben Weinreb and Christopher Hibbert: *The London Encyclopaedia*, © Ben Weinreb and Christopher Hibbert 1983. Reprinted by permission of Macmillan London.

H.G. Wells: *Love and Mr Lewisham*, © H.G. Wells 1900. 'The Argonauts of the Air' from *The Plattner Story and Others*, © H.G. Wells 1897. 'The Diamond Maker' from *The Stolen Bacillus and Other Incidents*, © H.G. Wells 1895. *Tono-Bungay*, © H.G. Wells 1909. Reprinted by permission of A.P. Watt on behalf of The Literary Executors of the Estate of H.G. Wells.

W. Wheatley: *History of Edward Latymer and His Foundations*, © W. Wheatley 1936. Reprinted by permission of Cambridge University Press.

The publishers have made every effort to contact copyright holders where they can be found. The publishers will be happy to include any missing copyright acknowledgements in future editions.

INDEX OF AUTHORS AND EDITORS

INDEX OF AUTHORS AND EDITORS

INDEX OF AUTHORS AND EDITORS

INDEX OF AUTHORS AND EDITORS

INDEX OF STATIONS

INDEX OF STATIONS

INDEX OF STATIONS